THE
READING GROUP
HANDBOOK

The
READING GROUP
HANDBOOK

EVERYTHING YOU
NEED TO KNOW
TO START
YOUR OWN
BOOK CLUB

Rachel W. Jacobsohn

HYPERION

NEW YORK

For information address: Hyperion,
114 Fifth Avenue, New York, New York 10011.
Book design by Margaret M. Wagner

Library of Congress Cataloging-in-Publication Data
Jacobsohn, Rachel W.
The reading group handbook : everything you need to know
to start your own book club / Rachel W. Jacobsohn.—
1st ed.
p.   cm.
Includes index.
ISBN 0-7868-8324-3
1. Group reading—Handbooks, manuals, etc.   2. Book clubs—
Handbooks, manuals, etc.   3. Forums (Discussion and debate)—
Handbooks, manuals, etc.   4. Books and reading.   I. Title.

Revised Edition

10 9 8 7 6 5 4 3 2

To Helen Weiss—
my mother—
for nurturing my sensitivities
and imaginations

The lake reflects the mountain.
The mind reflects the water.
What reflects the mind?

—written by Fredric Lehrman to
Howard Garb Jacobsohn
August 1993

ACKNOWLEDGMENTS

$\mathcal{A}$s humans, we reflect on the beginnings of things, laws of first causes, and the ever-constant influences of time and change. In one respect, the origin of this book stems from the mid-eighties when my brother, P.J. Weiss, suggested that I use my knowledge of literary criticism to publish a newsletter. Or it may have been my parental nurturing, or the position of the planets one day, or it may have germinated from Christine Archibald, and then Lisa Hudson, two enterprising, visionary editors at Hyperion who asked the question, "Could I write...?"

I am grateful to my dad, Marvin Weiss, for supporting the inception of my *Reading Women* venture and for believing in me. My friend and colleague Sandy Brown, friend Marla Gassner, and word wizard Barbara Wohlstader, remain remarkably instrumental to the success of the first edition, and therefore intrinsic to the revised one. In 1993, when I was writing the initial edition, my nuclear family was intact; my daughters, Dara and Lela, and my (then) husband Richard provided constant and valuable support. The forces of time and change, my heightened consciousness and personal will cushioned the processes that led to this revised edition. I need to acknowledge the power of the stories that I was reading; I heard them, and have embraced the next phase of my life: children out in the world; alone by choice for now. I truly appreciate the fusion of the past with the present and future; I relish all three, the one sweet and salty flow of life.

Portions of this book are generated from phone conversations and lengthy questionnaires that enthusiastic reading group members known and unknown to me took time and effort to complete. This book, drawing on many women and men willing to share their experiences, has truly been a cooperative effort. I want to thank them for what they have taught me and hope their experiences too will benefit others. I wish them all well, and earnestly hope that those whose names I inadvertently have omitted from the list will forgive me. Isabel Soffer, Meredith Mullins, Carol Baldwin Slocum, Cleta Schmitt, Penny Reick, Marcy Smith, Patsy Biddinger, Ruthie Wander, Marci Smith, Shirley Erwin, Judy Robeck, Marla Green, Linda Projansky, Carol Kaplan, Bonnie Phemister, Carol McKegney, Beverly Pirtle, Pearl Levine, Julie Shapera, Kathy Sackheim, Jacqui Kohn, Barbara Alexander, Margaret Griesbach, Kathy Laws, Mary Ellen Coviello, Sandy Liszt, Susan Pristave, Marcia Levy, Marci Whitney-Schenk, Connie Zukowski, Jeane Lumley, Nancy Zuraw, Patricia McDowell, Judy Simpson, Joy Kealey, Nancy Feingold, Lucille Berger, Don Welshon, James N. Elesh, Barb Loevy, Ann Goldman, Sue Beauseigner, Donna Bass, Karen Green, Sue Stefancik, Liz Greengold, Pat Henning, Valda Pancost, Marjorie MacLean, Rena Cohen, Sherryl Engstrom-Somerville, Tom Sheehey, Florence Kane, Jolynn Huffman, Madonna Hayes, Madelaine Sargent, and five individuals who chose to remain anonymous. I'd also like to thank Jeffrey Liss and Judy Uhlmann for their contribution to syllabi in Appendix A.

Input from other group leaders is very much appreciated. I give special thanks to Roberta Rubin, Janet Stern, Carol Friedman, Allen Schwartz, Barbara Nelson, and Judith G. Palarz for sharing their wisdom.

CONTENTS

INTRODUCTION

$\mathcal{B}$efore an athlete performs in a competitive event, she visualizes the physical movements her body will execute in order to win—she mentally prepares herself by visualizing every step about to occur. After all the time and training and history that she has devoted to that moment, she stands ready. She pictures the future.

I have never been trained in this manner, and yet, right away, I see the distinction between the forces of hindsight and foresight in the books I read.

In 1992, when I was asked to write a user-friendly guide about book groups, who thought that *The Reading Group Handbook* (first edition 1994) would be one of the first of a handful of books about reading groups to proliferate in the ensuing few years? Lucky for me, my special-focus book would demand four printings, and now is in a new revised edition. No one could have predicted the cultural sensation that book groups (reading groups, book clubs, whatever you want to call them) would constitute as we moved toward the next millennium. Reading groups are trendy, all the rage, and, together with media coverage of them, are popping up all over, like pins on a sales-reporting map of a suddenly successful manufacturing company.

Years ago, one of the books discussed in groups was Laura Hobson's *Consenting Adults*, (Doubleday, 1975). It begins with a mother observing her life before the day she received the letter from her son announcing his homosexuality, and her life thereafter. The image, not the issue, that Hobson created of a defining moment resonates as I analyze other fictions, and other lives. More days than not shuffle unnoticed into life's deck, but some become landmark dates on which significant and irrevocable change occurs.

Whereas, by 1992 I had established myself as a Chicago area book-group leader, and one of three contributors to *Reading Women*, a nationally distributed newsletter "of literary ideas," I still perceived myself as just an individual bibliophile nurtured in my own small sphere by my work. I was experiencing the Zen of "is." With the writing of the book, I was thrilled to think that two decades of working with book groups had provided me knowledge of the process, and that, curiously enough, it was information worthy of organizing into a book to help others.

Then came the book. The athlete stands in readiness for the starter gun or the first serve or the kickoff—in order to effect what she had only visualized. Conversely, like the mother in Laura Hobson's novel who opened the letter to an unexpected reality, I never anticipated the "after" of April 1994, the debut of *The Reading Group Handbook*.

I now find myself well prepared to ride the wave of attention that reading groups receive. Since the first edition of Ellen Slezak's *The Book Group Book* (Chicago Review Press, 1993) was published, the reading-group movement has mushroomed and is being researched, dissected, and documented by the American-style media, the academics, and the publishing industry. It enriches my life to be part of it.

After peeling away the national hoopla, the feverish search for empirical data, and the "How-to" books, like-minded, curious humans—all over the world—will read a book and want to discuss that reading with others. Discourse. Interchange. Social intercourse. Shared inquiry. Whatever it is called, it always will exist in a natural state propelled by human curiosity and creativity: the students sitting around Socrates and Sappho; Anne Hutchinson in 1634 on the overseas journey to religious and intellectual freedom (researched through archival documentation as *the* first book group); the fashionable and free-thinking upper-crust engaging in the European literary salons, late-19th and early-20th century; the sensitive elite characters in novels such as *Mrs. Dalloway* and *Howards End* being paradigms for the twentieth century.

The burgeoning interest in book groups snared them from the select, educated elite and rested them squarely in the hands of the middle- and upper-middle-class, high school, and, perhaps also, college educated. As if a fuse were lit just a few years ago when my book appeared, book groups began to erupt into being, propelled by word-of-mouth, publishers' marketing skills, and the news media.

In 1994, I "guestimated" for inquiring journalists that there were conservatively 250,000 book groups in existence. Now, because of the Internet, the *Book Club of the Air*, a monthly part of Ray Saurez's National Public Radio show, *Talk of the Nation*, and *Oprah's Book Club*, also a monthly segment of her television talk show, the fuse has ignited an explosion of interest and participation. Ray and Oprah, or just Oprah for the masses (her audience is vastly larger than Ray's), have taken the work that I and others do on a small scale, and unfurled it over the airwaves and over the countryside—the word is out! At this point, I could easily "guestimate" that book groups now number twice the 1994 figure. Over a half-million groups from five to twenty-five members engage in critical and social discussion of a shared reading. Anonymous Internet users join chat rooms for discussions. Listeners call into Ray's show. Viewers read Oprah's selection and send in their comments, then a few of these people are invited onto her show to appear with the author. Think of it! Literary criticism was previously reserved for the learned academics and elitists; now the book group sensation celebrates the ideal of free thought, American self-determination, and grassroots fervor. Anyone who can read and think can critique a reading selection. This absorption and outpouring of knowledge and wisdom confers new status on the ordinary citizen.

Americans are, hopefully, returning to reading for illumination and pleasure. Because of the reading-group phenomenon, more people are thinking about what they are reading, seeking out others with whom they can share an intelligent and comfortable discussion of a book. The opportunities to participate in this activity are varied and numerous. Readers thinking about being in a reading group, wondering how one works, how to get one started, and how to keep it going, will find a wealth of suggestions and information within the following pages. Readers presently participating in a book-discussion group will discover many tips for varying syllabi and improving group dynamics. For die-hard solitary readers, this guide offers paths for you to follow on your individual journey into literary analysis. I have been gifted with letters from readers everywhere extolling the benefits of this book. I am grateful for this feedback. Whatever your particular needs or wants may be, this book offers suggestions for getting more out of your reading experience.

"*[G]*etting more out of your reading experience." This seems to be my catch-all phrase that resonates in book groups in this country, the world, for that matter, as the book-group phenomenon continually gains attention from the media. How *can* one get more out of that good "read"? You can listen in to Ray Suarez's show, or watch Oprah's. You can find groups in your local areas (see Chapter 1) or connect into a chat room or reading group on the Internet. More now than ever, real bookstores and libraries, and on-line bookstores and publishers' websites, are affording a myriad of opportunities to get you going, offering endless bytes of information for you to savor.

The desire for intimate, ongoing organization still exists. After the first edition of *The Reading Group Handbook* was published, I was contacted by so many readers seeking title suggestions, locations of groups, the whys and wherefores of critical reading skills and literary analysis, and information on group dynamics, that I founded the *Association of Book Group Readers and Leaders (ABGRL)*. Membership details about this cooperative information clearinghouse can be found on the final page of this book.

To my knowledge, ABGRL is the only organization registering existing book groups in this country. Its number remains small (700+ at publication time). I do not advertise, devoting most of my time to my groups, the writing of the association's newsjournal *Reverbera-*

tions, and traveling to conduct workshops and panels for varied audiences. The flourishing reading group movement continues to stymie the media and academic community; it remains impossible to empirically document because book groups exist as independent free-flowing organisms—everywhere. A well-run book group is the model of democracy—minimum administration, the majority rules, policies evolve as needed, and the group exists solely for the benefit of all the members.

Journalists continue to ask about the trendy book-group explosion in the nineties. "Why?" Below are some appropriate responses for you to consider as you embark on your journey:

- Outside of formal schooling, book groups function as continuing education. No grades are given. No didactic professors need pleasing. There's an opportunity to read all those "important" books that were never read, or read them again with adult perspective.

- Title selection usually exposes members to books that they would not have chosen themselves, another opportunity for expansion of knowledge.

- The opportunity to belong to an accepting, validating, nonjudgmental group of people distinct from any other cultural institution is attractive. A book group is comprised of people you *want* to be with, not *have* to be with. This "congregation" has the potential of becoming a nurturing and an empowering force for each individual.

- Meetings provide social settings in which friends or colleagues connect, nurturing gossip is shared, and networking occurs. Whether the group is within a neighborhood or within corporate home office, the positive results are the same.

- Group participation hones group dynamics skills, and increases critical reading and thinking skills.

- Ongoing groups create a fertile atmosphere in which self-reflection and personal growth can flourish in both public and private venues. Most groups' spoken or unspoken confidentiality policy allows for personal applications of the reading matter to be aired and shared in comfort. (Journalists have dubbed this the "support group" or "consciousness-raising group" of the nineties. We kid ourselves about the process being "cheap therapy." It sounds demeaning but book groups are a satisfying, enriching source of comfort.

- Reading challenging texts that stretch your reading capabilities can happen within a nonthreatening setting. (I call this "group grope.")
- Through the literature and through hearing others' responses, group members "walk" in another's shoes. The readings and the discussions are eye-openers as to diverse ways of living and thinking.

I believe a good book is a gift to be appreciated by the mind, the body, and the soul. It is ours to explore with the excitement of a child, the clarity of a scientist, the spirit of a priest or priestess, and the intensity of a creator. To be able to enhance these pleasures in the company of others is better than a gift—it is a treasure. Enjoy your readings, enjoy your book-group experiences, and don't be a stranger. Write to me. Let me know about your organizing efforts, group policies, reading choices, stumbling blocks, and your successes. Your experiences can help others. Soon we'll be one huge, inspiring network of readers and thinkers. Ah, the splendor of it!

OPRAH DID IT

*Y*ou may be holding this book because of Oprah Winfrey. If she's succeeded in convincing you of the joys of reading and book groups, then she's marketed, sermonized, and proselytized well. *Welcome to the club of book-group people.* We in book groups are all over the world, in all walks of life, in all sorts of skins. I welcome you with the excitement of a teacher who basks in the glow of students who've mastered challenging new concepts and skills. I welcome you with the passion of a veteran enthusiastic to be helping others get the hang of something new. And, I welcome you with the acquired wisdom of a crone who knows that much that happens in the universe occurs because of the principle of cause and effect, one event a propelling force for subsequent events. Oprah's inauguration of her book club constitutes a propelling force. Take this thought with you as you observe the behaviors of the characters in the books you read.

This book is written out of respect for the individual's ability to think, learn, analyze, interact with others, and grow in wisdom and resiliency from each new experience. Despite differences among us, all readers, think, and feel, and bleed; we all read a book, and discuss that book bringing a network of complex and common human experiences to the activities. These have the capacity to connect us. Because I was a child, I can sympathize or empathize with fictionalized children. Because I am a woman, I can recognize the issues of other women in fiction. Because I am human I can transcend the details of my life to sense what it means to be someone else. We enter other people's stories as they unfold on the pages of fiction, or nonfiction. If you've read any of Oprah's book choices you have already been transformed in some way, just learning about others' realities depicted in a variety of times and places and situations. When you look over the list of her selected titles, take some time to jot down the time and place of each book, the characters' dilemmas, the ending created by the author, and, perhaps, take some time to think about how your perceptions may have been altered by being exposed to other lives through fiction. Put a date on this paper, and stash it away somewhere. One day you'll find it, then you'll have a record, not of the books, but of you, in accordance to your perceptions of tales told by skilled storytellers. Note the transformational power of education through reading.

You may have read these books seeking a pleasurable reading experience, not noticing the narrative voice, character development, use of adjectives, thematic visions, etc. With the help of this guide you can begin to think about the books you read in expansive ways, and enjoy the pleasures of the text evermore. Start here, and proceed, hopefully, to learn more and love the process. Hooray for Oprah if she sent you to this book, and book groups. Beyond all this hoopla, the new and old readers of America watch with anticipation; history books will record how Oprah took advantage of her popular position to advance the cause of education and social and intellectual interchange via the reading and sharing of books. Amen.

*W*hat books does Oprah choose? Most of them would be called popular fiction or general fiction; some are fine modern literature. They read fairly easily, engage the reader emotionally, and have an identifiable beginning, middle, and end. In addition, and most significantly, each selection focuses on at least one social issue of our time. It has been said that we read other people's stories to learn ways in which we can better lead our own lives. More than just "engage the reader emotionally," we are drawn by the author's renderings into worlds of pain and hope, of secrets that weigh heavily on minds and souls, of disappointments and how they are coped with. The struggles with personal moral choices reveal the ways the characters, (and thus "we") conduct ourselves in a world with others, with our God, and with the physical universe we inhabit.

Each of Oprah's choices depicts a journey of a character on his/her life's path. Some of the tellings confirm our belief in the healing power of story. The telling of a story is said to carry transformative power—for the characters, for the reader. Each book has the capacity to affect us in all the ways described elsewhere in this text. Allow these stories and words, images and feelings, to flow through you; process them and open yourself up to being changed and enriched by them. We connect with the characters' lives, and their lives intersect with ours. They and we are the same, only the circumstances are different. Enjoy!

*H*ere is an annotated list of the Oprah titles from the beginning of her Book Club through November 1997.

1. *The Deep End of the Ocean*, by Jacquelyn Mitchard (Viking hardcover; Signet paperback; large print, F.A. Thorpe, 1996; unabridged audio cassette, Books on Tape, 1996)

The story of a child disappearing is all the more heartwrenching because, quite frankly, we are more and more aware of how tenuous is the cement that holds our daily lives together. *The Deep End of the Ocean* plays out a domestic nightmare none of us wants to experience. The plot may not be seamless, but this popular fiction page-turner depicts defining moments and the principle of cause and effect as it tracks an American family touched by tragedy.

2. *Song of Solomon*, by Toni Morrison (Alfred A. Knopf, 1977, hardcover; NAL paperback; large print, Curley, 1994; Random House abridged audio cassette, 1985)

The intent to hide or retrieve one's history is laden with land mines along the path of good intentions. This multigenerational family tale begins in 1931 when a "colored" baby is allowed to be born inside Mercy ("No Mercy") Hospital for the first time ("inside its wards and not on its steps"). Morrison rewards the reader with a novel teeming with intrigue, violence, turmoil, danger, and despair, and a novel brimming with hope as mysteries transform to revelations. This winner of the 1993 Nobel Prize for Literature is one of today's most celebrated authors. Enjoy her sophisticated narrative devices, shifting perspectives, and magical use of our language. Her penetrating view of the unyielding, heartbreaking dilemmas which torment people of all races will spur you to read her other books.

3. *The Book of Ruth,* by Jane Hamilton (Ticknor & Fields hardcover; Anchor paperback; large print, Thorndike 1997; Recorded Books unabridged audio cassette, 1997)

Winner of the PEN/Ernest Hemingway Foundation Award. We hope for the beautiful, some suffer the ugly more than others, and most of life is somewhere in between. Ruth's first-person narrative emerges from a mysterious source ("[W]e had no words for savory odors or the colors of the winter sky or the unexpected compulsion to sing") as she begins, with simple language, to reclaim herself—by recording herself. Ruth's life has exaggerated dramatic tales we expect of nineteenth-century English literature, plus the banality essential to postmodernist writing. The relationship of the tragic ending to the happy one, the romantic hero's life to that of the mundane, the presence or absence of eloquence, are themes that exude off the pages of Ruth's story. Readers will recognize the tragicomic quality of life in Hamilton's (sometimes) zany characters; as told by Ruth, in her book, everyone deserves a bit of hope and grace. (I know some readers who could not relate to Hamilton's novel. Others swooned.)

4. *She's Come Undone,* by Wally Lamb (Pocket Books paperback, 1992; large print Compass Press, 1997; Simon & Schuster audio cassette, 1997)

Wow, did Lamb (a teacher of writing in a private academy in Connecticut) in his first novel hit a sensitive chord! His book was recommended to me five years ago when it first appeared. No wonder this is an Oprah selection. Poor Dolores has more catastrophes on her plate than most people in three lifetimes. And even though her weight is proportionate to her problems, she manages to barrel into a state of resilience. Lamb's finely honed narrative tone allows readers to gasp at the melodrama or chuckle at the satire.

Note: Because the issue of women's body images and the mother/daughter, surrogate mother/daughter themes are quite strong in this book, I find it appropriate to suggest as supplemental reading a book that my daughter Lela gave me, autographed by one of the authors when she came to speak on her university campus: *When Women Stop Hating Their Bodies*, by Jane R. Hirschmann, and Carol H. Munter (Fawcett Columbine, 1995).

5. *Stones from the River*, by Ursula Hegi (Scribner paperback 1994; large print G.K. Hall, 1997; Simon & Schuster abridged audio cassette)

I heard without verification that this book did not receive as much praise from Oprah fans as the others. Its vision is deep, dark and mighty. Place: small, fictional town of Burgdorf, Germany, outside of Düsseldorf. Time: 1915–1952—before, during, and after two world wars. Not only human nature but external circumstances tested everyone during this cataclysmic period in world history. Hegi's art transforms history, hearsay, and the subsequent silences into a story about ordinary community members, like you and me, who had to respond to an alien chaos and moral trials that descended on their ordered lives. Hegi's poetic title and invention of a female dwarf as main protagonist will propel discourse of the novel for a long time.

6. *The Rapture of Canaan*, by Sheri Reynolds (G.P. Putnam hardcover, Berkley trade paperback, 1997; large print G.K. Hall, 1997; Books on Tape unabridged audio cassette 1997; Recorded Books, 1997)

The demands of church doctrine (the Church of Fire and Brimstone, no less!) and parental authority figures conflict with young Ninah's emerging self. The struggle is timeless and universal, and Reynolds's contribution to contemporary Southern fiction approximates literature.

7. *The Heart of a Woman*, by Maya Angelou (Random House hardcover, 1981; Bantam paperback, 1997; large print by Wheeler, 1997; abridged cassette Random House, 1997 (read by the author—a special treat)

If you loved this, Angelou's fourth volume of her autobiography, you're in for a treat when you seek out her other books. Definitely try to get hold of her audio tapes, her voice has a goddess-like magical quality. *The Heart of a Woman* takes us into the New York scene when Angelou gets involved in the arts and the Harlem Writers Guild. Angelou rubs elbows with some famous personalities, has interesting stories to tell, and a fascinating way of telling them. Her words pop off the page as if on fire.

8. *Songs in Ordinary Time*, by Mary McGarry Morris (Viking hardcover, 1995; Bantam trade paperback, 1997; unabridged audio cassette, Brilliance Corp., 1997)

When secrets fester among those who know and when they manifest a tainted aura among the unknowing, the atmosphere lies ripe for disasters to strike. In a small, primarily Catholic town of Atkinson, Vermont, in 1960, a plot unfolds supporting the above statement. Human longings, familial love, and hope fill the pages of this graceful novel.

9. *A Lesson Before Dying*, by Ernest Gaines (Alfred A. Knopf hardcover, 1993; Vintage Contemporaries paperback, 1994; unabridged audio cassette, Books on Tape, 1994)

By virtue of a believable plot line, a young African American man makes one mistake early in his life and finds himself on death row. While there, he is under the tutelage of a man instructing him about the meaning of heroism, manhood. Gaines's tender tale has the ability to ask and offer possible answers to age-old questions of personal conduct.

10. *Ellen Foster* and *A Virtuous Woman*, both by Kaye Gibbons (*EF*: Algonquin of Chapel Hill, 1987; abridged audio cassette Simon & Schuster, 1996; *AVW*: Algonquin of Chapel Hill, 1989; large print, G.K. Hall, 1991)

My groups and I loved *Ellen Foster*; Gibbons created a strong Huck Finn–like voice in an 11-year old girl who experiences much of life's uglier realities and needs to make choices. This is a beautiful little gem; I'm glad Oprah brought it to public attention. It should be in high school English reading curricula. Even though crudeness exudes from its pages, the ultimate message is, well, I'm going out on the limb defining a message—that each of us has the capacity to define a right and moral behavior that may be outside of community standards. We are truly responsible for our souls and choices that maintain our sense of humanity. Young Ellen is a valuable priestess. Recipient of the Sue Kaufman Prize for First Fiction and special citation from Ernest Hemingway Foundation.

AVW depicts how a woman "escaped" fates that we know exist and found a contentment and love that varies from the ideal but contains all that is deemed hopeful. This short novel contains a male and a female character worthy of men's, women's, and coed groups' discussion.

If you've read any of these contemporary, mainstream novels, I shall now attempt to elevate your level of thinking about what you read and, hopefully, show and prove to you that you know more than you think you know. And show you that you *can* easily think at higher levels, if you allow yourself to, and are introduced to these ways of thinking. Below are quotes from two famous philosophers of Western civilization that I offer you as different ways of seeing the stories about the human condition in the Oprah books. Let me know if and how you react.

What a chimera then is man! What a novelty! What a monster, what a chaos, what a contradiction, what a prodigy! Judge of all things, imbecile worm of the earth; depository of truth, a sink of uncertainty and error; the pride and refuse of the universe!

We desire truth, and find within ourselves only uncertainty.

We seek happiness, and find only misery and death.

We cannot but desire truth and happiness, and are incapable of certainty or happiness. The desire is left to us, partly to punish us, partly to make us perceive wherefrom we are fallen. —*Pascal*

On a closer examination it seems as though, in the case of a genius, the will to live, which is the spirit of the human species, were conscious of having by some rare chance, and for a brief period, attained a greater clearness of vision, and were now trying to secure it or at least the outcome of it for the whole species . . . so that the light which he sheds about him may pierce the darkness and dullness of ordinary human consciousness and there produce some good effect.

Arising in some such way, this instinct drives the genius to carry his work to completion, without thinking of reward or applause or sympathy; to leave all care for his own personal welfare; to make his life one of industrious solitude, and to strain his faculties to the utmost. —*Schopenhauer*

THE
READING GROUP
HANDBOOK

CHAPTER 1

WHAT IS A BOOK GROUP?

"I will nourish with it five thousand souls, a
hundred thousand souls, a million souls . . . all
humanity."
                                        —*Hugo*

All of life is a story, and daily each of us collects stories. We
share them at the dinner table at the end of the day, with friends
or relatives, with colleagues in the workplace. (Isn't that what
Monday mornings are for—to share the stories you lived and
shaped over the weekend?) We live them, we tell them, and we
read them. Put this guide into practice and remember the adventure. By forming a book club for the purpose of discussing other
people's stories, you will be creating a story of your own.

What Is a Book Group?

Reading groups in the United States date back to the early nineteenth century, when spirited New England women met to discuss
the issues addressed in serious poetry, nonfiction, and publications of the day. By the turn of the century, reading groups were
flourishing. Literary societies and book groups evolved from
women's reform groups, church groups, the National Council of
Jewish Women, and the American Association of University

Women. Women—and men—formed discussion groups because of a mutual desire to improve themselves and for the opportunity to socialize. Within a reading group, freethinking, aspiring souls not born to privilege could pursue knowledge heretofore reserved only for those who passed through the expensive pearly gates of higher institutions of learning. Through reading, the world of culture—and virtually the world in total—was available to all.

The catastrophic changes brought on by global events during the first few decades of the twentieth century—mass immigration, World War I, the Great Depression—had an impressive effect on the way people perceived their relationship to books. No longer were books a means to reinforce long-established traditional value systems or an escape route from everyday life into romance fiction with happy endings. New theories from Darwin and Freud challenged the equilibrium. Existence had become unsettling, changing in distressing and disturbing ways. Readers looked to writers for help to better understand what was happening in their own lives and were grateful to have books to help them to understand, to better incorporate their experiences into their sense of everyday reality.

Founded in 1947 as a nonprofit educational corporation, the Great Books Foundation developed a structured literature reading program for students from kindergarten into adulthood. Its founder, Robert Maynard Hutchins, president of the University of Chicago, saw a nation of individuals taught the mechanics of reading in the early grades, but lacking the skills for thoughtful analysis of reading material. In response, a reading program with a guideline for discussion was created to get the tired brain cells moving. "I think, therefore I am" was transformed into "I am, therefore I think, and I can think about what I read." The Great Books approach takes literary theory and analysis out of the sole purview of the academics and intellectuals, and gives it to the populace of national readers.

Today the Great Books Foundation groups attract men and women from all over the country. Discussions are led by laypeople who have attended training workshops, and center on interpretive analysis rather than modern formalist literary criticism. Everyone is welcome to join. In fact, the training program for Great Books leaders would greatly help any reading group, and its reading selections are carefully chosen and tested for their power to support lively, productive discussion. Call the Great Books Foundation at 800-222-5870 (fax: 312-407-0334).

Beginning in the 1960s, when energies were directed to social and political activism, this country has witnessed a return to and an increase in the number of book groups. Although women have primarily been the innovators and participants, there are also groups of men, couples, and mixed singles. Newspapers are including appropriate articles highlighting local groups and their participants, and showing the importance that being in a reading group has in their lives. In small rural towns across America, the book group has become a lifeline for people feeling isolated in their communities. Book groups are the evolutionary advancement of sewing bees, "meetings" at the corner tavern, or neighborhood gatherings on the front stoop. In this age of fast-paced lives driven into frenzy by "surround sound" and ubiquitous telecommunications, the presence of book groups provides positive reassurance of the value of human discourse and affords a place where the imagination is free to explore.

While book clubs are organized around a love of reading and lively literary discussion, they may evolve in various directions: some toward the interpersonal and social, some toward the scholarly, and still others toward the exploration of a particular subject or author. Some groups gather ostensibly to discuss the book, but the group structure actually provides participants with a means to promote new, or strengthen old, friendships. In this milieu, readers apply the text to their personal lives, and the book group provides adult conversation and social prestige (usually within a community). On the other hand, groups that read "quality" fiction and serious literature (more "difficult" books) tend to perpetuate an elitist attitude that strengthens their purpose of literary criticism. This identity both bonds them and elevates the structure and goals of their meetings. In addition, these groups that interact primarily for intellectual and educational challenge engage in little social interaction during the meeting; instead, their time is devoted to the "pure" literary criticism of a specific selection, genre, or author. Purpose, syllabi, and method of leadership separate one group from another and play an important part in establishing a group's tone and behavioral norm.

Nuts and Bolts: Basic Considerations

Starting anything new is risky. Even coming together with people you think you know well has risk, and seeking out acquaintances or strangers can cause trepidation. Let's suppose you're ready to take the plunge. The question then becomes, *How do I get started putting this thing together?* Grabbing people on the street might make for a funny scenario, but it won't get the job done. You need to find individuals who are a good match for you. I'm not necessarily talking about whether they like to read the same books you do. Don't let this be the primary issue (more on that later).

First, imagine yourself sitting in a group discussing a book—any book. What you need to imagine is the time of day and the people around you. This will help you determine some of the physical ingredients of your desired group. What time of day is it? How old are the people? Are they your age? Older, younger, a mix? Are they all one sex, or is your imaginary group coed? If all one sex, are they all the same marital status? If coed, are they couples or individual men and women? In this way, you can get in touch with your needs for your group. Gender and time considerations rank high with most participants; age and marital status concern some; and reading selections and "tone" of the meetings will always be a primary consideration.

Now let's consider time. During what part of one week of the month (let's say, for a monthly group) can you freely commit approximately two hours to this activity? And right at the outset, let me emphasize commitment. Once a time slot is chosen, you need to respect it. First requirement: your availability, then the availability of the majority of people. I don't have to tell you what your options are, but I will list them anyway. Morning, afternoon, evening. Weekdays or weekends. Some people want only weekend time slots—Friday nights, Saturday afternoons, Sunday evenings. There are Sunday evening groups that meet for dinner and discussion. There are weekday or Saturday afternoon groups that "do lunch" and have discussion. There is a Friday night group that serves a buffet dinner to tired working folk, and all unwind over a good intellectual literary discussion. This setup can happen any weeknight, too. Do you want your discussion connected to a full meal or only to refreshments?

I've brought up these several issues—gender, time slot (and food)—to emphasize the variations in organization that exist for reading groups. Once you've gathered together a group of interested people, these decisions need to be made, and you may find that you are disenfranchised by majority rule. So decide on the "when" before you embark. The more flexible you are, the easier the quest; the more personal qualifications you have, the more arduous the quest may become. Figure out what *you* want ahead of time—and then go after it!

Following is a list of ideas or methods on how to accomplish that desired end. Please understand that I'm basing these suggestions on a generic understanding of social communities in America. Your community, geographic location, or populace (rural, urban, suburban) may be so idiosyncratic that these suggestions are not helpful to you. If that is the case, try to vary them and apply them to your specific needs.

1. Talk to friends and relatives. If they are not interested, maybe *their* friends or relatives are. Enlarge the circle of personal inquiries as much as you can. Some groups have started with three or four interested people deciding to each recruit three or four more people. One group emerged from an idea thrown around at a birthday party when the conversation had turned to what books the guests were reading. One man sent letters to those he had carefully "selected" to be in his group, inviting them to meet at his house at a specified time.

Sometimes an already existing group can become a reading club. One woman told me that she belonged to a group of women who worked in the same professional field and who had agreed to get together for nonspecified discussion during after-work hours. When this loosely organized plan fell apart, they changed the venue to book discussion. This worked out nicely for them, especially since they were all in care-giving professions, and they chose their readings with that in mind.

One woman went to a bridal shower knowing only the bride and heard another guest talking about a reading group in formation. They compared schedules and books they each liked, and one thing led to another. This woman spoke to me of how excited she was that day—she'd been looking for a group for a long time and was a bit uneasy going to this shower not knowing anyone else, yet the day turned out to be a great turning point for her. So, what's the moral? Talk it up, ask, listen. Eavesdrop!

2. Ask the manager of your local bookstore. If the bookstore doesn't already have a reading group in existence, it may be interested in starting one, or lending you some space for your own.

3. Talk to community members, people you may see all the time but who are strangers or acquaintances—at the post office, the grocery store, the cleaners, the pharmacy. These people may be interested or know of others who may be.

4. Ask salespeople or the proprietors of local stores if you can put up a public notice. Any notice you put up anywhere needs to be carefully thought out. "Looking for people interested in starting a book group" will get a far greater response than "Looking for women interested in starting an afternoon reading group," or "Looking for coed weeknight book group. Call 555-5555 after 6 p.m." To get a response, you do need to publicize your phone number, and, yes, there is a risk in doing this. Obviously, anytime you leave your phone number in a public place, you open yourself up to the unknown, and we all know that "the unknown" can be irritating or even dangerous. You have to be the best judge of this plan. If you don't want to invite problems, try making an arrangement with the store's proprietor, perhaps giving him or her your name and putting on the notice that if anyone is interested, "See proprietor. Leave name and number."

If this is the case, then screening callers will be your next task. Have some questions prepared, such as: "What are your expectations of a reading group?" "Have you ever been in a book group before?" "How did it operate?" "Why are you interested in another?" "Are you looking for a soapbox or a discussion? I don't want one person to take over, do you?"

Be inquisitive, slightly confrontational, but not combative. View these questions as your screening process, but understand that this is your first (and maybe your last) opportunity to control this process. Of course, take callers' names and numbers to amass a prospective list, but if someone does not sound "right" to you, hedge or say whatever you want to protect yourself and your privacy.

5. Ask people connected with institutions of learning—school principals and English teachers, but don't overlook elementary or nursery school teachers. Professionals familiar with children's literature can be very insightful. Ask your librarian. "Hi, I'm so-and-so. I live in the community and I'm looking for a book group to join or perhaps to start up. Would you or anyone you know have knowledge of one around here, or be interested in getting together to start one?" "Is there a bulletin board that the teachers/customers/patrons see where I could put up a notice?" "Can I leave my name and number with you in case you think of anybody? Can I call you in about a week to find out if you've thought of anyone?"

6. Inquire of the membership of local community/volunteer organizations: PTAs; churches, mosques, or synagogues; clubs such as the Loyal Order of the Moose or Rotary; and charitable groups such as hospital auxiliaries. Do they run a book group? Could you join? Is there anyone from their membership interested in starting one—outside or inside the organization? Would they include your inquiry in their newsletter?

Does your area have a community center? A YMCA? Consider inquiring there. A volunteer group in my area started a book discussion group years ago. Some people have joined the organization just to have the privilege of taking part in the reading group. Both member and organization profit.

Make a note that some reading groups have links to national organizations such as Panhellenic, the American Association of University Women (AAUW), the League of Women Voters, the General Federation of Women's Clubs, Newcomers, and others.

7. Use local newspapers. A small ad in the classified or personal listings may get a response. A friendly call to a friendly editor may get you a few free lines on a page when space is available. Pitch the idea as a public notice or a community service. Maybe the editor will write up a little article for you, encouraging anyone interested to call the newspaper. Alternative presses also may have readers who would be good candidates for your group.

8. Put up notices in public places: train stations, bus stops, college campuses (on bulletin boards or kiosks), local restaurants, banks.

Be creative, and have fun with your project. Consider keeping a journal or notes. Your experiences will become fodder for stories to share with your group once it's formed; or maybe you will start writing one day. Once you begin your journey into the world of language and illusion, you never know where the muse may lead you. Alice started by reading a book, too, remember?

NUMBERS

How many is enough? As I see it, there are two questions here: How many people should you collect for your organizational meeting? How many people comprise a "good" group?

Sometimes a small group grows; sometimes a large group shrinks. Expansion from interest and attrition from lack of interest are uncontrollable variables that you should expect. The problem is: How can you know *which* variable to expect? You can't. Just be mindful of these possibilities when collecting your original group. Then time will provide the answer. Eventually, a group of committed participants will form your reading group core. When you feel that enough interest has been generated to get a group started, then call that first meeting, whether it's with eight, or ten, or six, or sixteen people. The numbers will take care of themselves. Get started. Trust time and the process.

A good group of committed participants can be as small as five or as large as twenty-five. In my experience, the optimum is to have twelve to fifteen members on a group list at all times; ten to eighteen would be my next high and low figures. Unless you are fortunate to gather an ardently committed, healthy group of individuals, the stuff of life may cause anywhere from a third to a half of the membership to be absent from any given discussion. Padding the list a bit will ensure an adequate number for an interesting discussion every time.

I can count with the fingers of one hand the occasions when the number in attendance has dropped to under five. At those times something special happened: Very small groups seem to take on a different atmosphere, one of intimacy and depth that may not be achieved with a larger group. Sometimes those normally reticent to talk feel more comfortable and articulate freely. Sometimes feelings about the group and the group dynamics come out. I learn a lot. And I have learned never to be disappointed with a small turnout. Those are wonderful times of possibility.

COMMITMENT

What does "committed" mean? Committed is putting the date on your calendar. Committed is making all the necessary preparations to clear that time well in advance—child care, family events, car maintenance, transportation—to assure your availability. Committed is planning business trips and vacations (when possible) around book club dates. Committed is—well, here's my all-time favorite: A normally outspoken woman was unusually quiet at group one night. When I called her a few days later to check if all was well, she told me that after the meeting she had gone home to tell her husband that she had filed for divorce that day. In her case, commitment to the group, the group process, and ultimately to the gift that she had given herself—a reading group—were her imperatives. She "didn't want to miss the discussion," she said.

HOW OFTEN SHOULD MY GROUP MEET?

The majority of reading groups meet once a month. Some noted on my questionnaire that they meet every four to six weeks, depending on everyone's schedule. One reported meeting semimonthly, which is quite ambitious for a group that discusses a different novel at each meeting. And one woman wrote that her group meets when all members have finished the book. (Now that's loosely structured!) Most of my groups that read and discuss novels come together once a month. And most groups noted that they break for the summer months, as my groups and I do.

The majority of groups reported that they meet for two-hour sessions, although others said anywhere from one and a half to three hours. Some built in social time before and/or after their meeting.

Very few groups reported that they spent more than one session on a book. However, several times my groups have spontaneously eliminated the next book from their syllabus to spend an additional session on their current selection. William Kennedy's *Ironweed*, A. S. Byatt's *Possession*, and George Eliot's *Middlemarch* spanned two sessions each. According to questionnaire responses, multiple meetings on one book were held for *Mating* by Norman Rush, mainly because not everyone had finished it. Shakespeare's *King Lear*, Smiley's *A Thousand Acres,* and the film *Ran* were the subject of multiple sessions broken up by themes and issues. David McCullough's *Truman* was divided into two sessions, with 500 pages required for each month's meeting. And *Oldest Living Confederate Widow Tells All* by Alan Gurganus and *Wings of Morning* by Thomas Tryon were both discussed by chapters.

I know of groups in which the facilitator spends at least a dozen sessions on one selection. As would be expected, her modus operandi is quite thorough and quite academic. One group of senior citizens who meet with me once a week for one hour has spent up to eight sessions on *Bellarosa Connection* by Saul Bellow and on *The Shawl* by Cynthia Ozick.

Proper discussion of a short story usually requires at least an hour. If you choose to discuss short stories, plan to read more than one for a two-hour session. However, you may not get to the second one, depending on the levels and depth of the discussion.

One of the joys of literary discussion is that it ignites thought, rather than tying up a work of fiction in a neat little package. Don't be surprised when, after a two-hour discussion of a piece, it lingers with you. Every reader has a unique list of influential books that never lose their status and place in her or his psyche.

When discussing frequency with your potential group, be sure to give yourself enough time to read the selection carefully. Be calculating with your calendar. I assign a somewhat longer book for September because most people have extra time to finish it over the summer months. I try to assign short books around the holidays because time then seems to be at a premium. (Some groups do not meet in December to alleviate that pressure. Some have just a holiday party with or without significant others to get together, but without the reading commitment.) The semimonthly group mentioned in the first paragraph of this section must be real bibliophiles. I admire their time commitment to their reading and their reading group.

Best suggestion for the frequency decision: Start with once a month at a designated time slot for two hours and see how that feels.

WHERE SHOULD MY GROUP MEET?

My extremely philosophical mother taught me that in the decision-making process there is no such thing as "should." According to her, "should" is only a concept within which man has built sets of rights and wrongs. So, in choosing where to meet, there are no rights or wrongs. You "should" plan to hold your meetings where it is most convenient and mutually agreeable for most, if not all, the participants.

There are two major possibilities to consider: outside and inside a private home.

Outside a Private Home

- A bookstore.
- In a room in a public building. This could be in a church, synagogue, or library, especially if that organization is the sponsor. Mary Ellen Coviello from Summit, New Jersey, said, "One library burned down, so we just shifted to another." She also said that one woman in her group works at the library and reserves the space for them.
- A public meeting room in a bank or a school building may necessitate acquiring permission and/or paying a small fee, but several groups mentioned that this is their location. Food service is sometimes an issue at these sites.
- Several groups said that they met in a private room in a restaurant, had a standing reservation, and were nicely accommodated. One respondent commented that she felt too old and lazy to fix food for a big group. She much preferred the treat of lunch out and a book discussion. Groups also reported doing likewise for a dinner meeting, with discussion either during or after the meal.
- The members of one city group live in apartments that are too small to accommodate a group of ten or more. Fortunately, two of the members own art galleries and graciously offer their work spaces for meetings.

Inside a Private Home:

- The majority of groups meet in members' homes. The determination of the home hostess/host is either on a volunteer basis or by rotation system.
- Some groups meet only in a centrally located home. They refuse to meet at any home that is outside a certain "convenient" driving radius. If space

requirements are a factor, or if one member has a perfect setup and is willing, you could agree to meet in one home all the time. Refreshment duties can be shared or money pitched in.

• Some members are more than happy to host multiple meetings. These are usually people who are hospitable by nature or who would rather entertain at home than travel elsewhere.

• Some members reserve a community room in their apartment building. One city woman reserved the party room in her mother-in-law's building. One apartment-dwelling woman hosted at her friend's home but prepared, served, and cleaned up all the food.

Parking can be an issue. Availability can be scarce in some city locations. Also, suburban homes may have parking problems during the winter when streets are icy and snow-covered. Many times I hear, "Give me May so we don't have to worry about parking," or "I'll take September when the weather is good."

Some members never volunteer to host. A few may need a couple of years before they are comfortable enough with the group to "let them in"; others may have hidden issues that prevent them from offering; and some are just lazy about doing their fair share. How you handle this is up to your group. Most groups that I lead or that responded to the questionnaire take turns hosting meetings in members' homes. It's fun going to everyone's house. Family pictures are surveyed; a very real sense of connection and intimacy is achieved. Each host or hostess may handle the refreshments differently, so personality and lifestyle are on display: bakers versus nonbakers; fat and cholesterol-conscious versus eat, live, and be merry; presentation-and-aesthetics-mean-a-lot types versus just-put-it-out types; sparse versus lavish; sophisticated palates versus plebeian tastes; and the anxious host versus the laid-back entertainer.

The factors of privacy, atmosphere, size of group, location/distances, weather/safety, children, rental fees, and of course personal desires all affect your decision on choosing a meeting site. And again, the decision is not permanent; it can be reevaluated and changed on a trial basis at any time. Have fun going out! And have fun straightening up when it's your turn!

CHAPTER 2

WHAT MAKES A GOOD MEMBER?

"Every man who knows how to read has it in his power to magnify himself, to multiply the ways in which he exists, to make his life full, significant, and interesting."   —*Huxley*

Who's a Good Candidate for Membership?

𝒢libly answered, anyone who can read. More specifically, I've prepared a list of what I perceive as qualifications for the *perfect* reading group member, complete with personal comments.

• *Interested, Willing, Enthusiastic*

You certainly don't want someone whose arm needs twisting, either to join or to participate.

• *A Certain Reading Level*

A good reading group member should be able to read at better than eighth-grade level, which is slightly above the level of most newspaper writing. But level of education achieved (high school, college, postgraduate) is not an important factor. Although many of the people in the groups I am aware of are college educated, this level or the degrees after one's name are not nearly as important as self-motivation and desire.

•Conscientious Reader

A person who has read the selection recently, finished it, and thought about it is an asset to any group. Many of my groupies say, "Oh, I can't remember. I read it so long ago," or "I didn't have time to finish." Others can muster up only "I liked it" or "I didn't like it." These members, and their comments, are always welcome, but contributions like the ones just cited are far from discussion stimulants. Those who have read the selection and come to book group with thoughts, feelings, opinions, criticisms, and/or questions bring much more than their bodies to a discussion.

•Committed

The ideal member is committed to the group and attends regularly. There's nothing sadder than a space in a group with a number limit occupied by an uncommitted, uninterested person who is absent more than present. Some groups have rules about how many meetings a member can miss before the privileged space is awarded to another.

•Prompt

Need I explain?

•Curious

We can learn much about the world in which we live and the people in it from many a fine book. The curious will question authenticity of information, search for the author's message, assess the characters' decisions and actions, and react to the literature as a puzzle to be taken apart and put back together again, and more.

•Sensitive

Those who can emotionally and psychologically "walk in others' shoes" have an advantage in understanding fictional and nonfictional characters' life dilemmas. Those having any experience or training in social science or social service fields will be a great asset to a group, but just having a basic empathy for and understanding of the human condition is quite adequate.

•Inquisitive and Flexible

Those who ask questions and those who are flexible will explore possible answers but not need *the* answer. The joy of literary interpretation is in the quest, not in reaching a destination.

• *A Good Listener/A Good Participant*

Somewhere between the detrimental extremes of absolute silence and frustrating, irritating loquaciousness lies the ideal. (More on these two points in chapter 6.)

• *Sense of Humor*

Oh, the benefit of comic relief! If only every group could have at least one quick-witted personality to help us laugh at ourselves. We need to not take ourselves so seriously all the time. Occasionally I envision the Watchful One above laughing at the efforts of us lowly humans trying to figure out all this stuff about existence and purpose and good versus evil and fate versus free will. The ultimate joke may certainly be on us, but still we keep trying.

• *Focused*

A person who can stay on track helps the discussion greatly. Indulging individual needs for attention and wasting time chatting about extraneous matters undermine the group process and goal. (Socializing belongs before or after the discussion.) Assembling a more or less mentally healthy group is definitely a plus. One person who constantly focuses on painful personal problems can throw a group off balance; so can someone who just doesn't take to the analytical process and open forum format.

• *Intelligent*

An intelligent individual enriches a discussion with knowledge in a variety of subjects. Those with expertise in history, current events, natural sciences, psychology, foreign cultures and languages, mythology, religions, etc., are great assets to the group. One woman I know has a law degree, a social libertarian's soul, and an impressive command of historical events and dates, especially those of America's tumultuous Kennedy-Vietnam era. Her passionately delivered perspectives enhance our discussions tremendously.

• *Eloquent*

The beauty and meaning of the written language are manifold when read aloud by the right person. In my groups, there are two professional actresses whose voices lend rhythm and magic to the spoken word.

Although this list may seem a bit enthusiastic, in essence it seeks someone of sincere intent, active intelligence, sensitive soul, and rational mind. Even if a minority of your members have half of these qualities, you have indeed gathered together a special group.

FRIENDS OR NOT?

Some questionnaire respondents suggested *not* asking friends to be part of the group. What's the message here? That the familiarity of friends may not create the ideal situation for a reading group. Recently a woman called to ask if I would lead her group. Her tale: Four out of the ten people who said they were interested in a member-led group came to the first meeting to discuss Marge Piercy's *He, She and It,* a brilliant and complex novel. Toward the end of the discussion, a member announced that they had discussed the book only superficially. With that proclamation, the group fell into social and personal chatter for the rest of the evening. Perhaps those who don't know each other very well can more easily focus on the literature because it is their common ground. Then friendships come gradually through this process, not vice versa.

Group Demographics

Many groups cull members from a neighborhood where members share similarities in lifestyle, income, and family goals. Often these groupings are continuations of already forged friendships in which like-mindedness is also well established. Other groups draw together professionals from the same field of work; others may be members of the same service club or organization, or live in the same apartment building or planned community development.

When forming your group, give some thought to its identity. Do you want similarity or diversity in membership? Homogeneity or heterogeneity? Narcissism and self-approbation are easy sins to fall prey to. As Charles H. Parkhurst said long ago, "The man who lives by himself and for himself is likely to be corrupted by the company he keeps." To the questionnaire query "What advice would you give to someone considering starting or joining a reading group?," one woman wrote: "Have a wide range of ages and backgrounds to provide a variety of viewpoints."

Below are two examples of groups with variations on these descriptive statistics: age, gender, nationality, race, citizenry, religion, education, lifestyle (socioeconomic), lifestyle (sexual orientation), geographic location, and marital status. When you read the following group descriptions, think about which one would carry on a more enlightening discussion and if that is the one you would prefer.

- *A fairly homogeneous group.* Ten suburban women, college-educated, white, Anglo-Saxon, Christian, fourth- or fifth-generation American, middle-class, twenty-five to thirty-five years old; seven married, two divorced, one single, all straight, half working outside the home, most with children between infancy and ten years of age. A fairly traditional, mainstream American group. Although each individual, of course, has a unique identity that will impact the group, this crowd is fairly uniform.

- *A more diversified group.* City-dwelling, college-educated, middle-class men and women, half married (none to each other), all professional, some with children, two men with grandchildren. One lesbian, one first-generation Irish-American Catholic male, two immigrant Chicanas (first in their families to attend college), one Jewish man, one black Methodist woman, three white Protestant men (one president of his own company, one an army brat born in China, one a social worker). The ages span twenty years; members are twenty-five to forty-five years old.

Obviously, these groups have been set up by me to make a point: The more diverse the population of your group, the more diverse the perspectives, the ideas, the experiences, and the fields of knowledge. And hearing those new and/or opposing viewpoints will either strengthen or alter your own. Even in the most homogeneous group, your viewpoint will be challenged. Obviously, the way one person interprets a book is only one perspective—one of many.

DON'T BE AFRAID OF THE STRANGER—OR CHALLENGE YOUR STEREOTYPES AND PREJUDICES

Only an idealist would envision a rainbow coalition—cross-leveled by socioeconomics, age, life experiences, and lifestyles—gathering in anyone's home for a free and open forum of ideas. Humans prefer to associate with like-minded, like-experienced people. People like us offer acceptance, comfort, security, stability, and reinforcement. And this is certainly one way to view a reading group—as a safe, non-threatening place.

On the other hand, inviting people of varying backgrounds into your group will expand your perspective of the literature and life, and teach you much beyond what the books themselves offer. As Kafka said, "A book must be an ice-ax to break the seas frozen in our souls." Stereotypes and prejudices may be challenged and may (or may not) begin to break down. Then, if the story ends well, strangers will become familiar, and those who were feared for their differences will become comfortable associates in the book discussion process. In this uniquely nonthreatening environment, all participants will become comembers.

> • A men's group in Evanston, Illinois, was begun by James Elesh, who asked eleven other men he felt were "compatible" to come along. One man in the group told me that because of the men's varying demographics, he has become friends with men he may not have had another opportunity to meet. He also told me that he has learned a lot about other people from this experience.

> • An opinionated, gruff woman in one of my groups often ruffles the feathers of other group members, yet her storehouse of information is valuable to all who listen to what she says, rather than the manner in which she says it. There's not only intelligence, but also a great deal of soul and sensitivity if one looks beneath the surface.

ORGANIZATIONS' MEMBERSHIP

Some groups operate under the auspices of organizations, such as the American Association of University Women, the General Federation of Women's Groups, the National Council of Jewish Women, the YMCA, or YWCA. These, in addition to churches, synagogues, Junior Leagues, and hospital auxiliaries, often sponsor book discussion groups that require organization membership as a prerequisite.

CANDIDATES FOR ADMISSION

Initially, organizing members for a start-up group has an element of chance to it, unless of course, you know each interested party personally. Deciding whom to admit is a difficult issue and smacks of control. One group joked about formulating a questionnaire to distribute among candidates for admission when a spot became available. But beware: A bad guest is only a temporary problem; a prospective member who seems inadequate can always be fed an avoidance line. But a newly admitted poor member is the stuff of tragicomedy, and not a laughing matter. Candidates are easier to turn away at the door than to "kick out of bed," and these are sticky situations to handle. One respondent reported that her group eliminated an undesired person by telling her that the group had disbanded, which it did for a few months and then reconvened. So, try to choose your charter and new members as wisely as you can, given the above suggestions. And good luck.

CHAPTER 3

BEFORE THE *REAL* FUN STARTS: COST AND ORGANIZATION DETAILS

"Business is business."
—*Octave Mirbeau (French playwright, 1850–1918)*

*C*hapters 1 and 2 are packed with things for you to think about. Don't worry! The hows and whens and the wheres will all fall nicely into place; the *who* has a bit more importance, but I gave you a lot to think about and that will fall into place, too. This section concentrates on what you can expect your venture into reading group membership to cost you in money and time, and it lays out a sensible approach to conquering the organizational details.

Organizing a reading group demands many of the same skills and attention to detail that other cooperative activities do—a school dance, a bowling league, a fund-raiser. These activities are dissimilar in specifics, but all require some joint decision making, some list making, paperwork, use of the mail and/or phone, and some attention to food and equipment. So it is with reading groups. Every group is basically the same in function but varies with individual specifics and needs.

After reading this section, make a list of the items that fit well with your needs for organization. Use your list as a guide as you proceed with your planning. Only through trial and error and trial will you be able to run a streamlined organization. Even our 200+-year-old government is still trying to get it right!

What Will It Cost Me?

The recent increase in interest in reading groups has generated a variety of phrases describing the experience. For example, one of my *Reading Women* partners, Kathy Gurvey, coined the phrase that being in a book club is the "intellectual sport of the nineties." Some hobbies, such as skiing, sailing, and knitting, incur costs and require advance planning. Yet all can be enjoyed solo or as a group activity. So it is with reading. The difference is that as a hobby, being in a reading group is a financially conservative choice.

YOU GET NOTHING FOR NOTHING

Could being in a reading group cost you nothing? Yes, conceivably. If all members lived within walking distance of each other and could communicate in person, the gasoline for transportation, postage for mailing notifications, even phone charges would be eliminated. If there are no children to consider, or if the meeting occurs when children are in school, or if the children are supervised by a different (and free) caregiver, *voilà!* No child-care costs. Now, if you lived within biking or walking distance of a library or a friend who owned the books your group was reading, and you could always borrow the book, the cost of book purchases could be eliminated. If you belonged to a member-led group in which no professional leader's fee had to be paid, and used the library to do some background reading about the author but never made photocopies of any material, your research would cost nothing. If your group decided to serve no food whatsoever (not even water), you could eliminate all food costs.

See how it can be done? Does that approach sound appealing? More realistically (and enjoyably), being in a reading group is going to cost you something. The scenario I painted above sounds like going on vacation in your laundry room to save the cost of coin-operated machines.

THE LIST

After reading the above you probably now have some idea about what costs you can expect to incur when you belong to a reading group: *Books* will be your major cost, then *leader fees,* if there are any. Those who host meetings will incur *food* costs. *Baby-sitter* fees may be part of your list, too. Others include the expenses of *notifying members, research/copying,* and any *transportation* (gasoline, cab, parking, public transportation). Several of these costs will vary by individual and by geographic location. The group and the policies you establish will determine others.

Food. Your decision about food—the kinds and the quantities—is cost variable. Some groups agree on a spending limit for refreshments. Members of other groups put money into a fund to cover the cost of refreshments for the year, and each host/hostess is allocated a certain amount.

You may want to eliminate food costs. This policy lends itself easily to groups that hold their meeting in public buildings, but the same policy can be extended to private homes. Don't feel that just because your group meets in a private home, you must incorporate food service into your plan. The idea of brown bagging or BYOF (bring your own food), so to speak, or no food at meetings, has some sound rationale to it. This is discussed at length in chapter 5.

Books. Total book costs will vary depending on whether you borrow from the library or a friend, or if you buy each book, and whether your group reads hot-off-the-press hardcover releases or waits for the paperbacks. There are readers everywhere who need to get their hands on those new releases ASAP. But for those whose priorities are ordered differently, they can wait in wild anticipation for the paperback release and delight in the financial savings. As well, individual likes and dislikes about hardcover versus paperback are a priority factor for some readers.

Many groups choose to read only paperbacks specifically because of the cost factor. My newsletter, *Reading Women*, features only works published in trade paperback for that very reason. Even so, I do hear complaints about the inching-up costs of paperbacks. For my own reading lists, I try to average $8 to $10 a book for a ten-month syllabus. Sometimes a paperback may cost a bit more, but many fine works of literature can be found for as little as $5.95.

Your group may choose to read only paperbacks that cost *x* dollars and not a penny more. Raise the issue of book costs at your organizational meeting. The objective is to reach a consensus on how much the cost of books will impact the choice of books. (There are other ways to save on book costs in addition to those mentioned here. See the section on book ordering in chapter 8.)

Caregiver/Baby-sitter. This is an issue appropriate to some groups and not to others. How you handle it will depend on the makeup of your group. Some groups hire a communal caregiver/baby-sitter for the children; others leave those arrangements to the parent. Every mother—oops, *caregiver*—has some little tricks up her/his sleeve to cut child-care costs.

Notifications. Sending notices to members is a cost. Some groups eliminate this by putting together a master list at the beginning of the season with member info, dates, locations, titles. Then everyone operates from this list unless otherwise informed.

Leader Fees. A member-led group eliminates leader fees. Groups that choose to hire a professional leader bear an additional cost shared among the members (more in chapter 9).

Location/Transportation. Traveling costs are a consideration for some—usually those in urban areas who incur parking fees, taxi fares, etc. How this is handled may be an issue for your organizational meeting.

One person should never spend another person's money, but I have to assume that if you've bought this book, you have the disposable income to cover the cost of a reading group's basic equipment—a book. So think of the cost of belonging to a reading group as you would the cost of participating in a sport, or taking a vacation, or getting a manicure or massage. Being in a reading group is a gift that you give yourself. Enjoy it. You, your mind, soul, psyche, and spirit deserve it.

Those Deadly Administrative Details

An up-to-date membership list should be in members' hands as soon as possible. This pronouncement may seem like I'm putting the cart before the horse, but a list gives a group a sense of reality, or order. Of course, changes will be made, but first there has to be a list to begin.

Some groups give the "keeper of the list" a title—secretary, leader, chairman, chairperson, cochair. On the questionnaire, Rena Cohen of Highland Park, Illinois, delineated her administrative duties: "Periodic updating and distribution of membership list and reading list. The president (that's me, and it's more of a joke than a title) does it." Donna Bass, in several different groups, wrote of the secretary of her neighborhood group: "She is most unusually organized; but for this individual, I believe the chores would be shared."

An updated, correct list of members with current addresses (with zip codes and apartment numbers) as well as home and office telephone numbers is a priceless gem. I can't overemphasize its importance. If you change your name, phone number, or address, be sure to tell your group's "secretary" and announce this information at a meeting so all can make a note of it. Keep your list current and correct.

The person who takes this job should be organized, patient, and, perhaps, have access to free copying or a personal computer. This job is not a life sentence. All the jobs that need to be done to make a reading group run smoothly can be designated as temporary or permanent, voluntary or elected, by group decision.

THINGS TO DO

Now let's put into list form what's just been described about reading group mechanics. These specific duties can be divided into as many individual jobs as your group decides. If you discover more, please inform me.

1. Organizing and keeping the member list
2. Selecting the books and recording that list
3. Determining rules and policies (some groups have written bylaws)
4. Distributing both lists to members
5. Determining the meeting place, time, date, and book to read for each month
6. Distributing that information
7. Disseminating any changes to that information
8. Checking on the availability of book selections, and/or the ordering of books for individual or group purchase
9. Paying for that book order
10. Collecting fees for books and other items
11. Deciding whether to be member-led or professionally led. If member-led, making other policy decisions; if professionally led, organizing a search-and-select committee
12. Determining a fee to pay a leader and collecting that fee from members
13. Collecting moneys for food and refreshments, if the group decides to pitch in collectively
14. Mailing timely reminders regarding meeting date, time, book, and location (and a food supplier if it's different from the host/hostess)
15. Purchasing postage, postcards or stationery for mailings
16. Hiring and arranging a place for the caregiver, and paying for services rendered
17. Paying any rental fees for meeting rooms
18. Notifying local newspapers or umbrella organizations (a church or synagogue, AAUW, Federation of Women's Clubs, etc., that may periodically publish bulletins or newsletters) of meeting specifics for timely publication
19. Mailing of copies of reading selections when appropriate
20. Collecting fees *may* necessitate the choice of someone to handle the money. Whether your group opens its own account or works out of someone's personal account is a decision you will need to make.
21. Keeping order at the meetings, if this is necessary
22. Having a person who will start the ball rolling to decide how all these decisions and more are going to be made

This may look like an overwhelming list of "to dos," but when you go through it as needed, you will see that what seems like a big chore now is really a small one that requires only a little time and organization. Again, trial and error. See what works right for your group. Every group, of what I guesstimate to be as many as 100,000 or more across the country, has developed some type of order and communication system. So you can, too.

Sometimes organizing a book group happens easily and spontaneously. You remember that old saying, "Where there's a will and there's somebody to get the ball rolling, there's usually a way to a reading group." Just for fun, let's eavesdrop on a small group of women who are in the early stages of reading group planning:

- "Okay, Laurie, you call the bookstore, make sure the books are available in paperback, and order a dozen each."
- "Sarah, can you line up a baby-sitter for two hours at Sharon's house?"
- "Is that okay, Sharon? You have that indestructible playroom that would be perfect for our kids when we're not around to watch them every minute."
- "I'll take the September meeting, so that won't be a problem."
- "Betty, can you take this list and organization letter and put them on your computer? Can you make copies and send one to all of us? Can you do it in the next two weeks so we can get an idea of how many people are willing to commit to this thing and are willing to pitch in $30 for the food?"
- "Who wants to hold on to the money and dole it out for the first four months? Karen, could you do that? Great. Anything else?"

Betty may ask, "What or who is going to cover the cost of mailing the letter and list? If I do it every month, which I'm willing to do for the time being, that's, let's see—$.29 times twelve—that's $3.48 a month for each member."

Back to the original speaker: Let's call her Sue. Sue says, "Then let's add a postage and handling cost to what everybody has to pitch in. That would make it, let's see—for four months, $3.50 times four equals $14, divided by twelve—that's a little more than a dollar more a person. Should we add that to the $30, or just take a dollar and some from the money for food?"

Sharon: "From the food money."

Maureen: "Why don't we reimburse Betty for the postage and see how it goes with the food for four months? Depending on how many people we have after four months, we'll be readjusting these figures anyway."

"Okay." "All right." "Good idea." And a decent beginning plan has been made by a handful of women.

At the September meeting this group will realize that they need a location for subsequent meetings. Some groups sign up for hosting well in advance; others take care of this spontaneously at one meeting for the next, notifying those not in attendance. All these details need attention, need a policy, or at least a precedent from which to diverge. Discuss, decide, revise accordingly. And have fun creating something out of nothing. If some of our national corporations ran as smoothly as some book groups, more stockholders and taxpayers would be pleased with bureaucracy. Reading groups work well under the democratic principles of one person, one vote—and policy for the good of the majority.

Perhaps you want to keep a little journal of your plans and their evolution over the years. A start-up group of young adults today could easily see the second quarter of the twenty-first century, and maybe even conduct a session on Mars or the moon. You could be the author of a book tentatively titled *The Oldest Living Reading Group Member Tells All.*

ASK AND YOU'LL GET AN OPINION

Here's what some of the questionnaire respondents said about their groups' administrative duties and how they were handled:

- "Both groups that I belong to have newsletters (not the book discussion groups but the parent organizations . . . i.e., Parker Newcomers and Mountain Pine Woman's Club). These newsletters contain information about all the club's interest groups, including time, place, book for book discussion, etc. Each year one group prints a booklet that contains each month's information. Members volunteer their homes and refreshments. Sign-ups are taken at the September organizational meeting. One member volunteers to take orders at the September meeting, collects all money, and then places our order with the local bookstore. We receive a 20 percent discount."—Jeane Lumley, Parker, Colorado.

Jeane started the Parker Newcomers Club Book Discussion Group eight years ago, and the other group has been a part of the local Federal Woman's Club for over a decade.

- A woman from Boston noted that in her group a committee of two or three people select the coming year's books. The group as a whole, at the end of each meeting, decides about the next meeting—who brings the food, where to meet, who facilitates, when it is.

- A very helpful Judy Robeck from Kihei, Hawaii, said, "Our library group was able to get books at special rates." Judy's group has a committed membership: "Distances are great. . . . [P]eople come because they are interested."

- Meredith Mullins of Melbourne, Florida, wrote, "Meetings are determined at the first meeting each year. We are given a schedule then. We order our own books and arrange our own child care."

- Anonymous: "Host of the meeting notifies anyone who missed the previous meeting. Everyone gets their own book."

- Nancy Feingold from Chicago said, "We decide when our next meeting is going to be held during the current meeting. . . . [D]ate changes are conveyed via a phone chain. . . . [N]o money is collected."

- A very helpful and articulate Rena Cohen of Highland Park, Illinois, said, ". . . [T]here is always a problem, especially in a group composed of friends, with *changing dates!!!* (Rena's emphasis). We have struggled with this several times, trying to accommodate members. But, inevitably, a change that allows one member to come makes it impossible for others to attend. So we try to stick to a simple rule: No date changes. We meet the third Thursday of the month unless it's a holiday or some other unusual circumstance."

- Sarah Simpson of Lombard, Illinois, said that any change in the set date and time is very rare, but is a group decision. "One person takes the [book] orders, orders and distributes the books. Children have access to nursery across the hall—no sitter. Women bring small babies. Notice of meeting in church bulletin and occasionally . . . in local newspapers." Sarah's female assistant minister started this group in 1988 for the young women of the church, but anyone is welcome.

- Madonna Hayes of West Milford, New Jersey, had a forthright answer. "She who chooses the book calls members [twelve to fourteen] to ask if they need a copy. She orders them from our nearby Annie's, where we receive a discount. The hostess calls all women a few days before the meeting to remind them where we will meet and to hear who can't attend."

Below and on the next page are some samples of a postcard and a computer printout that you might adapt for your group's needs.

BOOK CLUB NEWS

Book Club will meet
on Thursday, April 9th at 8:00 p.m.
We will discuss: The Things They
Carried
by Tim O'Brien

We will meet at:
Clara Red's
290 Branch Road
Buffalo Plain
633-1001

Take Route 6 1 mile South of Miller Pond to Newtown and turn left, go to Pineneedle and turn right. The house is on the right.

```
Book Group Thursday- Feb. 25 7:30
          Jenny Green
            4242 N. Dover
                 place

RSVP   476-0024

        Ceremony  by Silko
```

SOME JOB AND COST SPECIFICS

Secretary. A group "secretary" may be selected to send out the monthly postcards. Or each host/hostess may send them out for his or her meeting. Some secretaries or host/hostesses use cards previously self-addressed by each member, which saves time and work for the secretary. If this job is taken by one person for a year, you may consider making address labels or having each person address x number of cards or envelopes at a meeting early in your season.

Leader Fees. When a leader is hired by the group, the fees are divided equally among members. This is usually accomplished in one of two ways: The fee is divided among those who attend a particular session, or each member is responsible for her/his portion regardless of whether he or she attends. The second method is far superior in fairness to the first, and refers back to the issue of commitment. Being there, saying your fair share, and paying your fair share are the responsibilities of each member.

Treasurer. If a group decides to designate one member as treasurer, some headaches diminish. The treasurer can collect a fee from each person to cover the administrative costs of the group for an entire season. Moneys for postcards, food, leaders, child care, etc., can be kept in the treasurer's checking account or in a new book group account. Then the simplest method is for the treasurer to write a check to the secretary to cover the cost of the mailings and to the leader and caregiver to cover her/his fees.

Baby-sitter. Years ago I was part of a group that hired a baby-sitter for our preschool children. Sometimes the children were in the same home as the discussion; other times they were in a nearby home, depending on available space. Two methods of payment arose. In one case, only the mothers who shared the services of the baby-sitter split the fee. In another case, the sitter fee was incorporated into the membership fee for the book club, whether or not you needed to use the sitter. In this example, even though not everyone had a child to deliver to the sitter, there was always enough money in the kitty to cover the baby-sitter's fee without extravagantly burdening each young mother.

I feel archaic even bringing this up today. I have no idea what caregiver fees are or how much one would charge for a group of children. One thought, though: If group members do need a caregiver for their children, think about choosing a meeting time when preschool children are at their best. Years ago my group met from 9:30 to 11:30 A.M. and that worked out well—for the most part.

Additional Costs. At the far end of the reading group experience are costs for gifts members give each other for life-cycle occasions (weddings, births of children/grandchildren, contributions in memory of members' loved ones, or even in memory of a group member). And more extreme and expensive, but definitely in the realm of possibility, are the costs of trips that groups take together. Marcy of Western Springs, Illinois, recalled a bright book club memory. Hers was a member-led group, with each member taking a turn. When one member announced that she was moving to Phoenix, the rest kidded that "she was not getting out of taking her turn!" The more they joked, the more real it became. Eventually, everyone flew to Phoenix and discussed the book in the member's hot tub. This was a glorious week of being together (followed by years of fabulous memories).

I am the leader of a group that's been together—with minor additions and deletions—for fifteen years. For the last decade we have felt so closely bonded, even though our lives do not intertwine intimately on the outside, that we collect money periodically for the events noted above. Several times a year we may pitch in $3, $5, or $8 to celebrate or commiserate with a fellow group member.

Another peripheral cost sometimes occurs when a group member is vigorously involved in a charity and asks group members to contribute or to buy some fund-raising item. Over the years I've bought more mums, raffles, lox boxes, lilies, candy bars, and cookies, and written more checks to more charities that weren't on my priority list, than I care to remember. But I don't consider this a liability of my position. I see the group as a body of individuals who can impact some social cause through networking within the group. Occasionally, it costs some money.

So let's add it up. Averaging ten sessions over ten months, $10 for the book, $10 for the leader, $3 for refreshments, and $3 for a raffle or gift, and your book club adventure may cost you $260 for the year. If your group is member-led and gifts are not part of your style, your major cost is your book purchase—$100 or so a year, or less if you borrow from a friend or your local library. If your group sends out postcards, don't forget to include your $2.90 share for postage. If each host/hostess supplies food independently, when it is your turn to host, plan to spend anywhere from nothing to $20 for refreshments and up to $50 or more for a meal, depending on how elaborate you want to get.

Don't worry about getting all these things accomplished. And it doesn't matter how each is done—just work out a way that is best for you and your group.

I am reminded of a revelation I had when I was a young girl of about seven and just beginning to sleep over at friends' homes. Wow! The things you can learn about human nature at a friend's house! When Aileen and I sat down to eat breakfast and I was served my bowl of oatmeal, I thought the world had turned topsy-turvy. In my home we poured our own milk and sugar on an unshaped blob of oatmeal and stirred it through at will. At Aileen's house, the cereal was molded into a central hill with the milk floating like a moat around it. And they ate it that way—not mixing it together! That overnight and breakfast helped me understand that not everybody did things the way *we* did at my home, and that was okay. Now that I've told this, it seems like a dumb way to make an obvious point— that each reading group may do things differently, but all will, in the end, "eat the same oatmeal."

CHAPTER 4

RACHEL'S RULES OF ORDER

"The errors of a wise man make your rule,
Rather than the perfections of a fool."
—*William Blake*

$\mathcal{S}$ince one of the major themes in literature is the concept of order, we should not be surprised that order is important in our group reading experience as well. *Lord of the Flies, King Lear, A Thousand Acres, Nineteen Eighty-Four, My Son's Story, A Doll's House, Ordinary People* are literary examples of families or groups of individuals attempting—and experiencing the consequences of their efforts—to devise order. Societies and families run well, or not so well, depending on the way order is established, maintained, or imposed.

The Massachusetts Bay colony in its 1641 *Body of Liberties* set forth some rules, including "If any man after legal conviction shall have or worship any other god, but the lord god, he shall be put to death."

Now that's one way to achieve order—scare it into being with the threat of death. Although that method from our American heritage dates back over 350 years, we cannot deny that it still exists in societies today. But that is not the tactic I suggest using in your reading group. The best approach is a democratic one, whereby the majority of individuals agree upon those rules that are important to the maintenance of order and well-being in the group.

When I mention the word "rule," I don't necessarily mean one brought up, voted on, and then written in stone. I mean procedures that help establish foundations and set perimeters everyone is comfortable accepting. Of course, these rules can be changed or amended in any way the group deems appropriate.

Below are some rules, or "Rachelisms," that I enact within the groups I organize and that I suggest to you for consideration. Some are included because I have learned about them from other people's reading group experiences.

1. *No smoking.* This rule is important because smoke bothers some people, and because of all the fuss about secondary smoke and its effects. I play dictator on this one when I start a new group. Nobody has ever voiced objection. Those who want to smoke may do so outside or in an adjacent area, depending on the feelings of the host or hostess.

2. *No children.* This means children who could be a disturbance. Some questionnaire respondents said that children are welcome at their meetings because the atmosphere is very loose and informal. Consider what kind of atmosphere you want to achieve before setting a policy on children. I'm a purist on this one. I want to eliminate all possible intrusions to afford participants the best opportunity to clear their minds for discussion.

However, I am well aware that this ideal situation cannot be effected all the time. Carol McKegney from Petaluma, California, told me that children ages five to thirteen play while her group meets one evening a month. "The children are distracting at times, but usually they go off and play."

During many an evening group, the dad has brought the children home from dinner or a diversionary outing and put them to bed while the mom is hosting. The children's entrance calls for the discussion to be put on hold while they hug and kiss Mom and say good night to her and anyone else they know well.

Let me suggest to parents of little ones who may need attention during the discussion time: Teach them to respect your activity. "This is Mommy's/Daddy's meeting. Come in and say good night to my friends and me, and then off to bed with you. I'll come into your bedroom later when everybody leaves to kiss you again while you're sleeping" (or some variation thereof). Children coming in to say good night, waking up from a nap, coming home from school, or playing (and then crying) in the next room need a parent's attention. But a parent's involvement in a meeting at home is a good way for a child to learn respect for other family members' rights and the expected boundaries of his or her behavior.

3. *No tardiness.* Both in my private and professional life, I am an on-time person. If a group wants ten minutes to organize, get refreshments, or make announcements, that's fine. However, if a group wants to chitchat for longer than ten minutes, I suggest that they arrive earlier or stay later and socialize then.

Please note: Many groups congregate early to socialize before the discussion begins. Some of these groups send out reminder cards that specify this tradition. An example: "Coffee and . . . at 9:15 A.M. Discussion begins promptly at 9:30 A.M."

Whether you hire a professional or are member-led, members should know that the designated discussion starting time needs to be respected. You are starting on time—not when the socializing dies down and not when the last person straggles in. Latecomers should just quietly sit down and integrate into the discussion. When someone does arrive late, I usually say, "Hello, glad you are here. Please get a drink and a snack and join in the discussion." And when that person sits down, I say, "We're talking about . . . " and try to bring him or her into the discussion that is already in progress.

4. *No pets.* Unless everyone in the group agrees that pets are okay, I think they should be kept out of the discussion area. I've seen very large dogs lick and paw participants who definitely did not want that attention. I've seen fear activated in several folk. Some people experience allergic reactions because they weren't forewarned and didn't take the proper medication. Barks, growls, poking snouts, and swinging tails can be disruptive and annoying.

One woman always puts her dog in the basement, but we hear him whining throughout our discussion. One cat owner thoughtfully reminds the group ahead of time to alert the allergy sufferers and those who will carefully choose what they wear so as not to carry pet hair home with them. Let the group decide how it wants to handle pets.

5. *No extraneous noises.* These include vacuum cleaners, showers, music, and radios in other parts of the house. Turn them off during discussion time.

Scene: Tri-level home; our coats on bed in master bedroom; husband lying on sofa watching TV on the lower level; meeting in living room with food spread out on connected dining room table. All is okay here—the TV is not disturbing the discussion. However, when we were deeply engrossed in commenting on the father-daughter relationship in Barbara Kingsolver's *Animal Dreams* and had just taken a deep breath and given forth a sigh of recognition and resignation, in that very second of silence, the husband burst out with one of those hearty howls of laughter. We all knew it was in reaction to the television, but the moment was a curious one.

6. *No telephone.* Some people turn on answering machines. Some answer the phone, but leave the room to talk. Some say, "Can't talk now, having a meeting." Whatever your approach, just realize that the telephone and ensuing conversations are very disruptive to a discussion.

7. *Handiwork.* Some people are driven crazy by the distraction of another person crocheting or needlepointing during the discussion. The click of knitting needles happens to be *my* nemesis. One teacher always brings her papers to mark while she discusses. Bless her mind's ability to do both well.

8. *Movement.* Participants getting up, moving around, or refreshing their drinks do not bother me or the group process, if they stay keyed into the discussion. But if they move to a refreshment area and begin a private conversation, the group discussion suffers. I am firm on this one: There is no place for private conversation during a group discussion. Either move to another room, share your thoughts with the group, or save them for later privacy.

9. *Interrupting.* Groups handle interrupting differently. I've seen a "talking stick" passed around and have used one myself when the book demanded respect for each person's insight and response. Some groups encourage chaos, intense excitement, shouting matches. Some politely take turns. Some settle on a mixture of both. I hate to

miss anything anybody says, so when people start talking all at once, I usually say, "Wait, wait. Now remember what you wanted to say, but let's take turns." Sometimes thoughts are forgotten, but the discussion process does not break down. I have found that often my role goes beyond facilitator to parliamentarian, and my groups appreciate that egalitarian approach. I've observed other leaders handle this situation—one glares at the intruder; another tries to carry on more than one conversation. Take your pick.

10. *Atmosphere*. A cozy, well-lit area in which everyone has a comfortable place to sit and can see each other directly is the ideal setting. I prefer a circular arrangement because it is so conducive to conversation. One group with twenty-five members still meets in private homes. They usually set up chairs in rows to accommodate everyone. I try to place myself where I can see directly into everyone's face, but I still feel like a teacher in that setting. Some groups meet around a table.

11. *Reading the book*. Yes, the purpose of the reading group discussion is to talk about a book everyone has read, but occasionally this is not the case. What's your rule? Should that member come to the group or not? Some leaders say point-blank: "Don't come if you have not read the book." I don't feel the same way. I prefer that everyone come every time. However, if you have not finished the book, be prepared for the ending to be discussed in front of you; obviously the group cannot limit its discussion because someone has not finished the assignment.

Sometimes, when someone hasn't read very much of the book or if someone has read the wrong short story, I do a little exercise I call "fourth-grade book review time." I let people fill in the blank: "This book is about . . . " It's difficult to report a plot line objectively. Much interpretation, editorializing, and analysis come out of this exercise, and I find it a useful discussion tool when a member needs to be "filled in" on plot so that we can move on to form and function.

The people in my groups and I always have a good chuckle when, upon arriving at a location, I see someone sitting outside in a car or inside another room madly cramming in the last few pages. Ah, what busy lives we all lead!

12. *Guests*. Yes or no? "Yes" sounds hospitable and logical, but there are issues of confidentiality and comfort level to address. Who

would be welcome? A member's mother? father? sister-in-law? college-aged child? potential members? How many times?

I allow members to bring anyone they deem appropriate to be a guest, and I bend over backward to make that person feel comfortable. This reinforces the idea that everyone's opinion is important. Strangers who call me to inquire about my groups get invited once as my guest.

Once, however, when asked by a woman if her daughter could come, I ruled against it. The specific book to be discussed elicited personal and intimate responses and a guest, particularly a member's daughter, would have hindered free, comfortable expression. Another woman told me that a group member's mother visited her group once and continued to berate and argue with her daughter throughout the evening. Everyone was extremely uncomfortable. (As a matter of interest, mother-daughter groups do exist. The relationship is the prerequisite.) Discuss this question within your group.

Following are some questionnaire responses concerning the issue of guests.

- "They are welcome for one session. Then they have to join."
- "Anyone female who wishes to attend is welcome."
- "All members of [the umbrella organization] are welcome. Board could vote to accept member. No one has been turned down."
- "No rules. No guests have been invited."
- "We permit guests, but only if they have no intention of joining."
- "No rules, but they must pay in advance."
- "We require everyone, even guests, to have read the book."
- "Happy to have them and try to be on our best behavior so they'll come back. The group has been together for so long, however, that we have to make a real effort to include newcomers and not be insular" (thirty-year-old group, twelve to twenty members).
- "Out-of-town visitors are welcome, but we don't include others."
- "No rules—occasionally have a spouse sit in."
- "We welcome new members. People are encouraged to come even if they have not read the book." —Costa Mesa/Newport Beach, California, AAUW book group

One questionnaire response mentioned that John Blades, a writer for the *Chicago Tribune,* visited her group while he was writing an article on book groups. Another said that her group invites the author, if local, and when one accepted, it was very interesting.

13. *Taping the discussion.* Those who can't come to meetings will sometimes request that the discussion be taped. In this way, they feel they lose out a little less. Other members take care of this, usually placing the recorder close to me and I turn over the tape at the appropriate time. I will also sometimes tape a discussion for my own professional improvement. But the presence of a tape recorder can be unsettling to a group. If you want to introduce one into the group process, discuss it with the members. For some, anxiety is sometimes generated when speaking in the presence of a recording device. But this fear can be eased and members need not make a fuss. Plus, a recorder can be turned off and on at will for stories too personal to be granted recorded perpetuity. Once your group is in full swing, someone will come up with this idea. Make a mental note of how long it took for you to hear, "Oh, I'm so disappointed. I can't be at book club. Can you tape the discussion for me? I don't want to miss hearing what everybody has to say."

CHAPTER 5

FOOD!

$\mathcal{F}$ood service? Yes. Like weather outside, there is food at most reading group discussions. Let's begin with some examples on the lean end of the food service issue.

NONE OR ALMOST NONE

- An all-men's group in Evanston, Illinois, served coffee and cake at the end of its meetings. Coffee cups, plates, and cake were on the dining room table; the men were in the living room discussing the stories, without refreshments. Coffee and cake came only after the formal discussion ended, and the members considered those refreshments and the banter that followed a very important part of their evening.

- The discussions I facilitate at community centers, churches, and synagogues usually serve coffee only. In addition, some of these facilities will not permit beverages in their meeting rooms. The actual book group meeting then is held with no beverages or refreshments in hand.

- One group that meets in the library of the Saints Faith, Hope, and Charity Catholic Church in Winnetka, Illinois, serves nothing. But after their morning discussion the "core" group usually goes out to lunch and continues the discussion on a deeper, more personal level.

- At presentations in libraries or bookstores, coffee is also the standard and solo fare (sometimes cookies or a coffee cake will accompany).

- Private groups that meet in public buildings (bank conference rooms or university meeting rooms, for example) may encounter administrative policies concerning food. Check on this policy if a public facility is one of your ideas for a neutral meeting location. The Anteaters Readers Group that meets in a classroom or in the library or administrative building on the campus of the University of California, Irvine, brown-bags it and conducts its discussion over lunch.

A LITTLE BIT MORE

Obviously these meetings lack the glamour that accompanies food specially prepared and attractively served. But let me support this purist position. When deciding about food and the nature and quantity of it at your book club, be mindful that food really does *not* need to be present to meet the goal of literary analysis and/or social camaraderie. One woman said succinctly, "It wasn't necessary." Another told me she thought food was far too important an issue at her discussion group and that it took away from the main venue. She, like others, feels that the intellectual and mental stimulation, plus the social and interpersonal connections, can more than satisfactorily flow forth in an atmosphere where food is absent.

Also, criteria such as the economics of food purchases, shopping and preparation time, waste (okay, *waists*—I couldn't resist the pun), diets, social pressure, space limitations, and individual preferences may affect your decision about food at meetings and may influence your decision to eliminate the element altogether. This may seem a somewhat Presbyterian point of view. Here's the point: Food is an *optional* component of a book group. Assess the purpose of your group when considering the presence and amount of food.

If a new participant asks me what to serve, I suggest coffee and ice water, maybe some soda or juices, and perhaps fruit, cookies, or coffee cake. Maybe even cheese and crackers.

Why Food?

The truth as I see it: Food at meetings is a worthy addition. In some cases it is primary to the group process. Respondents in Virginia and in California spoke to the point: "I wouldn't want to be in a book club that didn't serve food!" Since most questionnaire participants said that food was *somewhat* or *very* important, I have a feeling that a majority of reading groups include food and beverages in their scheme.

Incorporating food into your group opens new dimensions. The presence of food creates a powerful dimension to a social gathering. Humans do not usually choose to dine alone; shared meals symbolically link, herald life-cycle events, promote stronger business associations, and welcome strangers. Also, food is emotionally bonding. If an event is important emotionally, symbolically, or spiritually, food will be present to confirm the event's ritualistic importance and inspirational essence.

Physical hunger has strong associations with the hungers of the mind. A mental tête-à-tête among intellectually invigorating men and/or women is a delicious appetite stimulant. Some foods may stimulate our natural endorphins, which give us a sense of comfort and calm. One professional woman always comes to my book group after work and dinner with some of the other members. Neat, tall, and trim, this woman is the epitome of professional success and exemplifies restraint. At one meeting, she devoured a dish of pistachio nuts with a sprinkling of chocolate candies and apricots. As she rose to leave, she said, "My whole life is based on control. Yet I come here every month looking forward to eating with wild abandon."

I try to create an atmosphere in my groups that allows each person to get in touch with that primal essence of her/himself that gets masked over by the demands of daily life. Food is an additional tool to delight the senses. The more stimuli provided at a meeting, the more accelerated and exciting the discussion. One woman called me the day after a meeting. The women in her group convene around a coffee table laden with an assortment of nachos, dips, veggies, fruit, popcorn, brownies, cookies, pretzels, etc. This woman couldn't stop laughing when she thought of the night before when every-body was nibbling and munching constantly throughout the discussion. "It was so noisy. Everybody was so busy eating and talking and reaching and chewing. I couldn't believe it," she said.

WHEN TO SERVE

Whether to serve food before, during, and/or after your meeting is an issue that will come up as you plan your group. I included this matter in the questionnaire and received varying responses.

- A brown-bag group eats during their discussion. Another group that meets at a restaurant to share a meal and a discussion talk about the book during and/or after their meal.

- Other groups that share meals together finish their meal before the discussion begins, bringing only coffee, etc., to the meeting area.

- Some hold their discussion around a kitchen or dining room table, enjoying the extra closeness and energy that seem to come to the discussion when seated that way, even though refreshments are not served at all.

- Some groups serve food and beverages before and after the meeting, but not during. One little story involved this procedure:

    I meet with a group of Chicago women who have been discussing books together for about six years. Ninety-five percent of the time, we discuss novels; this night we were discussing three short stories. Moving in and out of different pieces of fiction requires a greater amount of mental energy than staying with one piece for the whole session. Each separate discussion builds and peaks and cools down, and doing it three times is taxing for everybody. So I found it a humorous and telling moment when the hostess exited the meeting room and returned carrying the serving platter from which we had nibbled before the meeting began. As she plunked it down she said, "Okay, enough of that. What I really want to know is, what's your vote on this apple cake I made?"

    Certainly, the discussion was finished. The hostess was exercising her right to imply "enough mental exercise tonight." The group returned to its social chatter, all pleasantly satiated by the evening's literary/mental stimulation. What more could I hope for?

- One group of men and women in Hyde Park, a city neighborhood near the University of Chicago, takes great pride in the pomp and circumstance they afford literary criticism. They don formal attire and congregate for a grand feast over which they discuss their reading selection.

• In some groups certain foods, such as popcorn and veggies with dips, are served before and during the discussion. Then specially prepared dishes of some magnitude (desserts or hot, cheesy things) are served immediately after the discussion ends.

• Another group of women I dub my "gourmet luncheon group," with great homage paid to their culinary skills and resourcefulness. As this is one of the first groups that hired me when I turned professional almost twenty years ago, it holds a special place in my heart. In my experience this is a unique group, and I promised them I'd mention Sandy, the Barbaras, Judy, Lois, Royce, Jean, Ellen, and Ruth in this book because of our warm, close, and nostalgic association.

One Friday a month these women, all active in volunteer or professional careers, meet in their homes on a rotating basis to share a sit-down lunch. Never having more than eight members, because eight was the maximum that could fit around the smallest table when the group was in formation, the women serve a sumptuous formal repast usually with cloth, flowers, china, crystal, and silver, and going the full measure, with bread plates and butter knives, sometimes samovars. The meal is multicourse, the food is grand, and the scene is nothing short of old-world tradition. Sometimes I am invited for lunch, sometimes I join them after dessert for the discussion. These are local women whose children went to school with my children. We share community concerns and the concerns of life transitions. Coming to them gives me a chance to catch up on the local gossip that I miss because my head is stuck in a book so much of the time.

After such huge meals, it's amazing they can muster up brain power for a discussion, but most of the time they are able to cut right through to the essence of the book. The heavy meal takes its toll on the level of discussion, and even though theirs is not my most academic group, they read quality literature with me with a vigor surpassed by none.

However, a new member of this group *cannot* cook. She has broken the gourmet mold and, when it's her turn to hostess, serves trays of sandwiches and salads from a local store. Nobody cares, but she always gets a bit of kidding, especially when the frozen ice-cream bars are served for dessert! Maybe her actions are a hint of the future.

Let this little story be a lesson to those of you with visions of glorious, magazine-looking meals accompanying your book discussions. Too much food can dull the discussion and also can intimidate and/or tire group members. If you are uncomfortable with your group's food service policy, discuss it among the group members— as a group. Everyone should feel comfortable with the "level" of food served, and the food issue should not disproportionately overrun the purpose of the reading group.

As an aside, let me tell you that I have also heard of groups that take the exact opposite position on the depth of their book group discussions. They opt *not* to have a serious discussion at all. These groups eat and chat for half an hour before their fifteen minutes of extremely superficial discussion of the book that they all read. Then they return to food and social chatting for the duration. There is no "should"—only the desire for harmony. But I have been flattered by a lot of serious readers seeking me out to lead them after being intellectually dissatisfied with the too-social, not-serious-enough type of book groups.

THEMATIC FOODS

Several of the women in the "gourmet luncheon group" mentioned above plan their menu around the cultural influence of the reading selection. When asking her whether she would prepare Mexican food for Sandra Cisneros's *The House on Mango Street,* one member responded, "Oh no, we had Mexican the last time book club was at my house, or was it Chinese? What was the book we did? I do remember, I made something Chinese for the event." For the meal/discussion of Barbara Kingsolver's *Animal Dreams,* set in the fictional town of Grace, Arizona, Lois graced the table with a southwestern-colorful cloth and napkins, a bright flower arrangement, and a scrumptious shrimp-and-pasta dish (although I doubt the people of Grace would eat much shrimp). Even the salt and pepper shaker embodied the southwestern theme.

Madeleines have been served when discussing Proust. Custard and prunes when discussing Virginia Woolf's *A Room of One's Own.* Tea and scones for the English novel. Tea and fortune cookies for books with a Chinese setting. Southern food including fried green tomatoes for Fanny Flagg's popular *Fried Green Tomatoes at the Whis-*

tle Stop Cafe. Any book that has an ethnic or cultural identity could influence food choices, if your group is so inclined. This takes extra effort and extra creativity and adds a sensual, transportive element to the reading experience.

BEVERAGES

If your group decides to keep foods to a minimum, I still suggest supplying beverages. I've seen coffee (regular and/or decaf), tea (regular and/or herbal), punch, iced tea, lemonade, and carbonated drinks. I have seen wine and wine coolers, but no hard liquor and wouldn't suggest it. Water is an all-time favorite—and the price is right.

FOOD FAVORITES

Popcorn. Popcorn, popcorn—the all-time favorite. Cut-up or whole fruit. Cheese and crackers, breads and spreads, pretzels, nachos and salsa and guacamole, veggies and dips, brie with chutney and crackers, muffins, plus cookies, cakes, and pastry of any shape, size, fat, caloric, or sugar content are all common fare. Chocolate. Seasonal and holiday foods and candies are common. Licorice is also very popular.

Chocolate. If you're not allergic to it, any chocolate candy, especially those round little color-coated chocolate candies that are a standard at most meetings, constitute either an anticipated treat or an active temptation. Upon entering the meeting room, some women will unabashedly express their delight when they see a dish or bowl of them. One woman always has an emphatic remark: "Oh, I need my chocolate fix. I can't discuss my book without my chocolate." I remember when another woman offered the candies to her and she rolled over on her chair, pointed to her thigh, and said, "Why don't you just put it right there. It's going there anyway." We had a good laugh over that one.

One group that has dinner and a three-hour evening discussion serves "main dishes that will easily feed a large group (nine), like anything that can be served over rice or couscous. Often a Mediterranean theme exists." After dinner is the discussion, then dessert. ". . . Great desserts. The meal is definitely *not* low-fat!"

Paper and plastic products are easy and permissible, except to the conservationists in the group. Think about being prudently ecological and use regular silverware, plates, cups, or mugs. I've been in many homes where cloth napkins were used for just that reason. Paper plates and napkins, for that host/hostess, were an ecological no-no.

One evening I arrived at the meeting home at 7:58 for an eight o'clock meeting only to find the hostess walking away from the house carrying food packages. The woman's husband had arranged a business meeting at their home, so we were moving to another member's house. By 8:15, everyone had appeared at the new location, but I could not get the group settled down and the discussion convened because—all the food was not out yet! It kept coming out of the kitchen until the coffee table was filled with goodies: fruit plate, pretzels, popcorn, chocolate candies, licorice, and a beautiful chocolate-chip coffee cake (the recipe follows). By 8:30, we were on our way to eating and discussing—feeding our mouths, nourishing our minds and souls.

(Whenever there is a location issue for a meeting, I think of the musical *Guys and Dolls* and imagine a book group as a floating crap game. All we need is a place to gather roun' for a while.)

RECIPES

Following are some dishes that you may enjoy trying for your group.

CHOCOLATE-CHIP COFFEE CAKE

From Bobbie Michaels, Highland Park, Illinois

PECAN TOPPING
¼ cup sugar
1 teaspoon cinnamon
¼ cup chopped pecans

CAKE
¼ pound butter or margarine, room temperature
8 ounces cream cheese, room temperature
1 ¼ cup sugar
2 eggs
1 teaspoon vanilla
2 cups all-purpose flour
1 teaspoon baking powder
½ teaspoon baking soda
¼ teaspoon salt
¼ cup cold milk
1 cup chocolate chips

Preheat oven to 350°F. Grease 9″-by-3″ springform pan; set aside.

Prepare Pecan Topping; set aside.

In a large bowl, cream butter or margarine, cream cheese, and sugar. Add eggs one at a time, beating well after each addition.

Add vanilla, flour, baking powder, baking soda, and salt. Mix well. Stir in cold milk and chocolate chips. Mixture will be very thick. Pour into prepared pan. Sprinkle with Pecan Topping.

Bake 50 to 55 minutes or until wooden toothpick inserted in center comes out clean. Let cool 15 minutes. Remove outside ring from springform pan and cool cake completely.

Cake may be frozen.

COFFEE TORTONI

From Beverly Pirtle, Huntington Beach, California

2 egg whites
2 tablespoons instant coffee powder
¼ teaspoon salt
4 tablespoons sugar

2 cups heavy cream
½ cup sugar

2 teaspoons vanilla
¼ teaspoon almond extract
¾ cup finely chopped toasted almonds

Beat egg whites with coffee and salt until stiff but not dry. Gradually beat in the 4 tablespoons of sugar. Continue beating until stiff and satiny.

Whip cream separately. Add sugar, vanilla, and almond extract. Continue beating until stiff.

Fold cream mixture and one-half of the toasted almonds into the egg whites. Fold until well blended.

Spoon into 12 paper cups for a large dessert. Insert into muffin tins, or spoon into smaller decorative paper cups if you wish a "taste" portion. Sprinkle remaining almonds on top. Put in freezer.

HINTS

1. Tortonis can be made well ahead of time and frozen. When preparing for the freezer, wrap individually in plastic wrap and then place in a freezer container.

2. Tortonis can be placed in decorative paper cups depending on the occasion.

TACO DIP

From Madonna Hayes, West Milford, New Jersey

Spread an 8-ounce package of cream cheese in a pie pan. Spread one can of chili over the cheese. Grate sharp cheddar cheese on top, covering the chili completely.

Bake at 350°F until the middle bubbles. Serve with tortilla chips.

FRESH VEGETABLES WITH DIP

Twenty-four hours before serving, combine the following and refrigerate:

1 cup mayonnaise
⅛ teaspoon curry powder
2 teaspoons freeze-dried chives
½ teaspoon salt
2 tablespoons grated fresh onion

Serve with a variety of cut-up fresh vegetables, including carrots, celery, green pepper, mushrooms, zucchini, broccoli, etc.

MEATBALLS IN SWEET SAUCE

MEATBALLS:
1 pound lean ground beef
1 egg
⅓ cup flavored bread crumbs

Combine above ingredients, form into walnut-size meatballs, and brown in oven.

SAUCE
3 ounces grape jelly
¼ cup water
3 ounces chili sauce
1 teaspoon dry mustard

Cook in a double boiler until completely mixed. When meatballs are brown, add them to sauce and serve.

CHAPTER 6

GROUP COMPOSITION

$\mathcal{T}$hroughout the previous chapters I have emphasized the importance of group dynamics. Since lots of things can happen in a group experience, I have learned to expect the unexpected when putting human beings together. What would you answer to the question, What is the primary goal of reading groups?

I guess that most answers would fall somewhere between "literary criticism" and "being in a group." Those of you who may have answered "group discussion of a good book" are on target because that answer connotes literary criticism via group process. Whichever way you arrive at it, both parts—literary criticism and being in a group—are intensively intertwined. One could not be accomplished without the other. Discussing a book by yourself is analogous to the sound of one hand clapping.

In the first chapter I asked you to close your eyes and picture the people around you in your reading group, visualizing their gender and marital status. These categories of group identity are very important to most group participants. "I want people my own age." "I want an all-women's group." "I like a chance to talk to men on an equal footing." "My wife wanted me to come to her book group but I refused, so I said I would go see a movie with her and then come to this discussion." "The women excluded the men from their book groups, so we started our own." (Although this book focuses on reading groups, I've included some comments from film discussion groups, because they seem to attract men more easily than a reading group.)

Below is a list of some of the gender and marital status book group variations I've experienced, and some comments.

ALL WOMEN

This grouping comprises the vast majority of reading groups around the world. We have *Reading Women* subscribers in foreign countries. Several of their groups are comprised of professors' wives who group together to form a good old American book club; several are military personnel or wives craving intellectual stimulation. Call it part of the tide of history, a sociological phenomenon, a female bonding, or a feminist reclaiming of empowerment accomplished through group processing—all-women groups are increasing in numbers. After asking respondents to check off gender groupings (female, male, coed, or couples) on the first page of the questionnaire, I later asked them if they had ever discussed changing the gender character of their group. The vast majority said no. I asked why they had chosen a group of their gender structure and received the following responses.

- "AAUW is open to men. However, no men have come to [any] meetings." —Beverly Pirtle, Huntington Beach, California

- "I enjoy the all-female camaraderie and discussion. Bright, funny women who like to read and be around other women." —Carol McKegney, Petaluma, California

- "For me, an all-female group is very supportive, and we are all interested in similar books." —Anonymous

- "A male component would be interesting, but not all the time. This is simply where my interest lies and I feel men and women have frequently differing interests that would limit my total enjoyment. We started as a feminist 'action network' . . . [then] we dramatically decreased the size and turned into a reading/discussion group [because] we wanted a more personal slant to our meetings." —Ann Goldman, Oak Park, Illinois.

Ann commented further: "This group is very diverse—ethnically, economically, and in terms of age."

• "We have always been clear that we wanted this to be exclusively a female forum. Most of us figure we spend enough time with men elsewhere. My husband wanted to join for years, and he finally started his own." —Marla Green

• "I have heard of a couples' group, but the dynamics of the group are very different from that of our all-female group. We do not have to contend with sexism." —Anonymous

An elderly city woman, a Great Books group participant for nineteen years, chose her group (a class at a community center) because of availability and convenience. The majority of women in that short-fiction class are widows, which speaks to another dimension of book group demographics.

Occasionally a syllabus will be gender-specific. Sarah Simpson's church group for young mothers and working women almost exclusively reads books about "the experience of women in different times and cultures." She stated, "We don't read about women in suburbia."

Other respondents noted variously that they were interested in reading only female authors, were not aware that coed groups existed, thought that only women showed an interest in reading groups, were interested only in a "friendly group [and] congenial people" and didn't care about the gender of the members, or have talked about including men but nothing ever came of it. Because women's lifestyles are radically different by generation and by financial necessities and by options available, women meet both in the daytime and the evening. All the men in my groups attend only evening time slots.

ALL MEN

I observed an all-men's group in the Chicago area and I've heard of another, although I'm sure there are more. Male bonding is as trendy today as women's. Reading groups operate for any population as one way of abating normal human feelings of isolation and loneliness. It's ironic that women are in the forefront of the reading group movement, when traditionally women were excluded from political, intellectual, and literary discourse. As far as men being included in women's groups, the women respondents (to the questionnaire) said overwhelmingly that their group never considered nor would ever consider turning coed.

I have seen men assume two different demeanors toward me when our group interaction first begins. They'll either give me a gender-blind chance or patronize and distrust me until I prove that I know what I'm doing and what I'm talking about. As for women and men working together in a reading group, sometimes old, ingrained prejudices get in the way of goal accomplishment. "My wife says I'm wrong, but . . ." "Maybe I shouldn't say this when men are present, but . . ." "You wouldn't know this because you are a man/woman, but . . ." Nonetheless, it has been my privilege to discuss film and literature with sensitive, intelligent, and introspective men. I have learned new ways of seeing the literature because I have gotten to see it through the eyes of men, each of whom is also an individual, bringing individual insight as well as gender-oriented perspectives to our common, shared reading.

James Elesh of Evanston, Illinois, who started his own all-male group, responded, "The women's book groups seem to exclude men. [It was] easy to find men who missed using their intellect." I like that comment. It reminds us that literature serves as a release from everyone's daily grind, whatever that daily grind may be and whoever may be grinding it. His group discusses two to four short stories per meeting, and meetings occur every four to six weeks depending on collaborative scheduling. The short stories are selected by the host, and copies with reminders of necessary information are sent to each member with ample preparation time. The host leads the discussion. The night I observed this group, they discussed stories from an Irish collection, perhaps because the host was Irish. One story was by a female author; two were by men. The participants couldn't have cared less about the sex of the authors.

COUPLES

I lead a film discussion group made up of couples who are friends. They have a great time. The men want to discuss the *Raging Bull,* macho-type movies; the women lean more toward gentler films. I assigned them *Thelma and Louise* not long ago, but several "macho" men had headaches the night we discussed it. Those present generated a superb discussion of an extremely important film. Several other professional leaders in this area facilitate discussions of films with couples. It seems to be the popular intellectual and social thing to do around here with one's spouse or significant other. I have also led a couples' group that discussed only short stories. Once I was asked to lead a couples' discussion as after-dinner entertainment, similar to a salon-type discussion of bygone days, and a stimulating time was had by all.

COED

Coed basically translates to anybody—singles, couples, or one of a couple. One man in the coed group I lead can attend only if we don't schedule the group on the third Wednesday night of the month, because that's when his wife's reading group meets and he's needed at home with the children. Adult singles seem to enjoy the intellectual element mixed with the socializing. My current coed group is fairly tame, although I know of coed groups that are raucous events.

In answer to my questionnaire plea ("Please relate a particularly humorous, startling, or sad vignette about your group"), one woman wrote of her Chicago coed/couples crowd of nine: "What is most startling and/or humorous about our group is the fact that this collection of otherwise mature, professional intellects can also be downright raunchy. It is not unusual for us to discuss sex for a good part of the evening, or for certain members to make noises with various body parts. [However,] a certain element of levity is present during every evening." She also notes, "Some romantic pairings have developed as a result of our association with one another. Also, those who started out as mere acquaintances are now much closer."

This is the joy of being in a book group that I want to emphasize. Everyone—man, woman, parent, teenager—has an equal standing in the process of literary analysis. I would like to think that as a professional facilitator I am identity-factor-blind, but I know that I, just like everyone else, has a set of prejudices subconsciously or consciously operating. Humanitarian acceptance of all participation is the order of the day in reading group discussions.

Personalities: Love and Hate

This section may be redundant to your knowledge of human beings and different personality types. However, as you identify certain personality types in your group, you will note those who appear on my list of the imagined "perfect member" and those who may prove otherwise.

The Verbose One. Verbosity is okay if others also have ample chance to speak. If discussions are dominated by a few, generate ideas within your group about how everyone who wishes to speak has that chance. The chair of one New Jersey group has addressed problem verbosity by determining that every member has ten minutes to present a part of the discussion.

The Interrupter. An irritating variation of the Verbose One. In these cases, I break in. "Now don't interrupt. What were you saying, Natalie?" Or, "Wait, let Michael finish." For the most part, interrupters are enthusiastic rather than rude. Try to discern the difference and maintain everyone's right to complete his or her thought.

The Reticent One. Some personality trait prevents some members from jumping into the discussion process. It may take a while for the "blockage" to disappear, or it may never do so. Perhaps a directed, proactive move on your part, or general words about freedom of expression, will be helpful. At least this person is engaged in the process; that's a big first step, whether or not she or he is verbal. I encourage you to try to bring out the quiet one. You may be helping to give birth to a new voice, one never tried out before. But be careful. Deep-seated poor self-concepts or just plain timidity are exorcised very slowly. A comfortable, accepting atmosphere is the best beginning.

The Rambler. This person makes great (or not-so-great) points, but stacks so many of them on the table that they crash from their own weight. Nip this in the bud and simultaneously control the speaker: "Whoa! You're making a lot of points. Let's dig in on one point and go from there." These members are assets; you need to use their ramblings to the group's advantage.

The Self-Deprecating One. "Well, I'm probably wrong, and I don't know if I should even bring this up, but, well, maybe . . . " Old negative self-perceptions may be difficult to break, and breaking them is not the purpose of the group. Reinforce the legitimacy of this person's comments.

The One Who Doesn't Get It. Yes, ladies and gentlemen, we will find those who enter into the discussion group process but, for any number of reasons, shouldn't have. Several respondents made note of those who "just don't get it," and their group's ensuing acts of forbearance and extraction.

The Silent One. There are those who like to attend—and listen—and that's all. My place as a paid facilitator is more tenuous on this issue than for those of you starting or joining a member-led group. I feel that if a person pays his or her money and just wants to listen, that's his or her prerogative. But, if you're in a member-led group, you may find that a continually silent person may affect the group process. If this is a problem, talk about it.

The Angry, Troubled Person. Those who constantly carry their emotional baggage on their sleeves may let their personal problems color everything they see and read. These members need to be gently handled, but handled nonetheless. Grief can create a similar syndrome. Be mindful and sensitive. Sometimes a private suggestion of professional therapy can help. Loving, supportive book group members may be the perfect catalyst for a person who feels unloved and overwhelmed with life to seek help. For your group's sake, remember that the group goal takes priority over individual needs. The process needs to run smoothly for all.

The Logical One. Anyone with a background in science, math, or music can bring a logical perspective to a discussion. This is the pragmatist/realist of your group. Embrace this person and incorporate her or his vision.

The Laugh-a-Minute Person. Quick-witted, satirical, intelligent, doesn't take anything too seriously, and doesn't impede the group. Be joyful if he or she shows up at your group.

The Ever-So-Earthy, Honest One. A relative of the Laugh-a-Minute, this person usually says the things that you are thinking. What a delight and a relief.

The Philosopher. May quote the theories of great thinkers and great philosophers (Nietzsche, Plato, Kierkegaard, Buber, Santayana, y Gasset, Mao, Marcus Aurelius, Whitehead, Emerson, Marcuse, Buddha, etc.); will insert abstract perspectives.

The Social Scientist. Always nice to have an educator, therapist, psychologist, etc., in the group. He or she has an uncanny ability to synthesize into concrete terms what you fumble to express about human behavior and the mind.

The Humanist/Moralist. Carries the banner of progressive moral humanism; could also be called the theosophist, if your group sees morality through the filters of organized religion; should not be confused with the social scientist whose passions may have been dampened by academic studies.

The Devil's Advocate. Say one thing, he or she will debate the opposite viewpoint. Why? Why not?

The One Who Is Always Right. There is no one right way of seeing, interpreting, or analyzing literature. Extreme pedantry and didacticism are out of place in reading group discussions. Sometimes this person will verbally attack another member for the stand taken, and the atmosphere can fire up to boiling level. I've heard of physical as well as verbal blows.

The Egoist. Too many egos spoil the discussion. I like to remind those in my groups that egos "need to be checked at the door." One woman from New Jersey who describes the tone of her discussion as casual/controversial added that in her group, *"no one* tries 'one-upmanship.'" (She proudly listed the academic credentials of some of her comembers: two Ph.D.s, two retired English teachers, two with literary degrees [one French, one German].) As this woman notes, "One-upmanship has no place in a reading group discussion. The individuals of the group, and the group as a whole, never win when 'winning' is the goal of one participant."

The Bigoted One. Get a life, Archie. Wake up and smell the multi-culturalism before the twenty-first century arrives! There are fifty-eight languages spoken in the schools of California; we don't look like the founding fathers anymore, and don't forget that they came here because of their own desire for freedom and civil liberties. Reading groups can open the American mind.

The Pollyanna. American writer Eleanor Porter (1868–1920) created her, and now some groups get to enjoy or tolerate or shatter her (or his) outlook. Cherish the optimists; our bright and cheery future needs every one it can get.

The Digresser. This person plunges into an unconnected or extremely tangential story, and usually for an inordinate amount of time. Make a rule: All personal stories should be relevant to the literature and limited to five minutes. I call these "episiotomy stories" because of their perceived urgency according to the speaker. My groups and I usually listen politely, but when too much has been said about too little, it's already past time to look at my watch and say, "You have sixty seconds to wrap up."

The Imaginative One. Don't fence this one. Just tag along and have fun getting your mind stretched.

The Parliamentarian. If you need one, hope that one naturally emerges from your rank-and-file membership. If not, the person could be member-designated on an annual basis. Listen to this "leader" to maintain order; otherwise, you'll have to end up with something like the ten-minute policy they're trying in New Jersey.

*I*n summary, try to find people for your group who enjoy a good debate and who also respect the opinions of others. As one woman said, "[M]ake sure the members of the group have the potential to get along." Problems arise, not so much from opposing viewpoints, but from frictional personality types, problems in members' lives external to the group, and any number of other reasons. I as the leader, and you as the member, have the right and responsibility to define your goals and to act accordingly. Conflict that creates tension and discomfort erodes a group's unity and purpose. Frankly, if adults cannot control themselves long enough for an intellectual or social discussion, then perhaps the group would be better off without them. The majority of questionnaire respondents commented about the absence of decorum problems and their good fortune at having members who get along. So the odds are with you.

CHAPTER 7

THE ART OF DISCUSSION

"One of the more enlightening truths one learns
from books is the exacting presence of the mystery
of life."   —*Unknown*

"If a book comes from the heart, it will contrive to
reach other hearts."   —*Thomas Carlyle*

Our Experiences with Discussions

As described in chapter 6, the aim of a discussion is twofold, as
"literary criticism through collective action." Our understanding
of the reading material is initially governed by the subjectivity of
the isolation in which we originally encounter the book. In other
words, we all read alone. And while we are alone reading, each of
us "sees" the text through a complex set of very personal images,
and each of us brings our own strong social identity to our encounter with the text.

In the group discussion process, members work together as a
close-knit team. By combining individual strengths in personality and areas of knowledge, the group becomes smarter and more
effective than the sum of the individuals. Yale psychologist Robert
Sternberg has called this unification of traits a "group IQ." When
individuals are harmoniously combined, the result is a smoothly
working, powerfully effective group.

Following is an exercise your group can try to emphasize the value of team effort. This exercise does not negate the existence of individual differences; instead, it utilizes varying personal traits as the primary means to goal achievement.

Take an ordinary rectangular or square piece of cardboard (something like a shirt board will do). It should be at least 8½″ by 11″. Cut it up into at least fourteen or sixteen pieces, in odd shapes like puzzle pieces.

Scatter the pieces on the floor. Then ask four group members to get on the floor and put the pieces together. Have the rest of the group sit back and observe silently. Varying dimensions of domination and cooperation will surface, each affecting the ease and speed with which the task is completed. One team member may begin to question methodology, assign tasks, and direct others. Another may willingly take orders, while the third may refuse to complete the task. Another may want to take over the whole task, and then want all the credit.

I've done this with several small groups when I have become their facilitator. Much about the goals of a book group discussion can be learned from this exercise. Obviously, the most effective way to complete the puzzle exercise is via enthusiastic cooperation among the team members, perhaps with the addition of verbal encouragement and reinforcement. This applies to a book discussion as well. In your book discussion group, *be supportive.* If you encourage and help each other, then the performance level of each participant improves significantly and the level of discussion becomes more exciting and rewarding. The value of participation, the longevity of a group, and the bonding that is an outgrowth of participation are results directly proportional to the care given to the spirit of the discussion.

LISTEN—PARTICIPATE

It's been estimated that we spend nearly half of our waking hours listening, but that our efficiency rate is only 25 percent! Being a good listener is a very important and powerful component of being a reading group member. If everything that is said in your discussion applies in some way to the book subject, you don't want to miss hearing any of it.

The following are key elements of effective listening. To polish your listening skills, in anticipation of your participation in a reading group, pick one or two things to work on during encounters with friends, family members, and coworkers.

1. Look at the person who is speaking. Maintain eye contact. Try to concentrate completely on the speaker.

2. Fight the tendency to interrupt. Practice totally listening while avoiding mentally formulating a verbal response before the speaker has even finished. Just listen and allow the other person to talk and finish what he or she is saying.

3. Stay relevant. When the speaker says something that triggers an unrelated subject or idea in your mind, squelch the desire to express it unless it relates to the core of the discussion at hand.

4. Perhaps give the speaker some subtle signs of being heard and understood—little nods, *mmmm's*, etc.

5. Ask questions.

6. If your mind wanders, refocus, ask for repetition: "I'm sorry. I heard you say 'food' and my mind wandered. Would you please repeat the point you were making?"

I have developed one way to begin a discussion that affords everyone an opportunity to listen and to speak about whatever ideas have been brewing in anticipation of the meeting. As I sweep the room, everyone is given a moment to articulate his or her reaction to, and analyses and criticisms of, the book. Often comments go flying, and I'm not sure how much everyone else hears or understands, but I listen carefully, ask clarifying questions, and write down key phrases the speaker has used. Many times this rapid flow of ideas and gut responses becomes a primary working agenda for group discussion. Ideas grow from this technique, and the group comes to life.

You may want to try this procedure with your group. Perhaps a designated leader can be the secretary and record what is being said. Listening is crucial in this exercise. Once the volcano of spontaneous responses ebbs, the discussion can build from that foundation. Any generative method your group develops to begin a discussion is fine. Heed the words of Horace: "He who has begun has half the work done."

My method for beginning a discussion, and my procedures, vary depending on the desires of the group, the demands of the book, and my mood. Usually I let the book dictate how the discussion begins. A new author may need introduction. An unfamiliar genre may need background. The setting of the book (the time and place in which it was written) may need explanation. These procedures are leader-directed. But turnabout is fair play, so many times a discussion simply needs a kick-start question such as "So, what did you think of this?" or "Well?" or "Did we like this book?" to become member-directed. Sometimes asking, "Is there anyone who didn't like this book?" creates the perfect entrée into a controversial discussion on its merits. "Has anybody been to?" elicits members' verification of the novel's place. And we go from there.

You are beginning a collaborative give-and-take that supports, challenges, and expands thoughts and responses of each group member. Remember, your questions and responses should emerge from the text, and discussion should be redirected back to the text.

To analyze a text (its form and function) and discuss its personal applications, I offer the following guidelines: *Clarification. Penetration. Assessment.*

Frequently in group participation, comments are in direct contradiction to the facts presented in the text. If you need to, go back into the text and search for the words to achieve validation or correction. *Clarification* of members' understanding can be gained by asking questions with only specific answers. "What does Snow White take a bite of?" "Who gave it to her?" "What happens to Snow White when she bites the apple?" "Does she take only one bite?" The collective substantiation of facts is a continual process in my groups. Vacillations in memory, fact retention, and personal recoding are caught and corrected in a nonjudgmental manner; usually jokes are made about brain cells failing, and we move on.

Ask questions that substantiate and enlarge comprehension of the action and embark on *penetration* into meaning. "Why did the woman give Snow White the apple?" "Why did Snow White take a bite of it?" Answers will easily be forthcoming but may vary from person to person as ways of comprehension are expanded. "The stepmother gave her the apple because she didn't want Snow White to go hungry. She said so." "No, she gave her the apple because she wanted to do away with her. She was jealous of her beauty after the mirror told her that Snow White was prettier than she was." The more your members penetrate into the possibilities of interpretation, the more expansive the comprehension.

All of the above becomes more significant when you begin to assess meaning. Appraisal or *assessment* tends to illuminate the perceptions of each member, and probably takes up the majority of discussion time. Assessing action engenders value judgments—ethical and moral evaluations that are all dependent on individual personalities, experiences, mind-sets, and knowledge. "Was the stepmother wrong in giving Snow White the apple?" "Does this symbolize an evil act on her part?" "Does this mean that she was an evil woman?" "Does this story or myth influence the way we perceive stepmothers?" By turning reactions or comments into questions, discussion of meaning can be extended almost limitlessly. Asking "How?" in regard to the last question addresses the influence that "story" has on our lives.

When a forceful participant announces an evaluation as the *only* interpretation possible, I clarify with the query, "Perhaps you are projecting your own opinion? Let's hear from others." Projection of self is quite distinct from interpreting causality of character action. Be careful.

The fairy tale of Snow White can foster discussion of the origins, mutations, rationales, and uses of fairy tales. The beautiful adolescent girl in her emerging stage can be discussed in terms of her need for a man to save her or in terms of the feelings of her disenfranchised, aging mother. (In this case, stepmother—why?) With these few examples you can see how the discussion can flow from the history of the genre to the author's intent, to the flow of the plot, to the reflection of the human condition that every participant has experienced in some variation. And we haven't even discussed those seven adorable little guys (men, dwarves, monks, isolates, spirits, eunuchs?) in monklike robes who find her, succor her, abide with her, but "save" her for the handsome prince. Themes of good and evil, reward and punishment, cycles of life, prescribed gender and hierarchical roles, and more may emerge in the discussion.

The more "lenses" you look through, the more you can see. But take heart. This requires time and effort, and for some, learning new skills.

I recall one group that was meeting for the first time. Although some of the women were strangers to each other, the coordinator knew everyone, and the meeting was at her house. She and I had had several previous phone conversations, and I had assigned Nadine Gordimer's *My Son's Story* for our first discussion. That evening, after explaining the dynamics of discussion and literary criticism, we began to talk about the book. Predictably, as first meetings go, the participants' remarks centered on emotional responses to characters' actions and reactions. This epitomizes first-level literary criticism—"It feels right," and "I know that to be true," therefore, "this author has portrayed human nature as I too have observed it and experienced it." However, the women also expressed some good insights into behavior motivation, and the better part of an hour went by.

When I felt it was time to introduce another level to our discussion, I pointed out that Gordimer's intent may be more ambitious than to create merely a story of familial relationships—that her family story is intended to be viewed as a political analogy. I suggested that perhaps Gordimer designed impure father-son, mother-husband, mother-son, brother-sister relationships to represent the South African government's relationship with its citizenry—or "children,"—under apartheid, and that she uses the familial to examine the political. In doing so, she inextricably connects one to the other. The more corrupt the "father" (the government), the more corrupt the "children" (the people) become. I raised the ultimate question that Gordimer asks: How do we maintain normal, loving, private lives when we live under debasing political doctrines? I put forth that Gordimer's authorial skill provides her readers with a story both recognizable on human, universal, and mythic levels, and forceful as an exposition of the corrosive political climate in her homeland.

I had everyone's attention; no one stirred. When I finished talking, there was only a delicate silence . . . broken by the woman sitting to my left who leaned forward and emphatically stated, "I don't buy that!"

Talk about having the air let out of your balloon! I waited for other responses, but no one came forward. The woman had the right to her response, but others did, too; yet, they didn't know they could exercise that right after so impassioned a declaration. No one made a move to reexamine the point, so that was the end of that. I had to go back to the drawing board and develop a new strategy for exploring varying levels of interpretation. I also learned to watch out for the unexpected crushers!

This demonstrates an important requirement for those who join discussion groups. They must join with a curiosity and a willingness to work with others on an explorative journey to understand and appreciate the literature. Comparing ideas and individual reactions and interpretations—not crushing them—enhances the richness of a discussion. The freer the atmosphere, the more expansive the flow of ideas.

TENSION—YES!

Picture this. You get on an airplane, bus, or train, sit by the window, and are joined by a seatmate—a loquacious one. He/she articulates a strong opinion about a politico—her position, her power, her plan—that is in direct opposition to your also strongly held beliefs. Do you listen and stew? Do you move to another seat? Do you counter with your opinion, arguing in an effort to change this seatmate's viewpoint? Do you just listen, perhaps merely saying, "Gee, I disagree with you on that one"? Or do you, metaphorically of course, steady both barrels and "blow this one away"?

This scenario is actually similar to ones that arise in book discussions. In all likelihood you will come to your reading group with an opinion, perhaps a strong one, about some aspect of the book. Most likely, some or most of your fellow members will disagree with your idea or opinion. What will you do? Options to retreat or to retaliate are available and represent two very real and natural responses to challenge, but these responses negate the concept of an ideally constructed reading group.

The *wrong* way: "I think Rachel Kinsella (the protagonist in Jane Smiley's novella *Ordinary Love*) was really stupid. I can't believe that she would just blurt out to her husband that she was having an affair and did not once think of the consequences."

Now, this is a strong opinion. However, the issue is not *why* this group member can't believe Rachel Kinsella's actions; the actions are as Jane Smiley created them. The issue is the fact that Rachel Kinsella did, in fact, shamelessly blurt out her indiscretion to her husband. That behavior and the author's intent deserve examination, and so does any controversy they engender. Use this member's viewpoint. She or he has raised an important issue concerning personality, behavioral motivation, marital communication, gender roles in a historical perspective of specific time and place, and the expansive perimeters of self-knowledge. Explore the provocation of this significant moment. Ask evaluative questions. Ask why. "Why?" is the perfect question to delve deeper and deeper into analytical criticism. "Why did Rachel Kinsella do that? Does Smiley succinctly offer us the answer on a platter?" No. Authors like to show and not tell; readers put together details and arrive at perspectives and truths. These permutations from using the same specifics generate the richness of a discussion.

Tension is healthy in group process—if it's responsible, thoughtful, and not created from silent hostility or one-upmanship. After all, a reading group is an intellectual sport. If you follow my suggestion and "leave your ego at the door," you will more easily understand that your opinion is being attacked, *not* you. Support your case as best you can, using additional details. Of course, by bringing up certain points, you will be offering a stack of ammunition to another participant who has arranged the same identical points in a contrary fashion to reach a different conclusion. These are the events that grease the wheels of a rich discussion!

MIRROR, MIRROR ON THE PAGE

Concepts of "self" do interfere with the ideal of group collectivity, yet there is a commonality about life, and that's why we can all be nourished by literature—we see the universal application to our own lives.

Let's suppose you hear these statements about a certain reading: "That girl was wrong to have sex with that boy she hardly knew," or "Her mother has every reason to tear up her photograph; she's a bad daughter." These are moral judgments that have as much to do with the personal life of the reader as the fictional life of the characters. Here are the same responses with self-reflection incorporated: "I think that girl was wrong to have sex with that boy. I was born and raised in a strict Catholic atmosphere. My attitudes about everything are colored by that." "My father left my mother and me when I was six. The sick feeling of being abandoned never seems to go away. Even though I moved away from my mother when I married, I talk to her twice a day. I can understand the pathology and obsessive reaction of that mother when her daughter abandoned her. I would never do that to my mother. It would kill her."

Why not? Anybody can say anything in a discussion, although what is said needs to be contributed with responsibility and respect for self and for the group. Each life is fashioned by so much outside stimuli, and when they can be connected to the fictional lives on the page, a fascinating process is incorporated into the discussion, and we are enhanced and validated and changed. Immersion into fiction can be liberating. For, in the "pretend" lives of the characters, authors depict the struggles and conflicts of life—the quests, the questions. Through their perspectives we confront the possibilities of our own lives that might have remained forever hidden from our vision.

A significant moment for me during a discussion: A woman stood up and said, "I never said this out loud before, but when I was little my father abused me. This story made me realize how many other people have had this happen to them, and they just hold it inside." She sat down and crossed her arms over her chest, holding on to her shoulders as if she were hugging herself.

Truths about the dark side of human nature frequently emerge as painless confessionals in group discussion. While contemplating self-centered and selfish character motivation in Muriel Spark's *Symposium,* a woman openly revealed her own calculated plan for acquiring the man of her choice as a husband—a plan conceived while she was convalescing in a hospital around the time of the attack on Pearl Harbor, in December 1941. She told us that she assessed her attributes ("red hair, big boobs"), considered that she had reached the age she needed to be married, and mentally went through a list of men, crossing them off as candidates until she reached the name of the one she eventually married! "I hadn't thought of what I did quite that way until today," she said.

At one time we were discussing a short story in my own special group. As Judy tells it, "An odor of sweat was described in a story, which evoked an epiphany for me. It triggered a memory of my beloved father playing handball and the smell of his gym clothes following these workouts. As a young girl I connected to this odor which later permeated my reminiscences of my deceased father. Also, [I] realized that I actually like the odor of sweat, since it connects me with my dad."

Judy's advice to anyone starting or joining a reading group is to come with a "willingness to listen, share, and preserve confidentiality." I clearly remember the house where we met, where everyone sat, and the suddenness of Judy's realization of the meaning of her attraction to "earthy" men. She was overcome with emotion, part of which was joy at the process that allowed her to reach that understanding. Several years before that day, Judy and the group were discussing the film *Moonstruck*. Once again, Judy had been attracted to the underworld character of Ronnie Camararo, the baker who wore a black rubber glove over an artificial hand. She was chided by some for this sexual attraction to men "with dirty fingernails." We talked about the dimensions of the character, but Judy's epiphany was not to come for several years, not until after her father's death.

All serious literature is concerned with the subjects, material, ethereal, and spiritual, that touch our lives. Through the course of your reading and seeking the truths about the nature of story, the creative intelligence, and the human condition, you will discern that everything is connected and that our world is actually a dynamo of animate nature. And when you collaborate and connect with others in the process, anything is possible. The power of a group is an awesome thing.

Why?

To reiterate, group discussion of a book is designed to:

- Enhance understanding of the book and appreciation of the art of writing—akin to learning the secrets of performing a magic trick that has previously amazed and confounded you. "How did he do that?" transforms into "Wow! Look how well he did that!" The childlike perplexity transforms into a sophisticated appreciation of skill.

- Examine human motivation by reading about how other people respond to internal and external circumstances, and how they act and react. Characters in literature are reflections of us, as we are of them. Dilemmas that happen to them and their array of choices for solutions, or absence of them, reflect their time and culture.

- Explore human nature and meanings of our own life experiences. The very act of discourse increases our sense of self-worth and the nature of commentary and interpretation.

- Expand awareness of the world around us and enhance our understanding of the relationship of time and space and light, and the elusive nature of reality.
- Expand intellectual horizons, establishing strong connections among individuals through the exploration of the literature.

CHAPTER 8

YOU ARE WHAT YOU READ

"Reading is to the mind what exercise is to the
body. It is wholesome and bracing for the mind to
have its faculties kept on the stretch."
—*Augustus Hare (English writer, 1834–1903)*

*L*et's get right down to the central issue that brings everyone together—the books.

After having given great attention to who will be in your group,
you will want to apply the same scrutiny and care to your book
list. Definitions of "a good book," "a good author," or a "book
worthy of discussion" vary broadly. Whatever your group's procedure for choosing reading selections, you will most likely find
that you want to actively promote a book you liked or want to discuss with the group. If somewhere along the line this doesn't happen, mark my words: You will leave that group *or* you will be
called upon to stretch the limits of your tolerance.

Many a member has dropped out of a group because its reading list included too much "fluff" or, conversely, too much Shakespeare. Some people have mentioned to me that their friends do
not read the esoteric books that we discuss at book club and that
they come to book group alone because their objective is, simply,
mental stimulation. One woman said, "My friends read the latest
Jackie Collins. Maybe I'm an intellectual snob, but I need my
feminist fix. This [group] is all mine. I love it."

Most of the people in my groups and a large percentage of the questionnaire respondents noted that being in a reading group has exposed them to reading and discussing books that they otherwise would never have picked up or even heard about. Finding pleasurable and challenging reading material, plus finding compatible people with whom to discuss it, are the two magical components of a successful reading group formula.

This chapter deals with reading choices—namely, yours. What forms of literature/fiction are available to you, ways to perceive the complex field of potential selections, and methods to consider using for your group's decision-making process are discussed. The final sections introduce the idea of focused reading lists, offer suggested titles from my personal syllabi and those sent to me from readers nationwide, and provide book ordering information. (In addition, some syllabi are included in the appendixes.)

Highbrow/Lowbrow

In answer to my questionnaire query, "How has your reading group changed?," one woman answered that they'd discovered that they would like to read more challenging books. Among the authors on her current list were Ludlum, L'Amour, Bradford, Michener, Sheldon, Fulgrum, and Turow. Four of Jean Auel's books were listed.

This reader's desire seems appropriate, given the selection of authors. Some books, such as the fiction by the writers above, are very popular and generate massive sales. For the most part, however, their readers aren't looking for sophisticated plot or character development, and choose these books primarily for their entertainment. Many of my groupies read popular fiction in addition to our group syllabus. They readily agree that devoting a slot on the syllabus or an entire group discussion to these works may be good for very socially oriented groups, but more substantive and challenging works are most likely necessary for critically thinking readers.

A contradiction to this statement occurs when a group decides to critically study a genre, such as romances, westerns, thrillers, mysteries, or science fiction. In addition to being pleasure reads, these genres can also be explored for their form, development, and place in literary and popular culture. For example, one year several group members requested a mystery, so I selected a well-crafted one that could well stand alone as a novel, and with which we could discuss relevant cultural issues. If your group enjoys the above genres, try to find examples that combine the elements of the genre with literary merit.

Don't listen to book advice that smacks of cultural imperialism. A good storyteller's story is good no matter what its cultural orientation. We invite books into our nonliterary lives to provoke meaningful and pleasurable experiences, so be open-minded. To quote an original middlebrow American folk hero, former Chicago Bears football coach Mike Ditka: "Whatever it takes." That's what you and your group should read.

Scientists claim that we cannot dream that which we haven't experienced in some form. If we could experience firsthand every square inch of land and water on this planet, every life there is to be lived in every variation of gender, nationality, health, and religion, and if we could live these lives in every different era of recorded history, then our dreams, our imaginations, our horizons of knowledge would be vast indeed. But the nature of existence does not allow us limitless experience. So we read.

By nature, humans are inquisitive, and by virtue of the free access Americans have to printed materials, limitless opportunities for expansion of our knowledge and imagination exist—through reading. We cannot overestimate the public library's actual and potential contribution to American society and its long-term effect as a stimulus to the reading group movement. As an instrument of our free society, the public library assumed responsibility for providing citizens public communication of new ideas and insights, however crude and dangerous they may be.

Your reading choices will expose you to hidden doors far beyond what your present consciousness could ever reach. The entire scope of the world's literature lies at your feet. Reading newly published books increases your sense of the world today and clarifies your place in it. Reading yesterday's books opens up, like the folds of an accordion, the layers of thought and history that have laid the foundation for today's writings. I am a major proponent of reading books of the past, for they give us clues to understand the present and help us prepare for the future.

Choices

Form is a frequently discussed and variously defined term in literary criticism. You and your group members can have some semantic fun discussing whether a piece of writing qualifies technically as a novel, a novella, a short story, a prose poem, a narrative, a vignette, a memoir, a biography, a historical novel, etc., etc.—and what the differences may be among these forms.

NOVEL

Novels include a large variety of writings that have in common some mode of storytelling (i.e., narrative), usually prose as opposed to verse, that relates an extended, amply developed, and sustained story told in a specifically styled way. The novel we read today is most often considered a form of fiction, which means a feigned or invented story.

The picaresque narrative, or episodic story, of sixteenth-century Spain is widely accepted as the original structure for the novel form that emerged in England in the early eighteenth century. *Robinson Crusoe* (1719) and *Moll Flanders* (1722) by Daniel Defoe are picaresque novels. Samuel Richardson is credited with introducing in *Pamela* (1740) the character novel, this one being the story of a proper, calculating young woman. Both forms of novels have character and action, but the emphasis varies.

NOVELLA

Novella (Italian, meaning "little new thing") and *novelette* are terms describing works of middle length. Joseph Conrad's *Heart of Darkness* is an example. Most novellas are about 100 pages in length. Academics sometimes disagree about the distinction between novellas/novelettes and short stories.

SHORT STORY

Again, the terminology connotes length. All three of these forms—
novel, novella, and short story—contain the same components but
in different degrees and perhaps in different organization. Today the
short-story form is enjoying a renewed attention, and readers will
find a plethora of anthologies from which to choose reading materials. Many new writers start with this shorter form as part of their
learning experience. Some stay with it exclusively and are renowned
as masters of the form.

PROSE

All of the forms described above are written in what is called prose
form, and the majority of our daily reading and writing is in prose
form. The term *prose* includes anything spoken or written that is *not*
fashioned with recurring metric units, which we call verse, or poetry.
The term is mainly used to distinguish this narrative style from poetry.

POETRY

Poetry is any variety of deliberately and technically organized phras-
ing of language and vocabulary. Poetry comprises some of our greatest works of literature, although many mainstream American readers
do not choose poetry as their usual reading fare. However, many
reading groups enthusiastically include poetry in their syllabi. Prose
fiction is not always easily discernible from poetry; by virtue of
artistry, the boundaries can blur with the fused form, sometimes
called a "prose poem."

NONFICTION

Nonfiction works are texts of narrative prose that offer opinions or
statements based on facts, reality, and verifiable information. Forms
of nonfiction that are popular with reading groups include biographies, memoirs, essays, and treatises on science, history, philoso-

phy, politics, and sociology. Recently, books dealing with ecology, anthropology, self-improvement, and spirituality joined this list. Our insatiable quest for truth and expert advice these days continues to regenerate a growing demand for this genre.

ESSAYS

Essays are nonfiction—brilliant, fine thoughts dealing rather loosely with a single theme. It is an essayist's intent to remold familiar theories and facts of the day into heretical, whimsical, serious, or intimately personal visions. A group could limit its entire focus to essays and never feel at a loss for something powerfully thought-provoking to read.

HISTORICAL FICTION

Historical fiction and *nonfiction novel* are both terms for a genre of novel that borrows events, facts, characters, or settings from history and selectively incorporates them into a fictional narrative. Classic historical novels are Scott's *Ivanhoe* and Dickens's *A Tale of Two Cities*. In 1965 Truman Capote's *In Cold Blood* revamped the form into a fictional rendering of recent historical events, in this case a brutal murder. Capote and other writers felt, and many still do, that the actual events of ordinary people's lives may far exceed in intrigue, drama, and curiosity any plot that a fiction writer could invent. Nonfiction novels as a study of life and personality have been called the "new journalism."

PLAYS AND FILMS

The structural design and intent of books and films and plays are comparable. Groups read aloud and discuss plays, compare novels to its corresponding movie, and discuss the art of film and a particular film. Play discussion groups and film discussion groups are equally as popular as reading groups, but not as numerous.

CLASSICS

The term *classics* most often refers to the literature of ancient Rome and Greece, always admissible candidates to any reading list. But not all classics were written centuries ago; *Ceremony* by Leslie Marmon Silko is considered the classic Native American novel, and it was published in 1975. Most readers think of a classic novel as being of the first or highest class—the best—and will fill their reading lists with them. There is guaranteed cultural value in this decision, but not necessarily a most satisfying reading experience. Some classics are flawed novels.

CONTEMPORARY

Books written in the nineties will be contemporary in relation to the books of the eighties, the writings of the post–World War II era are contemporary when compared to those written before the war. Most reading groups consider the term to connote those books written in the last few decades, if not the very last. I consider books written after World War II as contemporary, because after this event the world and world of literature changed vastly.

List Selection

List selection is vitally important. But what determines desirability? What books or kinds of books make that final cut? What do the reading groups in this country read?

Defining what one considers to be a good book needs intense deliberation. A work meets the requirements for my reading list if it is entertaining, educating, well executed, and deemed to have lasting or universal application.

Based on responses to the questionnaires regarding the book selection process, it is clear that groups have engineered a variety of methods to handle this most important aspect of the reading group experience. The procedures described below should give you some ideas for your own group. But remember, "trial and error" can just as easily mean "trial and success." Meredith Mullins of Melbourne, Florida, wrote on this topic: "The two organizers set up original procedures three years ago. Over time, we have fine-tuned them. Each May the group discusses the changes we want to implement in the coming year." She makes it sound so easy—and it can be!

Meredith continues, "In May, members give their suggestions for the next year. The two organizers cull from the list. We have several categories of books, and we try to read one book from each category. We really like a variety of types. Categories include Pulitzer Prize winner, nonfiction/historical novel, southern writer, foreign writer, short stories, biography/autobiography, classic, contemporary, and books made into movies. Often we attend the movie after reading the book."

This list excellently illustrates my remarks about trying various forms, seeking quality selections, and employing books to expand your horizons. Plus, the list gives some structure to the book selection process.

Meredith did not mention how or why the two "organizers" maintain the power of decision. Several groups reported having committees of two or three members that select the books for the coming year. No respondent explained how his or her committee was selected.

- One woman wrote that each spring, group members of the University of Illinois Woman's Club give lists of books that they've read or would like to read to their committee members. This committee comes up with an eleven-month list, "which changes as the year progresses."

- Marcy Whitney-Schenck's University of Chicago alumni group selects by general discussion after their regular book discussion four times a year. Whoever is present makes the decisions for the next few meetings. Their only rule is that they read only one work by an author. I try to follow this guideline, too. I like to introduce my groups to new authors. Then they have the pleasure of further reading on their own. Repeat performers make up about 5 percent of my reading list.

"Cultural authorities," as well as other reader recommendations, aid many groups in their book selection process. The *New York Times Book Review*, the *New York Review of Books*, *Hungry Mind Review*, *A Common*

Reader (which is really a mail-order catalog of select books), book review columns from national magazines and local newspapers, and *Reading Women* serve, for many groups, as authoritative voices in their selection process. Also, many libraries publish suggested reading lists.

• Several respondents reported that the one who hosts the meeting gets to pick the reading selection. Some groups vary this by having a rotating list of hosts and "choosers." Think about one more variation: Rotating the host, the chooser, and the member-leader, if there is one. In this way, no one has to host and lead at the same time. Some groups double up responsibilities like this, and it seems to work for them. I know several women who, when it is their turn to lead and hostess, become very stressed.

I'm continually compiling a list of potential candidates for each year's syllabus. I read many of the valuable "cultural authorities" cited above and receive publishers' press releases. Fellow readers, friends, and relatives are always telling me, "I just read a great book." I jot down the name, do my research, and if it passes my criteria for candidacy, I put it on my master list. But when someone tells me about a "good" book, I always ask, "Is it a book worthy of group discussion? Is it rich enough to sustain a two-hour discussion?"

Each April and May I pass around the list I've compiled to my group members. Each has the opportunity to comment and add suggestions. At the June meetings I pass around a semifinal list for votes, and then go into seclusion to come up with a ten-month syllabus by July. Quality, form, length, theme, narrative style, price, availability, author, world/current events, and connections to past works read are some of the criteria I use.

Once I send out my annual ten-month list in midsummer to individuals invited into my groups, that list gets sent around the country. How do I know this? People tell me. They send my list to their friends or relatives so they can do synchronized reading. From the little spaces in which we live, we impact others' lives in many ways. In Native American mythology, the spider is the female energy of the creative force that weaves beautiful designs of life, "carrying creation in its web, waiting to be unfurled!"

Recent articles in national newspapers and magazines report bookstores and publishers citing book groups as a prime factor in the increase of sales of certain books. Word of mouth has great power. John Grisham's books, Robert Waller's wild sensation *The Bridges of Madison County*, Kazuo Ishiguro's finely crafted *The Remains of the Day*, and Jill

Kerr Conway's *The Road from Coorain* are examples of this. Titles that are "spread" by groupies may increase sales by as much as 15 percent or more and literally assure the books' success, as well as cause book sellers to become more attentive to the power of reading groups. Many times sales will markedly increase when a paperback edition is released and waiting book group members snap it up to read.

• Sue Stefancik of Hancock, Michigan, is a member of a university women's club. "Our membership is international. Because of a local university, we have people from Britain, Poland, India, etc., who offer excellent comments and book selections." Sue's group decides by discussion at their last meeting in May about the September-to-December books and home locations. Then in December they fill in the gaps for the remainder of the year. She is the one in her group (the "secretary") who checks on book availability, orders the books (in paperback only) from the local store, has them held for group members, notifies members of details, and, as she said, "takes calls from members who can't find a book." In Sue's group, as in others, the person who suggests a book usually gets to lead its discussion. Sue's advice: "Don't narrow your selections. Our group has a wonderful, varied agenda. We love to jump from the classics to nonfiction to biographies."

• Jeane Lumley of Parker, Colorado, wrote, "All members are supposed to use the summer to find a book to bring to our September organizational meeting (a potluck dinner and business meeting, not a book discussion). We go around the room and everyone who has brought a book shows it and gives a brief synopsis. All books are put on our ballot."

Several groups reported procedures similar to this in which potential books are read by someone in the group before being selected for the syllabus. Although it seems as if that person is getting cheated out of a fresh reading experience, think of it this way: Your group decreases its chances of choosing a "dud," and rereading is not necessarily a disadvantage.

• After members in Nancy Zuraw's group build a suggestion list, "two members make sure each book is available, get reviews, and send them out. Members then vote." I like this because members are reacting to the opinions of "cultural authorities" as well as to group members.

As you can see, selection policies tend to fall into four categories: by committee, by members, by consensus or vote, and by leader. Each has advantages and disadvantages. Your group may have to experiment with different methods until you find the one that works best. Remember, if you or any member is dissatisfied with the system you are currently using, or the majority of the reading selections, speak up. This is your group, your time, your investment. Even if the books that are chosen are not the specific titles that you wanted, at least campaign for the level you desire in a reading selection. Or you may have to consider finding another group. There's a lot of territory between William Shakespeare and Sidney Sheldon.

DO YOU WANT A FOCUS TO YOUR READING LIST?

Groups view their meeting schedule as an opportunity to introduce a focus, or a concentration, or a specific genre, to their reading list.

- The Langley, Washington, group makes sure to include northwest authors as well as South American and women authors in its syllabus. Judy Robeck in Hawaii and several others reported highlighting local authors. Jeane Lumley's Parker, Colorado, groups "always choose a pioneer or western setting in one book. One group has been partial to the western woman's diary-type book."

- Many respondents said that their list contains a concentration of local writers or resident university writers and that these writers are invited to their meetings (and sometimes attend, with invigorating results).

- One respondent reported that the only criterion her coed group follows is that the author must be dead! Fortunately, and perhaps a bit perversely, a new list of possible candidates is being created all the time. In truth, recent death is actually one of the criteria I consider when putting my list together each year. It is a bibliophile's fitting way of paying homage.

- Pat Henning of Crystal Lake, Illinois, reported that her group reads "women writers only, except for a token male once a summer." Donna Bass of Glencoe, Illinois, speaks for numerous respondents: "Many of the books have a particular appeal to women and since the group is all female, the discussions have a decidedly feminine influence." An anonymous respondent wrote that her group picks books that involve health, environment, and politics. Many groups choose a seasonal selection around Christmastime.

• Groups reported spending multiple months or even an entire year on a particular author or subject. The list of possibilities is endless. French writers, or Italian, or feminist. British or Chicano/a, gay/lesbian, new Japanese/old Japanese, African-American, Eastern European, the new Europe, South African, etc. Concentration can also focus on forms and genres: poetry or short stories, mysteries or westerns. Also, literature of a particular time period can be isolated: Victorian, the beat generation, modern, postmodern, or Revolutionary. The American Institute of Discussion, headquartered in Oklahoma City, coordinates multidisciplined works around thematic subjects such as liberty, reward and punishment, and mercy. (See Appendix D for further information.)

The reading lists I prepare are usually heterogeneous in nature, highlighting a variety of genres and authors that we can compare and contrast in various ways throughout the year. Feminism/humanism, spirituality/religion, classics, prize winners, multiculturalism/internationalism have been major themes in my personal and professional search for meaning. And I'm always seeking examples of specific and daring narrative styles and structures in order to meet the challenge and demystify it.

In my short story groups we sometimes use anthologies organized around a specific topic. I am an avid proponent of the short story form and its "bang for the dollar," as my *Reading Women* partner Sandy Brown says. "Minimum reading, maximum pleasure and discussion" is my campaign slogan to lure reticent readers. Currently I facilitate three groups that read and discuss short stories exclusively. For the past few seasons I've been including short stories in my novel groups' reading list for at least one meeting.

Examples of good short-story anthologies organized around a theme include the following:

Literary matters

• *Points of View*, edited by James Moffett and Kenneth R. McElheny. Mentor.
• *Look Who's Talking*, edited by Bruce Weber. Mentor/Pocket Books.

The wonderful, diverse stories in these two anthologies are arranged by narrative technique; that is, by the way in which we, the reader, are delivered the story. Interior monologue, diary, first person ("I went to the store"), second person ("You see bakery trucks loading their wares"), third person ("He picked up her pocketbook"), etc. These are packed with great stories and are excellent tools for groups earnestly wanting to learn some mechanics of literary criticism.

Women

• *We Are the Stories We Tell* (subtitled *The Best Short Stories by North American Women Since 1945*), edited by Wendy Martin. Pantheon. Here you'll find the female experience in all its multiethnic, multiracial complexity, drawing on collective and personal pasts. Stories by some of my all-time favorite writers: Alice Walker, Eudora Welty, Anne Tyler, Grace Paley, Margaret Atwood, and more.

• *The Maid of the North, Feminist Folk Tales from Around the World*, by Ethel Johnston Phelps. Henry Holt. Phelps actually transformed these traditional folk and fairy tales from their original sources. "They all portray spirited, courageous heroines," she states in her introduction.

• *Between Mothers and Daughters: Stories Across a Generation*, edited by Susan Koppelman. The Feminist Press.

• *Women and Fiction* and *New Women and New Fiction*, both edited by Susan Cahill. Mentor/Pocket Books.

• *The Experience of the American Woman* and *American Wives*, both edited by Barbara Solomon. Mentor/Pocket Books. Cahill and Solomon have put together hours of reading pleasure that show us the ways in which present-day sexual politics connect to the past.

• *Unholy Alliances*, edited by Louise Rafkin. Cleis Press.

• *Fathers and Daughters*, edited by Terry Eichler and Jesse D. Geller. Plume Fiction.

• *Abortion Stories*, edited by Rick Lawler. MinRef Press. These illuminate issues of womanhood. Some stories are better constructed than others, but all allow exploration of conflicting ideologies and identities for women today.

Men

- *The Graywolf Annual Four: Short Stories by Men*, edited by Scott Walker. Graywolf Press. Offers great exploration of sexual identity. I was introduced to author Tim O'Brien (*The Things They Carried*) by reading this anthology. Stories by William Kittredge, Stuart Dybek, and Charles Baxter are unforgettable.

- *Men on Men 2*, edited by George Stambolian. NAL/Penguin. Testimony to the renaissance of gay letters and to this new and vital contribution to American literature. Allan Guganus, author of *Oldest Living Confederate Widow Tells All* (1989), has a great story in this book.

- *The Coast of Chicago*, by Stuart Dybek. Knopf.

- *Lives of the Poets*, by E. L. Doctorow. Random House.

Age Perspectives

- *20 under 30*, edited by Debra Spark. Scribner. Young American writers provide new energy and perspective. Reading young short-story writers is like reading America's future novelists.

- *Point of Departure: 19 Stories of Youth and Discovery*, edited by Robert Gold. Dell. Written in the thirties to the sixties, these stories elicit the pain, confusion, and excitement of American adolescence. I've used this little prize in workshops with teenagers and parents. (Parents of teenagers may find this a useful tool for better communication—if they can get their young adult to read it and discuss it with them.)

- *When I Am an Old Woman I Shall Wear Purple*, edited by Sandra Martz. Papier-Mache Press. An anthology of works that evoke midlife and later years.

- *Songs of Experience: An Anthology of Literature on Growing Old*, edited by Margaret Fowler and Priscilla McCutcheon. Ballantine. The subject of old age depicted by a variety of fine writers.

- *First Sightings: Stories of American Youth*, edited by John Loughery. Persea. Twenty stories by mostly noted writers exploring coming of age in America.

Japanese

- *The Showa Anthology (Modern Japanese Short Stories)*, edited by Van C. Gessel and Tomone Matsumoto. Kodansha.

•*A New Chrysanthemum*, translated by Lane Dunlop. North Point Press. Reading these stories expanded our understanding of Japan's tumultuous and arduous twentieth century. (Donald Keene's *Japanese Literature: An Introduction for Western Readers*, Grove Press, was a great aid.)

New Age

• *The Fireside Treasury of Light*, edited by Mary Olsen Kelly. Simon & Schuster. Contains excerpts from writings of the New Age and gave us insight into this exciting, transformative field of writing.

Love

•*Love Stories for the Time Being*, edited by Genie D. Chipps and Bill Henderson. Pushcart. "Presents the state of love today." Of the twenty-six stories, only a few were forgettable, which speaks well of this large anthology.

International

• NAL, under its Signet Classic label, publishes anthologies of British short stories, continental European short stories, etc.
• *Great Modern European Short Stories*, edited by Douglas and Sylvia Angus. Fawcett.
• *Eye of the Heart*, edited by Barbara Howes. Avon. A good anthology of Latin American stories, new and old.

Fabulation

Not exactly science fiction and not exactly reality, but marginal to both, fabulation, metafiction, fantasy, irreality, or whatever you want to call it is a genre worthy of attention. Fabulation exists in many cultures' literary heritages.

• *Superfiction or The American Story Transformed*, edited by Joe David Bellamy. Vintage.
• *The Book of Fantasy*, edited by Jorge Luis Borges. Viking. Superb international, multicentury anthology that portrays the labyrinthine strangeness of the world in which we live.

Regional

• *Southwest Tales,* edited by Jonathan Miller and Genevieve Morgan. Chronicle Books. Introduces readers to a variety of styles and experiences in the cowboy, Native American, rough-and-tumble region of this country.

• *In the Center of the Nation,* by Dan O'Brien. Atlantic Monthly Press; Avon paperback.

Recommendations are a natural part of our discourse with others. Who among us hasn't praised a restaurant, a film, a vacation spot, a beautician, a pizza parlor? Or received recommendations from others? Curiously, a vile restaurant, a grotesque haircut, or an unenjoyable film can be more easily forgiven than a book recommendation that brings no pleasure. But what gives one person pleasure may not have that magic for the next. And book selections, like quarterbacks and coaches and teachers, are constantly under scrutiny.

Why? Ask someone what he or she looks for when choosing a book, or what elements a good book should contain.

The common response "I like a book that holds my interest," isn't precise enough. What interest? Interest in a love story? And would that be one with a happy ending or a sad ending? And what constitutes which? Interest in stories of people learning to cope with adversity, family idiosyncrasies, childhood traumas? Interest in science fiction? Interest in the visceral experience that a book can provide? Or the intellectual experience? Or the spiritual? Interest in the nature of the art of fiction itself? In authenticity, fabrication, biography, historical fiction? Interest in the classics or the myths, or in their contemporary feminist and multicultural revisions? This list could be endless and presents a conundrum for the one making recommendations, or in my case, selections. What constitutes a good read?

Several years ago I included in my usual ten-month syllabus a novel by Italo Calvino entitled *If on a Winter Night a Traveler. . . .* Calvino is one of Italy's most brilliant modern writers, a wizard with literary form. In the novel, his fictional characters become mired in their own labyrinthine pursuit, but no more so than us living, breathing, bewildered readers on a parallel journey to understand Calvino's multilevel writing. Brilliant Calvino, of course, illuminates the mystery of life and our (his characters' and his readers') ignoble and floundering efforts to make sense of it all.

Great writer, masterful novel—terrible response. I walked into meeting after meeting greeted by angry members ready to tar and feather me. "Terrible." "Frustrating." "I didn't know what I was reading." "I'm so angry with you." "Why did you pick this book?" "How dare you make us read this garbage when there is so much good stuff out there!" "Why is this book in our syllabus? Why?"

Of course, I've experienced negative reactions before. A love-hate reaction to a selection is often the perfect catalyst for a healthy discussion and causes readers to articulate why they liked or did not like a book and what can be learned from that, and so on.

But the response to Calvino's piece was overwhelming. One woman voiced the majority sentiment: "My life is so busy, so filled with stuff I have to deal with every day, that I didn't need this aggravation. That's not what a book is supposed to be for! It's supposed to be a pleasurable experience, not a chore." Then Beth spoke. Beth, the struggling single mother who recently remarried and became the stepmother to a troubled adolescent daughter; the teacher of mentally retarded children lost in the Chicago school system; an only child who flew back and forth to Florida to tend her dying father. She said, "With all of this going on in my life, it was really nice to escape into someone else's troubles. For a while, I forgot everything happening to me and just enjoyed reading about these characters trying to figure out what was happening to them."

What does this show? The obvious—that the definition of "good reading" varies from person to person, moment to moment, need to need, perspective to perspective. So what can you do to set up a syllabus that will be pleasing to the majority, encouraging to the most hesitant, and challenging to all? Try your best, and then cross your fingers.

AND NOW FOR THE ENVELOPE, PLEASE

After sifting through all those thoughts and organizational directions, I hope you are not disappointed in the suggestions I have for you. But if my experience serves me well, some of you will like the picks and some of you won't. To borrow and alter the words and wit of Abraham Lincoln, "You can't please all of the people all of the time."

For your consideration, I've developed a few lists with various permutations. One author may appear on several syllabi, but I've attempted to keep that to a minimum. My intention is to emphasize talented writers more than specific titles. I consider everything listed worthy of consideration, reading and study time, and discussion. More suggestions are listed in the appendixes.

FAVORITES

Once I've "lived" intimately with a text in preparation for discussion with a group, I fall in love with its attributes and forgive its flaws. Therefore, choosing favorites is an arduous task. The titles listed below as part of my first list have received accolades from the majority of my several hundred reading group participants, and are referred to often in later discussions of other books.

A person new to the book group experience will find these selections very accessible. The lengths are not demanding, and the literary and personal rewards are great. I emphasize *personal*. Every one of these books engendered an intense visceral response from my groupies; they "give the heart a little squeeze," as Tim O'Brien said of his authorial intent when I met him at a book signing.

Books indicated with an asterisk (*) have also been read and discussed by other groups across the country.

- *So Long, See You Tomorrow,* by William Maxwell
- *Frankenstein,* by Mary Wollstonecraft Shelley*
- *Ordinary Love and Good Will,* by Jane Smiley
- *A Thousand Acres,* by Jane Smiley* (Pulitzer Prize winner)
- *Oh What a Paradise It Seems,* by John Cheever*

- *Pride and Prejudice*, by Jane Austen*
- *The Heart of Darkness*, by Joseph Conrad*
- *The Shawl*, by Cynthia Ozick*
- *The Things They Carried*, by Tim O'Brien*
- *A Summons to Memphis*, by Peter Taylor* (Pulitzer Prize winner)
- *Beloved*, by Toni Morrison* (Pulitzer Prize winner)
- *Animal Dreams*, by Barbara Kingsolver*
- *Crossing to Safety*, by Wallace Stegner*
- *Angle of Repose*, by Wallace Stegner* (Pulitzer Prize winner)
- *A River Runs Through It*, by Norman Maclean*
- *The Color Purple*, by Alice Walker* (Pulitzer Prize winner)

MORE

Again, with this list I am using the same formula for quality: entertainment value plus intellectual stimulation. Most of these books were written in the twentieth century.

- *Fahrenheit 451*, by Ray Bradbury
- *To Kill a Mockingbird*, by Harper Lee*
- *Lord of the Flies*, by William Golding*
- *Call of the Wild*, by Jack London*
- *Jane Eyre*, by Charlotte Bronte*
- *One Day in the Life of Ivan Denisovich*, by Aleksandr Solzhenitsyn*
- *The Adventures of Huckleberry Finn*, by Mark Twain*
- *The Joy Luck Club*, by Amy Tan*
- *In Country*, by Bobbie Ann Mason*
- *The Great Gatsby*, by F. Scott Fitzgerald*
- *Love in the Time of Cholera*, by Gabriel García Márquez
- *One Hundred Years of Solitude*, by Gabriel García Márquez*
- *As I Lay Dying*, by William Faulkner (actually, any Faulkner; some groups read *Absalom, Absalom* or *The Sound and the Fury*)

• *The Chosen,* by Chaim Potok*
• *Madame Bovary,* by Gustave Flaubert*

MORE, AGAIN

• *All the King's Men,* by Robert Penn Warren*
• *Cry, the Beloved Country,* by Alan Paton
• *Consenting Adults,* by Laura Hobson
• *Being There,* by Jerzy Kosinski*
• *Caine Mutiny,* by Herman Wouk
• *Crime and Punishment,* by Fyodor Dostoyevsky*
• *Confederacy of Dunces,* by John K. Toole*
• *The Handmaid's Tale,* by Margaret Atwood* (also, *Cat's Eye, Wilderness Tips*)
• *Middlemarch,* by George Eliot* (also, *Adam Bede, Daniel Deronda*)
• *Age of Innocence,* by Edith Wharton* (Pulitzer Prize winner)
• *I Know Why the Caged Bird Sings,* by Maya Angelou*
• *The Awakening,* by Kate Chopin*
• *The House of the Spirits,* by Isabel Allende*
• *Uncle Tom's Cabin,* by Harriet Beecher Stowe*
• *Dinner at the Homesick Restaurant,* by Anne Tyler
• *Breathing Lessons,* by Anne Tyler* (Pulitzer Prize winner)
• *The Remains of the Day,* by Kazuo Ishiguro*

NONFICTION

These books will encourage discussion. Again, I have placed an asterisk beside those also mentioned by questionnaire respondents.

• *On Violence,* by Hannah Arendt
• *Keepers of the Earth: Native American Stories and Environmental Activities for Children,* by Michael Caduto and Joseph Bruchac. Don't be put off by this title. This book is most illuminating, especially in conjunction with fiction by Native American or southwestern regional writers, such as Michael Dorris, Louise Erdrich, Barbara Kingsolver, or Leslie Marmon

Silko. Parents as well as children can learn together some of the seminal myths that are the foundation of the Native American belief system.

- *The Road Less Traveled: A New Psychology of Love, Traditional Values, and Spiritual Growth* and *Different Drum,* by M. Scott Peck*
- *Fierce Attachments,* by Vivian Gornick*
- *The Chalice and the Blade,* by Riane Eisler.* Theories of social relations linked rather than ranked; life-generating powers replacing power to take life.
- *Power of Myth,* by Joseph Campbell.* Themes and symbols that comprise the fabric of our myths and religions. Valuable as a reference to enrich any book's discussion.
- *Medusa and the Snail,* by Lewis Thomas and his other volumes of essays.
- *Natural History of the Senses,* by Diane Ackerman
- *Confessions of Saint Augustine*
- *Incidents in the Life of a Slave Girl,* by Harriet A. Jacobs
- *From Beirut to Jerusalem,* by Thomas Friedman*
- *Backlash,* by Susan Faludi*
- *Truman,* by David McCullough*
- *A Room of One's Own,* by Virginia Woolf*
- *The Woman Warrior,* by Maxine Hong Kingston
- *China Men,* by Maxine Hong Kingston
- *Chaos,* by James Glieck
- *Iron and Silk,* by Mark Salzman

SHORT STORIES

Some authors are masters of this form, and their opus is made up almost exclusively of these stories.

- Alice Munro portrays rural and urban Canadian lives with a feminist/humanist vision. *Friends of My Youth* and *Something I've Been Meaning to Tell You* are two of my favorite collections.
- Flannery O'Connor's early death ended a brilliant writing career (one novel, *Wise Blood,* and two volumes of short stories in total). "The Displaced Person" and "A Good Man Is Hard to Find" are famous.

- Eudora Welty, a writer's writer, penned "A Worn Path," "Why I Live at the P.O.," and "The Petrified Man," three of her more famous stories. Groups will also enjoy her novels, *The Optimist's Daughter* and *Robber Bridegroom*, and her autobiography, *One Writer's Beginning*, which teaches us to see our lives as an art form.

- Edna O'Brien's stories are set in the heartland of Ireland and almost always depict women.

- Anton Chekhov is a must for any reading group. The book *Metaphor and Memory* includes Cynthia Ozick's essay, "A Short Note on 'Chekhovian'," which shows us how universal his influence has been. As Ozick states, "An adjective that had to be invented for the new voice Chekhov's genius breathed into the world—elusive, inconclusive, flickering; nuanced through an underlying disquiet, though never morbid or disgruntled, unerringly intuitive . . . he teaches us us."

- Tolstoy's and Dostoyevsky's stories have the veneer of old mahogany and the freshness of this morning's rye bread. One group discussing Tolstoy's novella, *Kreutzer Sonata*, became embroiled in a heated discussion about issues prompted by the text. *Kreutzer Sonata* is about a man who kills his wife out of jealousy but is acquitted in a court of law because her actions were deemed more criminal. So intense were the clashes after I left that several of the members ended friendships and never came back to the group. (Tolstoy would have loved to have known that his art could generate so much emotion.)

- David Leavitt's collection, *Family Dancing*, knocked the socks off my group members. How can someone so young write so well and know so much?

- Grace Paley possesses a unique, unmistakable voice. Her three collections of stories and volumes of poems and essays carry grace.

- John Cheever is an important influence. When he died a decade ago, I realized that I too loved my idols much the way teenagers love their movie or rock stars. Cheever's stories taught me vision, dignity, wit, and the awesome power of possibility. "Good-bye My Brother," "The Enormous Radio," and "The Country Husband" are among my favorites.

- Saul Bellow is an intellectual's soulmate. Almost all of his stories and novels are of superior craftsmanship, but one has to search for the hidden emotion. That's Bellow.

- Everyone should read and discuss Shirley Jackson's "The Lottery." When it was first published in the *New Yorker* magazine in 1948, readers sent in bags and bags of mail. Her novels are most enjoyable, satiric, and mysterious. Her untimely death left us scant too little to enjoy.

• Raymond Carver put the term "minimalism" on the map of American letters. Most of his stories are set somewhere in Washington State or California, but Carver Country is anywhere a character can gain dignity, no matter how impoverished his or her circumstance. He rose from lean beginnings and died in 1988 at age fifty with the reputation of being one of America's finest writers. Film producer Robert Altman based the 1993 award-winning *Short Cuts* on Carver's stories.

• Perhaps Edgar Allan Poe's personal life of despair was the catalyst for his cultivation of mystery and the macabre that fascinates us yet today.

AMERICANA

Each of these writers of the mid-to-late twentieth century portrays a particular lexicon of the American landscape in her or his writing. I highly recommend all of them.

• Philip Roth
• Bernard Malamud
• Joyce Carol Oates
• Anne Tyler
• Anne Rice
• Louise Erdrich
• Tony Hillerman (combines detective stories/mysteries with well-researched Native American tales)
• Barbara Kingsolver
• Larry McMurtry
• Susan Minot
• Ellen Gilchrist
• John Updike
• John Cheever (Cheever Country spread from Manhattan to Connecticut and into the dining rooms and bedrooms and souls of mid-twentieth century Americans, who were grappling with strange new icons of technology and prosperity. What a wit. What a Calvinist. What a pained, soulful voice in America.)

You probably had reactions to some of these titles and authors as you read them, and you could probably add suggestions of your own. I feel cheated from hearing or seeing your responses by the constraints of this one-way communication. Please write and let me know your thoughts, feelings, and suggestions. We get to know new writers, like new friends, by having others introduce them to us.

(*Note:* See appendixes for additional suggestions.)

How Do I Get the Books?

There are two ways to think about book acquisition—in terms of *I* and in terms of *we*.

If you were reading for private pleasure, how would you get your books? Bookstore? Library? Mail-order catalog? Sidewalk or fund-raising sale? Borrow from a friend? Individual readers use any and all of these methods, and reading groups use them too. The major difference between solitary reading of a single book and reading for group discussions is that several people have to read the same book during the relatively same short period of time.

It would be easy to instruct you simply to go to the local bookstore to buy the book your group selected. But in most cases, this is easier to say than to do. Below I have revealed some ins and outs of the bookselling industry, and made a few suggestions for book buying that I hope will prove valuable.

1. Bookstores are in business to make money and do not always carry a large quantity of every book—or even a single copy of every book. When your group forms, it is a good idea to get to know your local bookstore manager or owner and to inform him or her of your plans. If that person possesses even a modicum of business savvy, he or she will willingly accommodate your group's book needs. A good bookstore manager will ask for a copy of your syllabus for the year and order the necessary number of books for each selection.

2. To do this ordering, the bookstore manager calls the distributor. If the desired quantity of your book is in the warehouse, the bookstore will receive its copies within a few days. If the supply is low or nonexistent, the books must be ordered from the publisher.

This process could take several weeks, and the bookstore will handle it.

3. Sometimes a book is declared out-of-print by the publisher. This may occur for two reasons: (1) Demand has died down and it doesn't pay for the publisher to keep copies on store shelves, or (2) All copies of a specific title are called in because it is going to be reissued in the future. This is done when a novel has been released in movie form (*Howards End, Enchanted April, Accidental Tourist*) and has engendered new interest, or when a subsequent novel of a little-known author becomes a hot item and all of the author's previously ignored books start selling anew. Such was the case when the early books of John Irving became popular after *The World According to Garp,* his fourth novel, soared to the top. Barbara Kingsolver is another author whose earlier novels gained attention when *Pigs in Heaven* was published to acclaim.

There have been frustrating instances when in summer I've chosen a book for the season's reading list, only to be told that it is out-of-print by midwinter when the supply is needed. Roberta Rubin, my friend and bookstore owner, has helped me circumvent this problem by ordering large quantities of each book on the list well in advance of the month they are needed and placing them on shelves specially reserved for book clubs.

4. A bookstore manager/owner should be happy to stock the books your group needs. If your group orders ten or more of one title, I suggest that you ask for a discount. Roberta gives me and other professionals and teachers a 10 percent discount, which I pass on to my groupies. One respondent reported that she gets a 20 percent discount from her bookstore. If you can find someone connected to a school or bookstore to order for you, the Book Source in St. Louis sells at a 40 percent discount. However, the order must be placed by retail store or school. Write to the Book Source, 4127 Forest Park Boulevard, St. Louis, MO 63108, or call 314-652-1000 or 800-444-0435. Some public libraries have printed order forms from Books by Mail, a mail-order house through which you can also get your books.

5. Some bookstores require that you "make good" on your order—that is, buy every book ordered. This is usually the policy of a smaller store. Since I order a large number of books for my

groupies, I cannot promise Roberta that they will all be bought. However, she and many bookstore owners in the Chicago area happily service book clubs, realizing that readers often try to save on their book purchases by borrowing from friends and libraries or sharing.

6. Roberta Rubin's store (The Book Stall, 811 Elm Street, Winnetka, IL 60093, 708-446-8880) received the American Bookseller Association's 1993 Charles S. Haslam Award for Excellence in Bookselling. This award is given annually to an outstanding independent bookstore. Others that have received this award are Tattered Cover in Denver; Books and Co., Dayton; Happy Bookseller in Charleston, South Carolina; and Square Books in Oxford, Mississippi. The Book Stall was the first midwestern store to receive this award. With the country being inundated with chain superstores capitalizing on the current resurgence in book reading and buying, try to give at least some of your business to the small independents.

Like many bookstores in this area, the Book Stall also sponsors in-store book discussion groups. Seasonally, I am one of eight leaders who come to the store to discuss a book of my choosing with store patrons. If you are having trouble getting a group going, want more intellectual stimulation, or want to see how different leaders conduct themselves, endeavor to convince your local store to initiate such a program. Barnes and Noble, Borders, Waldenbooks, plus the small independents in my area, are currently doing this. Many times in-store employees lead the discussion.

7. Some respondents and *Reading Women* subscribers live in small or isolated communities, and they lament over their inadequate libraries and/or bookstores. Libraries work under stringent budgetary guidelines and only buy popular books, not necessarily those recommended for the literature enthusiast in publications such as *Booklist* and *Publishers Weekly*. Small bookstores also will pander to mainstream popular demand, which leaves the thirsty reader adrift in a sea of saltwater.

Any of the stores listed in item 6 above, and the club and catalog discussed in Appendix D, should be happy to accommodate your book requirements via the mails. In addition, some libraries have purchase-request forms. One of my voracious reading friends regularly asks her library to purchase the newly released books reviewed on the front page of the *New York Times Book Review.* Make friends with your librarian, even invite her or him to join your book group. Then you have a better chance of getting your chosen books ordered for the library's shelves.

8. Some groupies tell me that they give their librarian the name of the chosen book and the date of their meeting. The librarian gathers copies of that book from the surrounding area's libraries for book group members to read in that short time frame when multiple copies are needed. This is called an interlibrary loan.

9. When ordering a book, make sure you know the correct spelling of the author's name. This is even more important than the title, because title listings can be confusing. A bookstore can more easily find the author's name on its computer lists than the title, but the best way to locate a book is to supply the author, title, publisher, and ISBN (International Standard Book Number—one given to each book in the world). If you are want to know when a hardcover will come out in paperback, author and title should be sufficient information.

10. Many book group members are concerned about the cost of books. Chapter 3 has some suggestions on ways to limit book costs. However, if you are like me and amortize the cost of a party dress over the number of times you wear it, use this same formula for a book—only amortize the cost against the hours and hours of enjoyment you get while reading the book, thinking about it, discussing it, and giving it to someone else to enjoy. You don't outgrow a book. A book may fade from its moment of popularity, but a good book never dies. A book is a steady friend and comforter that doesn't need special feeding and doesn't talk back, turn away, roll over, or go to sleep—it's there for you when you need it. The only thing a book can't do is solve your problems. Yet, a book's good story lets you know that you are not the only one in the world with problems. This connects you to other human beings, making you feel alive and good, even though you have problems, too. In these terms, a book is a real bargain!

Chapter 9

MEMBER-LED VS. PROFESSIONALLY LED

*B*eing a professional leader myself, I strongly believe in the value of the service I provide. Yet I'm well aware that the overwhelming majority of reading groups in this country, and probably the one you will be starting or joining, are member-led. I appreciate the specialness of each type, both as a participant in member-led groups and as the professional facilitator in many others.

What's a Member-Led Group?

As distinguished from a professionally led group in which an outsider is hired and paid to organize and/or facilitate group discussion, a member-led group is entirely organized and operated internally by participating members.

Based on your knowledge of group dynamics and from the group exercise in putting together a puzzle (in chapter 7), you can understand that a book discussion group can benefit from leadership. One type of leadership is the subtle, invisible variety that gently nudges or initiates. "Let's get started" may be all that is needed for everyone to refill their cup and leave the serving table to sit down ready to begin the discussion. Someone may even begin while walking over to the chairs. "Tell me what you think of that father. Wasn't he an ogre?" and off goes this group on a rich, open, and self-directed inquiry for a solid block of time.

If, in the course of things, conversation lags, irrelevant digressions ensue, or intense discussion ignites interruption, someone may gently nudge again. "What about the style of writing?" and "Why are most of Brookner's novels written in the third person?" focus conversation on a new tangent. "Wait a minute. We can't hear either of you. Take turns, then let's discuss what you're saying." This unofficial, unstructured kind of leadership encourages reason and democracy, and quietly secures a comfortable order within which all can freely participate.

To me, a reading group discussion with all members participating and contributing equally and freely has attained the ideal. To that end, many groups require members to prepare ahead of time, whether by bringing three questions to generate thought and discussion, by choosing a specific passage to read aloud to elicit pointed discussion, or by bringing applicable articles or information to enrich the discussion. In this way, everyone personally affects the quality of the discussion, and everyone "owns" the results. If you really want to have a cooperative effort, your members need to be involved in both the intellectual challenge and the emotional exploration that a book offers. Everyone knows that when we care about what we are doing, we do it better.

LEADER/ORGANIZER

All participants in reading groups, both professional leaders and members, should aspire to the goal described above. Realistically, though, we humans often fall far short of the goals we set for ourselves, and most groups do seem to need some element of leadership so that every meeting runs smoothly.

An appointed or designated leader can provide better structure when appropriately empowered to keep the ball rolling, maintain order, and keep the discussion on track. The more "help out," not "take over," a leader is, the better the overall results for your group. If you designate someone for this job who becomes dictatorial, and this does not suit the group, you have made a problem for yourself. Fix it before the group disintegrates from internal corrosion. How? Openly discuss and set guidelines and expectations of the leader. Delineate the job description to eliminate misunderstandings. A leader serves the group, not the reverse. Conversely, if the designated leader is not performing the job with enough forcefulness or efficiency, you may need to assign a more assertive person (or get one to volunteer).

Regarding maintenance of order, some groups just automatically incorporate policies into their plans. Examples of tactics used for better discussions include the following:

- The New Jersey group that initiated a ten-minute-per-person "speak" time is trying to correct two group dynamics problems—verbosity and interrupting.

- To combat several internal issues—verbosity, irrelevance, timidity, and interrupting—I often ask a question and initiate a "once around" exercise in which everyone takes turns and contributes before any one person speaks again. (A person has the right to pass.)

- When the sparks fly and all begin to talk at once, I'll quickly give people an order in which to speak. "We need to hear what you all have to say. Don't forget your point. Sue, go first. Then Michael, Laurie, Frank. Okay, take it away!" I do this as a professional, but any group member (whether designated as leader or not) can do this, as long as the group agrees to give this person the authority to handle this maintenance job.

- Another tactic that intrigued me was a group's use of a "talking stick." The stick is passed from person to person, as that person wants to speak. Its value is that it allows the first person to finish what he or she is saying before relinquishing the stick. It also gives a ceremonial importance to each comment, but self-control and spontaneity are optimal, so use the stick sparingly, if at all.

When I am the keeper of the order, I refer to myself as the "parliamentarian." My groupies are used to this title, but nobody who sent in a questionnaire mentioned this concept. If you decide to designate an order keeper, the actual title is insignificant. Call him or her anything you want, but get the job done. If your group gets too far off track, or if you all start talking at once, or if people monopolize the discussion, devise some system to correct these issues that grate on and corrode a good working group. The majority of respondents reported that their groups ran smoothly. But I would watch out for three things—irrelevance, interrupting, and verbosity—as problems that commonly arise and need attention.

LEADER/FACILITATOR

Each member, or those desiring to do so, can take a turn at being leader/facilitator. This person's job involves some preparation and research on the book before the meeting, perhaps formulating a list of questions or comments for discussion. In addition, this person would be expected to facilitate the discussion, get it going, and keep it going.

In many groups, members will bring biographical information on the author or professional reviews and commentary on the book to the discussion. Whether leaderless or member-led, these are an excellent asset to the group discussion. If you choose to be member-led, be mindful that not every member has the time, talent, or patience to do research and preparation, or is comfortable leading a discussion. In some groups, every member is required to take a turn; others ask for volunteers, and the timid or unwilling are let off the hook.

- An anonymous questionnaire respondent offered, "There's no pressure to volunteer to review, and many don't do it at all. Some do because they enjoy it and are good at it."

- Nancy Zuraw stated, "Everyone takes turns. At first we didn't have a leader, but we felt we needed someone to do research and provide a little structure."

- Patricia McDowell's St. Joseph, Michigan, group decides what books to discuss by members' willingness to lead. "You lead it, we read it" is their decision-making slogan. As Patricia states, "Members . . . read the book. Leader prepares biographical material on author, summarizes available critical material . . . and develops a few questions to start the discussion. Discussions are led by members who volunteer to lead the discussions of the books they choose. There is no pressure to lead, but over the past few years every member has led at least one discussion."

• Carol McKegney's group in Petaluma, California, enjoys its digressions. "Discussions digress but are usually redirected to the topic of books to read—if not the book read for that month. Some months we just don't pull it off—no one has had time, no good books were recommended, etc., so we just try harder to find something for the next month."

• An anonymous Chicago woman wrote, "Some discussions are great— others are so-so, but we always have a nice time."

• Donna Bass of Glencoe, Illinois, added some insightful remarks. "I used to belong to a member-led group and dropped out because it wasn't satisfying to me. While all the members enjoyed reading, their idea of preparation was to copy a couple of reviews and bring them to read aloud."

• Everyone in Ann Goldman's group in Oak Park, Illinois, shares responsibility for obtaining reviews, etc. She specified that her group was "free form," with only willing members leading a discussion. "Often a member will have a particular interest or expertise related to the book and will create a structured discussion."

• Jeane Lumley of Parker, Colorado, stated that everything in her group is done by willing members. "Some take hostessing duties, some bring refreshments, some do author research, some lead a discussion."

• An anonymous woman wrote, "[L]eader reads any biographical material on the author, book reviews, other books by the same author, or anything that she thinks may help the discussion. Members usually just read the book."

This was also the basic venue for member-led groups one hundred years ago. Members, except for the leader/facilitator who did advance preparation, just showed up having read the book (or not). As I perceive from my research, this is the modus operandi of the majority of member-led groups in the country today. The members of the member-led group in which I now participate are fairly serious literary critics. Each of us has our own slant on the way we perceive a book, and bring questions, thoughts, and secondary information to enhance the discussion in these various directions. The different personalities and interests of your members will play a great part in the quality of your discussions.

- Pat Henning of Crystal Lake, Illinois, wrote, "Anyone who finds related articles brings copies to the group. No person monopolizes. We go off on tangents, but then one of us, not always the same person, brings us back to talking about the book." Sherryl Engstrom was my contact for this group. She told me that the group began as participants in a course at a local community college. "It was called Women's Literature Discussion, and though the membership was not limited to women, women were all who came. When the course ended, we continued." That was in 1989, and today this group of eight women, high school and college graduates ranging in age from twenties to sixties, get together semimonthly on Wednesday nights for three-plus hours. Sherryl, who was the instructor for the course, now is paid to facilitate the group.

- Sue Stefancik of Hancock, Michigan, wrote, "Organization: 8:00–8:45 p.m., background on the author and discussion of book in general led by one member. 8:45–9:30 p.m., open discussion. Then refreshments. In May, when people bring suggestions for the next year's reading list, they usually volunteer to be the leader of the book they want. Leaders use libraries for reviews. Some leaders know the authors or have had some experience with the subject matter. Members only have to read the book. If they want to add any information they have found, it's always welcome during the talk."

Once you enter into the reading group process and begin to see the myriad connections that art has to life, you will look at our information-saturated world with different, more discerning eyes, and start to notice how current events connect to the reflective mirrors writers hold up to us, to society, in their literature. The wise Native American philosophy of Chief Luther Standing Bear, an Oglala Sioux, states that "knowledge was inherent in all things. The world was a library." Before bookshelves were invaded by insights and analyses of social scientists statistically recording "the activities of humans," it was the exclusive purview of journalists who traveled to exotic lands, diarists, poets, and novelists to record the life truly lived.

Magazines and newspapers are overflowing with stories that affirm the relevancy of, and sociological insights to, your readings. Examples of helpful supplementary information are feature stories on the author, news articles concerning social issues that the book addresses (such as AIDS, divorce, South African history and politics, or data on the passionate love affairs of married women). More academic supplements include nonfiction books (such as those on astrology, Native American cultures, the history of England, and myths). Dictionaries are often pulled off the shelves for reference. I often bring copies of relevant encyclopedia pages or poems mentioned in the text. I search for and bring pictures of any particular paintings or buildings the author references.

The book itself and the ideas and issues threaded through it will direct the scope of subject matter. Characters' names, specific constellations, trees, insects/animals, and historic events will offer you clues to guide you to more complete understanding. The title of Katherine Anne Porter's story "Flowering Judas" may prompt a religious perspective for the analysis, so biblical stories and reference material may be helpful. When discussing Jane Smiley's *Ordinary Love and Good Will*, I brought an article from *People* magazine concerning a man who plucked his family out of their affluent lifestyle and placed them on a farm in California. The parallels were significant in terms of paternal controls and the influence of social and historical forces on lifestyle choices. (For those of you who may not have read this book, the fictional protagonist grew up on a farm and was a Vietnam War veteran. These factors were discussed in my groups as strong influences on his lifestyle choice.) When my groups discussed *Jasmine* by Bharati Mukherjee and *Heat and Dust* by Ruth Prawer Jhabvala, I researched and made copies for everyone of five pages of notes explaining Hinduism, without which much of the value, or essence, of the author's intent would have been lost.

TONE

The tone of your discussion will evolve from the personalities and desires of your members. To discern their seriousness of purpose, I asked group members about the tone of their discussions in the questionnaire. Were they casual/conversational, structured/academic, intense/emotional? Whether member-led or professionally led, the answers were basically the same. Most indicated a casual/conversational tone. A few elaborated.

- "Our discussions are less formal as we come to know each other better. We discuss our books, but we also serve as an emotional outlet." (This comment is from a woman in a professionally led group.)
- " . . . the emotional factor plays a very significant role."
- "It's primarily serious, but a lot of fun, humor, and emotional intensity are there."
- "Good friends and very respectful of each other's ideas."
- "Varied casual and academic, as the leader suggests topics."
- "Unstructured. We often discuss the women's lives in the book compared to our own and women today."
- "This [casual] tone came about as the most natural. . . . [I]t was never discussed."
- "The tone is determined by the person's [leader's] personality and interests."
- "Friendly, safe. Members share personal stories and anecdotes when they are relevant to content material."
- "The original founders were serious, dedicated to discussing ideas as revealed in literature."
- "Although the discussion can turn very academic during the meeting, the overall tone is very informal. We are all friends, so a relaxed attitude carries into our discussions."

The Best of Both Worlds

As a segue into examining professionally led groups, let me share with you the comments of Marla, a woman who is in a group of ten that has been meeting for fourteen years. Marla's group currently has two of its original members, having gone through several dozen members in the intervening years. It is comprised of city (Chicago) and suburban women who are married, divorced, or never married, all in their thirties or forties. The group meets on Friday evenings for buffet dinner, discussion, then informal socializing. For years they were member-led, and as Marla says, "tended to ramble a bit. We often felt frustrated and that was when we lost members and enthusiasm. We do much better with structure." Marla's group hired a leader—me. Theirs is a classic story of a floundering group needing a shot of external leadership.

Many times someone will ask if I can take over leadership of his or her group, either from another leader or because they decided they needed one. If I can, I do, but when a time conflict prevents this, I suggest a single consultation meeting between myself and the group. At that time, we discuss a preselected book. As I lead the discussion, I try to teach them leadership and structural guidelines that they can put into practice or use when they interview another professional group leader. What makes Marla's group and one other special is that I only meet with them on alternate months; for intervening months they are member-led. This may be because, as Marla stated in her questionnaire, "Our leader doesn't want to commit to a Friday night every month," or for financial reasons.

Some groups hire different leaders for each meeting. One group hires a leader for three meetings, scheduling three different leaders throughout their season. Some groups alternate two different leaders on a monthly basis.

An outside facilitator does not negatively affect the intimate relationships within a group. If any of you have that misconception, please erase it. Yes, at times I feel personal information that would have been reiterated if I were not there is left unsaid, but for the most part a professional facilitator works within a group's already established atmosphere. Marla's is a group of confidantes, totally at ease with each other. In some groups, while a warm cordiality exists, I sense a protective tentativeness. In my special Friday afternoon short-story group, souls are bared at every meeting—there's no holding back—and most of these women are not friends outside the group. I, and other professionals, I am sure, lead according to the group's personality and desires. If a group wants a lecture for two hours, so be it. If a group doesn't want to pick apart the narrative construction, so be it. If a group wants to ignore author and only respond personally, so be it.

Fortunately, I am retained by many enthusiastic, thinking readers, but any group at any time could decide to go it alone. Years ago I was a member in a professionally led group that lost its leader to law school. We attempted to become a member-led group about the same time I was feeling my wings as a professional. I brought leadership qualities and extensive research and preparation to my turn to lead. Gradually, when it became obvious that others didn't want to expend the effort and that I loved what I was doing, the group hired me. I now facilitate that group monthly, and it runs smoothly.

Anyone in your group could emerge as your leader. If he or she enjoys it and is good at it, open your arms in appreciation. If it's money as well as love and admiration that he or she wants, give it gladly. A good leader is a blessing and a motivating force to a group. Marla's group wants her to take over the alternate months when I am not there. Enjoy, Marla.

By virtue of education in English literature, social work, teaching, or library sciences, or a blend of any of these, an individual will exhibit leadership abilities and mastery of fields of knowledge that lend themselves to reading group facilitation. Of the facilitators that I know, several have advanced degrees and teach or taught junior high, high school, or adult education courses. One began as a Great Books discussion leader at two Chicago-area libraries. All but one have gregarious personalities that lend themselves well to initiating conversations. The other individual is more lecturer/educator than facilitator.

WHAT DO YOU LOOK FOR IN A PROFESSIONAL LEADER?

Knowledge of the elements of literature and methods of critical analysis and commentary. A self-motivated, continuing education.

• A thirst for the research and preparation process.

• Time and dedication. Balancing the demands of my job (primary and secondary reading time, research and preparation time, travel and group time) with a private life is as challenging for me as it is for someone who works in the corporate environment. Professional reading group facilitators are self-employed and most are definitely not in it for the money. Several hold other jobs along with their literary pursuits.

- Leadership ability. This is not to say that group members are not leader quality; indeed, my case is a perfect example, as my career grew out of being a group member. But problems can arise when one member attempts internal control and leadership without group permission. As a hired leader, that's one of the items in my job description.
- Showmanship. Yes, it's true. And it's work. When I've felt ill or depressed, walking into someone's home for a two-hour session is the last thing I want to do. But I'm a professional there to do a job. I have a responsibility to the people who have prepared for and traveled to that moment in time and who expect me to lead them in an orderly, entertaining, elucidating, and stimulating discussion.

Groups that have been floundering may be rejuvenated under professional leadership. Others just forming may do best with professional leadership from the start. As with anyone in a professional field, the process of building trust needs time and takes effort by both parties. Once a leader establishes this with a group, it can flourish beautifully into the future.

- Judith Palarz of Los Angeles put together a sheet of information about her ideas for reading groups and now leads four of them. She is willing to conduct daytime and evening groups and designs "mini-courses" to suit a group's interests. Judith, a self-proclaimed bibliophile, also wants to open a bookstore with her husband. She is searching for a location.
- Allen Schwartz of Skokie, Illinois, currently leads more than a dozen groups and conducts "cultural caravans" every summer to Stratford, Ontario, theater and to London's West End theater in the spring. He states, "[W]orthwhile authors and titles give me continuous new insights." On why a group should have a professional leader, he says, "So that the members receive maximum benefit from the time they have invested in reading and then attending. The testimony of members from groups without a professional leader leads me to believe [there is] idle conversation, a flippant approach, a lack of seriousness, and little enhancement." Allen's advice: "Get yourself a professional leader! The sooner you do, the quicker and larger will be your return in terms of time and insight."
- Barbara Nelson, who leads fourteen groups in the Mill Valley area of California, commented in the same vein. "Professional leaders consistently put effort into providing information and a perspective that indi-

vidual members do not. If they're good, they should have a literary background the members do not have. But most important, they keep discussions on track. Nearly all of the book groups I have were in danger of disintegrating without a leader. People didn't read the books or discuss them when they got together." Her advice: "Be clear about the essentials when the group forms: number of members, cost, time (be firm!), how new members are added, responsibilities of members (read the book? come even if you haven't?), and schedule (can it be altered? how? why?)."

• Roberta Rubin, who now owns The Book Stall in Winnetka, Illinois, led a group of twenty to thirty women for seven years before buying the store. "I had been trained as a Junior Great Books leader. While doing that, I started a women's group. I selected the syllabus, usually on a theme—writers, British contemporary, etc. I charged them $25 for ten sessions, September to May. I led the discussion primarily as a Great Books discussion (Socratic method), but did quite a bit of preparation. I extended the concept into the bookstore, bringing in various leaders." Roberta started these Wednesday morning discussion groups in 1984, free to the public, but now charges $5 a session, which is credited to purchases. If bookstores in your area offer book discussions, this is an excellent opportunity to learn about new books and also observe different leaders.

• Carol Friedman has two graduate degrees and a Ph.D. in literature, eight years of college teaching, and twelve years of experience as a discussant. She currently leads five groups. "I take copious notes on each book and write numerous questions to ask regarding theme, style, the author's bio and previous works, and relevance to current events, etc." Hiring a professional leader "makes for a much more structured and cohesive discussion and is ultimately much more satisfying to the members. Try to formulate a book list and schedule meetings as far in advance as possible. Select a leader for each discussion and expect the leader to keep the analysis on track. Try to limit extraneous remarks."

These leaders reiterate what has been my experience, too. Member-led—very nice. Professionally led—even better. Most of the leaders commented on their efforts to promote maximum discussion and personal expression while controlling irrelevant and monopolizing conversation. Allen uses questions directed into "meaningful avenues." Barbara's insight: "People can be challenged to push themselves when they read if they are clear why they're in a book group. The facilitator's job is to articulate and remind people of the group's purpose."

HOW DO WE FIND ONE? WHAT WILL IT COST?

Most leaders are found by word of mouth. Again, if you know any, please send me some information on who and where they are. Since I'm anxious to help all readers, maybe I can become a matchmaker. If your group is contemplating this step, call friends who are in groups, local libraries, and local bookstores. Hopefully, you will soon be able to call me for assistance. If reader response to this book is good, I may start a national network for readers and leaders. You can contact me at Reading Women, P.O. Box 296, Winnetka, IL 60093.

INTERVIEW

Ask questions in person or over the phone. Ask about experience, book selecting, handling the discussion, handling problem members, starting/stopping on time, smoking—anything you want. Ask if you can observe the person "at work." I always grant this request, even encourage it, and go out of my way to seek permission from a group for "guests" to observe me. If a group then wants to hire me, I contract for three meetings, after which they can decide if they want me to continue. This plan gives each of us an opportunity to try each other out but not get married.

Barbara Nelson in Mill Valley, California, meets "with a group once at no charge and then allow[s] the people to determine if they want to make a commitment for further sessions." Barbara charges $15 per person per meeting for a ten-meeting session and asks for payment in advance. Judith Palarz tells me that she charges the same and that around Los Angeles the going rate is twice that much for a two-hour meeting. Carol Friedman charges $100 per person for the year of ten meetings.

I charge two separate ways, depending on the manner of group organization. For groups already organized, I charge $125 to $165 a meeting, and these groups have ten to twenty-five members.

Evening groups pay a premium for my time; I charge less for daytime groups. The individuals signing up for one of the groups I organize pay me $10 to $12 per person per session, and I ask for a ten-month payment in advance. Snowbirds pay accordingly, as do the financially strapped. Some groups I lead are under the auspices of nonprofit charitable organizations; I accept much less payment for my time and consider it community service. Sherryl Engstrom's group pays her the same as they paid to the local community college where she was the instructor—$80 per ten-month session. They meet semimonthly for three hours.

In the Chicago area I have heard of leaders charging $50 per session. Others are asking and getting $175 to $250 for one two-hour meeting. I think the price discrepancies are less a matter of "you get what you pay for" than "what the market will bear."

Leaders have different things to offer. Some are more pedantic/academic/structured; some are more therapeutic/group dynamics–oriented. Some are head cases and need adoration; some are humble and self-effacing. Some are incompetent; some are worth their weight in gold. If you are considering hiring a leader, do your research, observe, ask questions, and clarify answers. Hire on mutually agreeable terms. If you have complaints or criticisms, voice them. All employees need a job evaluation. I encourage my groups to evaluate my performance all the time. I want to nip complaints in the bud so they don't fester.

If the leader and the group come to an impasse, fire the leader. Say whatever you think appropriate. "We'll pay you through March and then we'll be doing something with our group leadership." Or, if the leader was paid in advance for the season, just don't have him or her come back in the fall. "We'll call you. We haven't decided what we want to do about next year" is adequate. More to the point, you could forthrightly inform the person of the reasons for dismissal. This might help in the leader's self-evaluation for the future. Remember, hiring and firing are normal business procedures. Groups are customers, clients, and consumers. Act accordingly.

To sum up about groups, here's a special message from Roberta Rubin, owner of the Book Stall: "As a way to get customers in the store, I decided ten years ago to start an in-store book club. It answered many other needs—a cozy place to meet people to talk about books, a chance to read books (often the classics) that you would not read on your own, a forum for intellectual stimulation, and not to be dismissed, a consciousness-raising group that might substitute for another kind of self-help group. Our particular reading group was bolstered by a wide range of ages of its participants. We had two stalwart eighty-year-olds who brought a keenness of eye, and experience, to the group. And we had several men in their sixties and seventies. And then we filled out with . . . women in . . . midlife who loved to read, loved to talk, or who just wanted to be there. The leaders were, and still are, wonderfully skilled at their craft, but the participants contribute greatly. Composition is something to think about.

"Without question, however—there are no *rules* in starting up a book club. Each group is different, and what is more, each discussion within each group is different. A book means one thing to me and another to you. A book may move you in an entirely new way when you discuss it as from when you last read it. Literature which had no relevance ten years ago may be achingly revealing now. That's what's so wonderful about books and makes discussion about them so exciting. Enlighten your life by joining a book club!"

CHAPTER 10

CHAT ROOM VS. LIVING ROOM

The compilers of dictionaries have difficulty keeping pace with the evolution of our language, which, being fascinating to me, seems to be driven by sociological and technological advancements that supersede language. When people began to build on that extra room to their homes that was bigger than a den/library and in addition to the living room, it needed a name. "Let's call it a family room," somebody said one day, and so it goes. No children can play in living rooms anymore: "Go play in the family room, please."

In the last few years, PC and internet users wanting to commune with others needed "places" to meet; these places created by the gods of websites needed a name, and voila! now we have *Chat Rooms*. Parlors, living rooms, dens, family rooms—now chat rooms. A curious handle for a place where nobody can hear each other but anybody who wants to can enter invited or uninvited, hang around, chat with the known and unknown, and leave (or disconnect) when the mood strikes.

As much as reading groups are a cultural phenomenon of the decade, I'd hazard to say that chat rooms win the intrigue prize.

Chat rooms are not "bulletin boards" or "forums" where internet users post a message which is listed for any future visitor's response. Those passive types of communing are done in isolation.

Chat rooms are visiting areas in cyberspace where (usually) anyone is welcome to come along and, for the purpose of this book, discuss a selected title, or any book(s) for that matter. There are chat rooms everywhere for discussion of anything (or nothing or sordid things), but many sites (publishers, bookstores) sponsor chat rooms for book or literary discussions. Some of these are scheduled (find events calendars on website menus), some are spontaneous. Chat rooms prescheduled for a book discussion are usually visited only by those interested. Usually. An intruder can be a momentary irritant, but so can one of the participants.

Here are some of the things I have learned from my experiences in designated chat rooms or prearranged virtual reading groups:

- You may have to LOG IN or "login." Devise a code name for yourself that you will remember; you can use this same password throughout cyberspace if it passes entry check as previously untaken.

- It's beneficial to read the FAQs, or Frequently Asked Questions, that some sites offer.

- If you enter a book discussion and haven't finished the book, be prepared for what's called a "spoiler," which is the person who spills the beans or the beans themselves, i.e., details about the end of the book.

- Because anyone can enter, homogeneity is almost always nonexistent.

- The identities of the participants are unknown so while you sense the mix, you can't "see" or "hear" the mix, only "read" everyone's comments.

- By the time I have written a comment or question on the keyboard and sent it (press "Enter"), the focus may have completely shifted onto another topic. Two or three threads of conversation may be going simultaneously. As a moderator, I can attempt to refocus but this may not always be the case in a random setup.

- Not everyone is bright; not everyone is nice; some are brilliant; some are brazen and forceful.

- Some friends meet and may monopolize the discussion; some may even send up secret, private, or personal messages.

- Chat-room discussions can be cacophonous yet organized free-for-alls with people talking over one another. That's the nature of the activity. Fast-paced, faceless, a bit frenzied, and fun. The facelessness may allow some inhibitions to come through. Given that at press time the government has declined to censor cyberspace, you take the chance of seeing anything in writing.

- Those of you who have fairly well-organized rules of order in your face-to-face reading groups may be in for a—treat?—surprise? when you enter one of these chat rooms.

- Suggestion: have your book handy so you can cite page references. Those that attended my virtual reading groups seemed to appreciate this as we discussed certain points that could be refuted or proved by the text.

- Conversing with a faceless stranger feels a bit alien at first. But chat rooms can extend my philosophy about book groups being the ideal of democracy. Every voice is equal, the will of the people is supreme, the right to "say" anything is fundamental.

- I can't help but think that chat rooms are the good news and the bad news. We individuals anywhere on the planet can commune faceless using only shared language, a thing of beauty. My first respondent on books.com was from Zaire! A woman (for almost a year I only knew her by her genderless code name) from Texas attends my virtual reading groups, so while she's at her monitor and I'm at mine in a suburb outside of Chicago, we exchange literary ideas and personal epiphanies that emerge from the texts. Yet the limitations exclude human contact. Well, perhaps it's a beginning, a continuation of dialogue and ideas between humans who could otherwise not connect at all, another and different thing of beauty.

Our technology allows us to expand our connections with each other, and we are given opportunities to create stories as we connect. I'd like to hear some of these stories. E-mail me at rachelj@interaccess.com with any you want to share. I may moderate more virtual reading groups in the future. Check simonsays.com and other publishers for the latest news on their chat rooms and events. Have fun; enjoy our global community of readers and thinkers.

Chapter 11

WHAT DO WE *REALLY* TALK ABOUT?

On the first level, we read a story, examining the concepts and details that bind the narrative and move it forward. On the next level, we read for meaning and thematic content and examine the structural techniques. Reaction to this reading activity is what I call "reader response." Whether the reader is a Harvard professor, a bookstore clerk, a cosmetician, a lawyer, or a homemaker with three children, each responds in some way to what she or he reads.

The academicians and the social scientists call it literary criticism, but we call what goes on in our book club, book group, or reading group a discussion.

To illustrate different levels of discourse on subject matter, let me use several reactions to a story that has received much critical attention. Charlotte Perkins Gilman's story, "The Yellow Wallpaper," written before the turn of the century, is about a young, new mother.

· Feminist scholars' perspectives for the most part focus on the diagnosis of hysteria and depression—conventional women's diseases of the nineteenth century—and the prescribed therapeutic regimen. Ellen Moers (in *Literary Women*) sees the story as a macabre, postpartum fantasy. The story has been noted as a valuable personal and historical document, evidence of women's illnesses and their writing for personal autonomy, and as a response to restrictive lives. The inclusion of academic and social scientists' writings will add a scholarly tone to your discussions, but finding this scholarly material takes time. Have your reference librarian help you. For the most part, literary criticism is found in the 800's of a library collection arranged using the Dewey decimal classification. Perhaps introducing these writings will expand your vision, as they have mine.

• A reading group member might say: "No wonder she went crazy. Her husband and doctor's 'cure' forbid her from talking, seeing her baby, or even writing in her diary. If she complained, her husband used her displays of emotion to build up his case. There's a joke in our house: When my husband says I'm a crab and I snap, 'No, I'm not,' he says, 'See, I told you so.'

"I wonder how autobiographical this story is. Boy, the message comes out loud and clear. These two guys, her husband and brother-in-law, both doctors, are cruel. Didn't they know what they were doing? Don't men know how they've mistreated women?"

• For me, "The Yellow Wallpaper" depicted a dark time that I did not enjoy upon the birth of my first daughter. In 1970 I wasn't in a reading group and didn't have the opportunity to openly share personal life experiences. I had not read anything by Gilman, since her works were not as yet unearthed by the feminists. (Remember, Marilyn French's *The Woman's Room* wasn't published until 1977.) If I had had this story as a reference to gauge my own pain, I could have saved myself a lot of confusing feelings. If I had read it before giving birth, I would have learned much from this protagonist's journey and been better mentally prepared and aware of postpartum feelings. Presenting this story to a group of young women on the brink of marriage and/or motherhood is offering a gift of knowledge, balance, belonging, and normalcy. It's a catalyst for discussions of intimate feelings that increase mental health and stability.

A reader in one of my groups might inquire, "Did Gilman intend for us to react this way? Was she telling a story or sermonizing?" Another reader may ask, "Why do you think Gilman chose this first-person voice? It's like a monologue." These comments concern structure, style, and tone that, for some groups, comprise a very substantial part of the group discussion and can be explored with or without scholarly supplements. Given the right atmosphere, a group can explore many different levels of interpretation and criticism. These could vary from the literal or surface story or the structure, tone, and style of the writer, to the psychological, sociopolitical, historical, metaphysical, mythic, metaphoric, anagogic, or ontological.

When you and your group enter into your book discussion, a spectrum of issues and ideas will emerge. A historian, for instance, would likely contribute an intellectual dimension to the discussion that would differ from that of a junior high school English teacher or a woman who watches "Oprah" daily and reports to us the applicable interviews. Such varying levels of discourse, if they exist in your group, will hopefully coalesce into a happy compromise level. I feel that anything that is relevant is an admissible contribution to the discussion, no matter on what "level" it exists.

Group Ambiance

The opening line of a Raymond Carver story states, "I've seen some things" ("Mr. Coffee and Mr. Fixit" in *What We Talk About When We Talk About Love*.) There are a few things I've learned about book groups and literary analysis I want to share with you, but I am no different than all of you who have lived and read and learned a lot and have a lot to share—I just may have eavesdropped on more stories, be they fictional or the ones I hear in the groups.

As a facilitator, one of my professional aims is to create a comfortable atmosphere in which the discussion will flourish. Once that comfort level is accomplished, a lot can happen. It's wonderful fun to sit with inquisitive, enthusiastic people and throw out ideas and watch them spin in the air.

Your discussion can whirl around in many ways. Some groups hold very structured, formal, orderly, and scholarly discussions—more academic and intellectual than social and conversational. In chapter 9 on member-led and professionally led groups, I reported that most groups noted in their questionnaire responses that the tone of their discussions was casual/conversational, which in no way should eliminate the relevance of those who responded "structured/academic" or "intense/emotional." Since some people marked all three categories, it is clear that within the framework of any group, the tone can shift at will.

Casual. You desire a relaxed atmosphere, a break from everyday tensions. You want to sit around and share with friends—whether you liked the book or not, how you felt about the characters, whom you liked and whom you didn't and why, what you thought about the ending, if you liked this book more or less than the author's others, and who would play what parts in the movie version (very important!).

Academic. As long as you put forth the effort to read the selection, you would like to know how others reacted to some specific issues: plotline development and credibility, moral/ethical choices that characters made, the authenticity of cultural or era representations, the author's message, and more. You came to learn and don't want the meeting to turn into a social get-together after an hour's discussion.

Intense. When you discuss, for example, why Codi Nodine (protagonist in Barbara Kingsolver's *Animal Dreams*) went back to Carlo in Telluride, you find yourself in a heated discussion about maturation possibilities in thirty-year-olds and issues of behavioral motivations and whether or not we can truly change our perceptions. You find yourself dead set opposed to what someone else has articulated, and an intense discussion heats up on definitions of "self." An explosion or debate ensues. Hopefully, this intellectual and emotional volcano explodes in the right spirit and is enjoyed by the entire group. Many feel exalted after having a chance to get worked up, to clarify and defend their philosophies. Much controversy also arose in group discussions of Jane Smiley's *A Thousand Acres* in regard to the verisimilitude of Ginny's and Rose's abuse at the hands of their father, Larry Cook. The tricky psychology of memory and revenge motivations spurred heated debate.

In truth, an active, vital book group engaging in criticism, analysis, interpretation, and commentary may encounter a combination of these three atmospheres at varying times. Eventually, the group's personalities will tailor an acceptable atmosphere.

What Do People Really Talk About in Reading Groups?

On the questionnaire, the inquiry read, "What aspects of a book do you usually discuss at a meeting?"

Most answers mentioned background of the author, purpose, style, stature, and focus. One theory of literary criticism purports that a reader need never be given an author's name or identity to appreciate the work. I will sometimes withhold biographical data about an author because the theory continues that a work of literature, by itself, exudes the essence of the author. "What do we presume to know about the author?" is an appropriate segue into the discussion on themes, message, or purpose.

I am continuously enthralled with the connection between life and the author's creation. What generates creativity? And what generates decisions about lifestyle choices? Regarding the connection between art and author and life, recluses such as J. D. Salinger and Thomas Pynchon intrigue me. Suicides are testimony to the theory that art is not always an adequate catharsis of painful experience. Writers such as William Wharton (*Birdy, Dad*) capture the imagination. Wharton is an American who became a painter living on a houseboat in France and conscientiously remained anonymous until a painful personal experience compelled him to go public with *Franky Furbo* in 1989: A multicar accident caused by smoke from a government-condoned field fire in Oregon in 1988 resulted in the death of his daughter, son-in-law, and two granddaughters. *Franky Furbo* had political and spiritual motivation.

The following topics were mentioned in questionnaire responses:

Characters and Story Line. The way the author develops his or her characters affects our responses to them; at the same time, our response to characters is driven by a myriad of personal experiences.

Why one person finds a character despicable and another sympathetic turns the wheels of a good exploratory discussion on character analysis. Since character analysis is the study of human nature, behavioral psychological motivation, and the development and actualization of self, how "self" is perceived and enacted is the subject of much discourse on every level of literary analysis.

Characters' Actions involve the relationship between fate and free will. Are characters' actions (and subsequently our own actions) the result of freedom of choice or destiny, some intangible, controlling force? Although this question of control can never be rationally resolved, it remains as enormously important in literature as in life. Perhaps part of your discussion can question why this is so. If nothing is in our control and all is fated or decreed, then why struggle to change any circumstances of life? But if we are free, then we can, by our own decisions, change ourselves and the world in which we live. The liberal (*liber* is Latin for "free") attitude has been dominant for roughly two centuries, since the French Revolution. But certainly much of human civilization bases itself on early concepts of Fate. One need only study early Greek literature and both New and Old Testaments to examine this line of thinking. The books of *Genesis* and *Job* and *Oedipus the King* are perfect examples. The late, great writer I. B. Singer said in his Yiddish inflection, "Of course we have free will. We have no choice."

Your attitude toward characters' actions will reflect the way you assign moral responsibility for what happens in the novel.

Social Implications. The changing circumstances of the external world affect characters' (and our) concepts of morality and humans' place in the universe. The questions raised in literature concerning moral responsibility connect to the events happening in our daily lives: euthanasia, genetic engineering, the allocation of tax dollars for space programs, welfare payments, AIDS research, immigration laws, the role of the United States in other nations' internal affairs, the foster care system, alternative coupling, child rights, adultery, tax evasion. These and more issues of responsibility motivate us to continue the dialogue. If we could answer questions of responsibility definitively, we would stop asking them, and life would stagnate.

Symbolism. Universal symbols such as a cross, a rose, and a flag connote Christianity, love, and a certain country. Apple pie, fleur-de-lis, and umbrellas are cultural symbols. Other symbols have specific political, religious, or cultural references that, unless you know "the code," may elude you in your reading. These are the ones I attempt to track down and, in the tracking, like Alice, fall down wells into rooms of learning experiences. I thrive on the doors that the decoding of symbols open for me. This pursuit opens up my world to new vocabularies, new frames of reference, and new modes of defining the universe.

Sometimes "symbolists" exploit private, intimate, coded languages known only to the author. Such hidden symbols may annoy the reader. One group member noted, "We become irritated with writers who make comprehension too difficult for us and do not let us in on the important secret." (This statement certainly extends to other elements of structure. Writers can be too evasive, cryptic, and enigmatic. "There are no secrets better kept than the secrets everybody guesses," said George Bernard Shaw.)

Author's Purpose. Searching for the meaning behind the story is one of the major goals of group inquiry. What is the vision displayed in words? Is it optimistic? pessimistic? prophetic? cautionary? humorous? satirical? venomous? cathartic? Always interesting questions to explore. Why do authors write? What is the author's purpose, other than perhaps money and fame?

"Writing is a dog's life, but the only life worth living," said Flaubert. "One ought to write when one leaves a piece of one's flesh in the inkpot each time one dips one's pen," said Tolstoy. For me, these writers ascend to the mountaintops of their breed. They communicate moral, ethical, spiritual, ecological, and sociopolitical consciousness and remind us of our lowly human status in this mysterious universe.

One of the great themes of literature is the meaning of greatness. Traditional understanding of it connotes a special power, usually ordained by birth or divine intervention. Biblical tales and Greek mythology examine greatness, and much of contemporary literature reworks these. Jane Smiley's Pulitzer Prize–winning novel, *A Thou-*

sand Acres, is a derivative of Shakespeare's *King Lear*—both about power, and each stylistic and structurally fitting in its time and place.

Greatness need not be of the public domain, and much of literature examines extraordinary, personal and spiritual, private individual accomplishments that help us redefine the concept of "hero." A perfect example is the humble servant Félicité in Flaubert's "A Simple Heart." Comparing and contrasting modes of greatness are achieved in discussing the roads taken by the two sisters, Codi and Hallie, in Barbara Kingsolver's *Animal Dreams.* Codi, the "fallen one," embarks on an arduous journey home to tend to her ailing father, to confront her past, and to search for balance and rootedness. Hallie takes off to help Nicaraguan farmers under Sandinista terrorism and to fulfill her ideal of a political, humane, connected self. Hallie dies in her quest. Decades ago, Hallie would be the great and idealized hero in the Hemingway and Melville tradition, and Codi would be the uninteresting "loser" sister. I questioned my groupies on why Codi in this 1990s novel was the protagonist, and not Hallie. Kingsolver, like many authors, begs the question, What is the meaning of greatness? The question is relevant for all time, and in our time focuses our attention on definitions of personal and public success.

Credibility. Some literature, such as Gothic or fantasy, asks that we suspend disbelief. Some novels are flawed because they ask too much of our indulgence; in others, it is to be understood as part of the form. For example, when Mary Wollstonecraft Shelley wrote her famous tale, *Frankenstein,* the mysterious, exotic, unexplained elements of the Gothic form were popular and quite accepted. During your discussion you will be able to discern the difference as well as the authorial reasons for stretching credibility.

Readers' Emotional Response. Most readers want to "feel" the book. How you feel at certain stops along the plotline is important. "How did you feel when . . . ?" actually is two questions: "How did you feel when Snow White took a bite out of the apple?" and "How do you think Snow White felt when she took a bite out of the apple?" The first examines your emotional reaction to the plotline action; the latter examines your intellectual response to the behavior of the character. By splitting the questions you can discuss, you and your responses separate from, but are emotionally connected to, the action in the novel.

Resolution. Does the plot ending meet your satisfaction? Endings are difficult to devise and somewhat artificial, since the characters' lives don't continue past the last page. However, the author does need to bring a sense of an ending. Popular among modern and postmodern stylists is the nonending, which they feel better represents reality. Generalization: Human nature seems to prefer art and life presented in neat little packages like a half-hour sitcom. When a novel doesn't offer that, we react. Something to discuss in your group.

Personal Reference. Personal references actually make up a large portion of reading group discussions. Our personal, real-life experiences are rendered important and meaningful in connection to the book and enlarge our understanding of it. The more this concept of the interconnectedness of life and art is part of your discussion, the more you can revel in its mystique. After a while, you may wonder if you are living life or art!

Literary Merit. What constitutes good literature? Which is a well-written book? To me, good literature glows with an incandescent sensitivity to its responsibility as history, morality, and affirmation of the human spirit and imagination. By virtue of its own presence in the universe, we are affirmed. Even the most horrid chapters of history are conferred with a veil of beauty through the artful act of writing. "Painful." "Depressing." "Disturbing." These are common reactions to some of the most beautifully rendered reflections of human experience. The telling itself is an act of redemption. Is there redemption? Is there morality in art? Some say yes, art flows from responsibility; some say no, art is pure form—art for its own sake. Think about these polarities when you discuss literary merit.

To be considered of merit, literature does not have to be understood; it has to mean something to you, although not always is that meaning clear. My mother, Helen Weiss, who has been studying literature for thirty-five years, remarked on the value of not understanding: "Sometimes when she [her leader] is very puzzled and there is no real 'Aha!,' we have to accept the fact that the story is going to be unresolved, and there will be no redemption. We might feel uncomfortable, but we do think about the work." My mother's experience is mine, too, and will be yours if you do not expect literature to *always* provide you with answers, guidelines, or strict codes that will assure order in the cosmos. Life, by its very nature, is in motion, and we wrestle with the moving forces continuously. This is what literature shows us; this is what we ponder. Literature of merit sets this as its task.

Work's Similarity to Other Readings. I've been part of discussions in which a purist attitude excludes mention of other works. However, comparing and contrasting the present work with other works or with other works by the same author is always appropriate. Recently, my groupies compared Virginia Woolf's creation of her "room of one's own" ideology with Sandra Cisneros's *House on Mango Street.* Cisneros transforms the metaphor of "room" into "house," and overlays it with strong Mexican-American machismo culture and our country's ethnic biases against immigrants. We've also compared the writings of Leslie Marmon Silko to those of Barbara Kingsolver, as they incorporate Native American thought and ceremony.

It's very natural for you to compare an author's earlier and later works. But be careful not to exclude those in your group who haven't read them. I usually ask for a show of hands to see how many would be excluded from the conversation before I continue with a compare-and-contrast discussion. You can always suggest another book on the same topic or by the same author that you think your comembers might enjoy. Such networking is common among readers.

The more books your group reads and discusses together, the more you will be collecting a storehouse of references. In not too long you will hear yourself saying, "Remember when we read _____ and we talked about _____?" Cross-references are one of the beautiful outgrowths of reading groups. Childhood friends share childhood experiences; reading group members share books and their discussions of them.

Narrative. An author needs to make two primary decisions: what story to tell, and how to tell it. Narrative concerns the process, the form, the technique an author employs to impart her or his story. Variant forms, of course, influence variant reader responses, and discussion of this is important to any analysis you give a book. How you receive your information has as much, if perhaps not more, importance than what information you receive.

Some examples:

- In *Animal Dreams,* Kingsolver has Codi tell her story in past tense to an attentive reader/listener. Unbeknownst to Codi, we are also privileged to the interior thoughts and memories of her father. Without Doc Homer's interior narrative, our perception of him would be based only on Codi's narrative. With both, we become active, involved listeners.
- In Fay Weldon's *The Hearts and Lives of Men,* an uninvolved, unidentified, omniscient narrator tells the tale. The voice is quite motherly, caring, sympathetic, and in fact pushy, telling us what to think about which character and when to think it.

Much attention is being paid to narrative voice today, and writers are self-consciously aware of its importance in their works—some going so far as to say in various ways, "I'm only the voice telling the story. Don't believe me. I lie." This arena of discourse leaves much for the reader to think about as we participate in the story. Think of a triangle: you, the story, and the storyteller. The interconnectedness is of paramount importance.

Theme. The question, What is this book about? does not address subject matter; rather, it addresses the idea that builds and drives the force of the tale. Sometimes an author incorporates leitmotivs (subthemes) into a story, and sometimes a story has multiple themes. Everything—language, symbols, form, character development, story line—should reinforce the theme(s). This, too, brings merit to a book. The "what" and the "how" should be in symbiotic relation. The antithesis of this would be a book like Toni Morrison's *Beloved,* in which the story of slavery and infanticide is so very painful that Morrison chooses lilting poetic language to convey the tale. As she said, poetry was the only palatable access route to the story, and the only way she found it could be told.

Point of View. Once the themes are identified, discussion will center on the author's or characters' point of view or angle of vision. The author's and characters' points of view may not always be the same.

Style. Style addresses not who tells or what is told but the language, diction, sentence structure, and syntax used. The language that I am using to write this book would be termed *middle* as opposed to *grand* or *base*. It is not in any dialect, but it includes the colloquial. It is not obtuse, oblique, glib, flippant, street, unintelligible, haughty, sarcastic, ironic, etc. Style has a great deal to do with the time in which a work was written. An eighteenth-century style does not fit an expository novel about contemporary Harlem street life. The purposefulness of Faulknerian language and syntax is interesting to discuss, as is Alice Walker's in *The Color Purple*. In many novels, the style of writing is of great significance and examination if it brings forth insight into the intent of the author.

A word on reading out loud. The act of reading aloud is a transformative one. Life is breathed into language when it is spoken, and new perspectives are attained where perhaps they were hidden before. Inflection, nuance, and cadence all enrich meaning. Try it and stop to smell the beauty of the language.

Setting. Setting—along with character, plot, and theme—is one of the basic components of a story. Often, in regional novels the land or town itself becomes a character in the story. Think of the New Hampshire setting of Russell Banks's *Affliction*; rural, backwoods Mississippi in Larry Brown's *Joe*; or Texas and Mexico in Cormac McCarthy's *All the Pretty Horses*. Setting, the combination of time and place, grounds the plot and the characters. Fantasy minimizes the requirements for specific time and place (examples: Peter Pan, Alice in Wonderland, Snow White). Much can be gained from examination of the setting an author has chosen. Authenticity and selectivity of detail can be an important part of your discussion. What is authentic and what is selected from other details to create the point desired by the writer?

Time and Memory. The effect of the presence of time, the passage of time, and the limitations it produces are of great interest to authors, and their exploration of it is increasingly present in novels. If Oedipus had known that that old man was his father before he met him on the road, Freud may not have had a theory, and we'd be free of that complex (though somebody else probably would have given it another name). In a story, characters pass through their present, carrying their pasts in their memories and their hopes for the future in their hearts.

In addition to those topics mentioned by questionnaire respondents, I'd like to throw in some ideas of my own.

Self. As a continuation of the idea about character development, it may help a reader to think about the ways in which authors explore the concept of "self." Is there an essential self? What effect do socioeconomic, religious, ethnic, cultural, regional, and gender factors have on self? What effect do birthmarks, scars, dates of or events at birth (such as curses and earthquakes) have on personality? What effect does the physicality or the nationality of a person have? What effect does the time in which one is born have on the actual self? Considering time in relation to self opens various doors: the viability of the astrological import of being born under a certain planet at a given second or minute and not another, or a specific planet or configuration of planets; the concept of one life continued into another by genetics, legacies, names, reincarnations. Multigenerational sagas, biographies, or antibiographies (as we could call Virginia Woolf's *Orlando* in this instance) create and explore the means by which life is continued from one self into another as a sort of moving force of energy. And, in regard to the view of self, explore the multiple and sometimes oppositional "selves" in each one of us, or in the fictional characters: the androgynous, the good/evil, the passive/aggressive, the selfless/selfish, the spiritual/materialistic, the leader/follower, the parent/child, etc., etc. Again and again—in *Orlando,* in Cynthia Ozick's works, in Cheever's stories, in Raymond Carver's stories, in Alice Munro's stories, in Amos Oz's *Black Box,* in Bharati Mukherjee's *Jasmine,* in Toni Morrison's *Beloved*—issues of self are explored. Authors show us the possibilities of *other* selves emerging with the right stimulus, and we read of change and/or variations. Discuss these ideas as you consider authors' depictions of a self.

Laws of Physics. Connected to the idea of *stimulus* mentioned above, a story line operates under the scientific notion of energy and matter interacting with one another. Otherwise, nothing would happen in a story. I'm talking about the application of scientific terms such as catalysts, inertia, organicism, repulsion/attraction syndromes, and principles of thermodynamics. These and other theories explain natural phenomena that logically include human behavior. Therefore, the laws of physics should be operable in a plot. Some catalyst is needed to get the ball rolling. It may have occurred in some form before the novel's action begins. One example: *A Thousand Acres.* If Larry Cook had not sexually abused his daughter, Rose, her reaction when he abdicates legal control may have been entirely different. His legal action at the beginning of the novel puts in motion an inevitable set of circumstances. A second example: *The Bridges of Madison County.* If Robert Kincaid had not been photographing rural bridges, what course would Francesca's life have taken? *Beloved* (Morrison) and *The Shawl* (Ozick) are wonderful examples of action and reaction, the effect of the passage of time and the effect one person can have on another. Both Sethe and Rosa, caught in their particulars of self, descend into private hells. The passage of enough time and the arrival of the right person for the job help them back to life. Cause and effect. Causality. One body's actions affecting another. Authors experiment and theorize like scientists. Enjoy.

Design. In mathematics and in music, as in science, the design is carefully balanced and controlled. Visual and literary art operate under the same requirements. Watch for ways in which images frame a novel, appearing in the beginning and at the end. Watch for balance in the speed of action; introduction of characters; tension and release patterns; interweaving of themes, images, and symbols. Within the whole of the novel or short story lie hidden the preconceived formulations of design. *The Counterlife* by Philip Roth is an extraordinarily balanced, orchestrated novel, like a superb symphony.

The Concept of God. Whether through a strictly metaphysical or strictly ontological perspective, much literature (art) argues for or against the existence of God, as being, as supreme being, and in what form. High-minded philosophical arguments get boiled down to characters in novels who are acting and living within a universe in which God does or does not exist, and what effect that has on human behavior. Godlike or satanic figures constantly appear in novels, in the authors' vision of the universe. Our moral codes of behavior are strongly linked to these ideas. Although not a novel, Woody Allen's film *Crimes and Misdemeanors* finely examines and argues, with no conclusion, the existence of God. No conclusion, but it forces us to think about codes of morality and the meanings they have on our lives.

Translations. The absolute best way to appreciate the beauty and the idiomatic nuances of the language in a foreign work is by reading it in the original language. The next best, with great variations in quality, is through the English translation. We are captives of the timely arrival of translated publications and their quality. This is an interesting field of study, worthy of note when discussing any translation.

Following are some other comments about topics discussed in book groups across the country, as mentioned by questionnaire respondents.

- "Everything, and I mean everything. We change topics many times." — Sue Beauseigneur, Chicago

- "We talk about the plausibility and depth of the characters, the believability of the environment the author has set up, whether or not we thought the characters were likable, and broader social and political issues the book may have touched upon, and we compare the book to others the author has written and to books written by similar authors." —Nancy Feingold, Chicago

- "The whole book, beginning to end." —Madonna Hayes, West Milford, New Jersey

- " 'If' questions, and why or why not this book would become a classic." —Marjorie Maclean, Langley, Washington

- "The spiritual dimension of being human." —Penny Reick, Winnetka, Illinois. Penny belongs to a group of practicing Catholics who meet every Friday and call themselves "Friday Morning Theology," or as one member put it, "God seekers," because, as Penny says, "We are about the business of discovering or uncovering God in our lives as well as revealing God to each other and the world at large."

  I was the guest moderator for this group when they discussed a book about a woman who lived through the Holocaust. Past the framework of organized religion lies the focus of literature that contains varied elements of positive, life-affirming values. Books can be viewed as transformative journeys—both the stories in them and the discussion of them.

- "Focus on the author; the political and social significance." —Anonymous

- "Today's society, man/woman relations, morals." —Anonymous

- "Relationship to medicine." This comment comes from a medical school resident I met. It exemplifies how individuals apply their own focus.

- "Anything that comes to mind." —Beverly Pirtle, Huntington Beach, California. Good answer!

By quoting my seventy-three-year-old mother, I pay homage to her and the role she has played in my exploration of literature and life through literature. She never did get that questionnaire filled out, so I took down what she dictated on my recent visit:

"Without our group leader, we could not continue our discussions. She's irreplaceable. We spend two hours stimulating our minds as she points out a particular passage and asks the right questions. We've talked about black holes, quarks. She brings in how mathematics and music are so closely connected.

"Quality of light that comes through stained glass windows came out of a discussion of a short story that only peripherally mentioned stained glass windows. A couple of women are artists, so Edith [her leader, Edith Wegman] asked questions to pull out this idea that folds back onto the story—the issue of light and seeing life at angles. Light is the most important."

My mother mentioned that this particular discussion brought up the paintings of Mark Rothko in the Rothko Chapel in Houston, and in New York's Metropolitan Museum of Art, where his paintings are exhibited. Various group members had visited the exhibits and brought to the discussion the issue of how light gets played with in his dark colors. "Half the time I don't know what they are talking about. The discussion goes from one thing to another," my mother continued. "It's a very enriching experience. Besides learning, it opens up your heart and your mind. It isn't that you think 'I didn't know that,' but we've all had our prejudices in the group and now we have tempered them or are at least aware of them. And we don't mind saying vulgar language anymore. Every person has grown. Some grow and go away—to law, to get degrees in psychology. Some didn't dig it even though we tried; they couldn't see and crack the code of the process of the group."

CHAPTER 12

PAST FEAR

We are born, we live, we die, and some of us pay taxes; it *is* conceivable and possible to exist without ever reading a book, for pleasure or reflection, for any reason. My work, as well my being, epitomize devotion to the reverse; my life overflows with art and images. I can't get enough.

When my groups and I convene each September, and when we disperse for the summer months, I thank them for coming along with me on life's reverberating path that is bordered on one side with experience and on the other, literature. I can't imagine existence without these two dimensions. What *would* "being" be like if there were no reflecting mirror? The brush strokes luxuriously and carefully applied in the opening scene of the film *The English Patient* have their fictional or factual origins on cave walls in northern Africa, and create a mystery, an exposition, a version of history, and subsequent fiction. Rudimentary markings reverberate into reflective narrative, into quests for stories of life in different places, different times. Every brush stroke may provide clues, truths.

Some humans, called "readers," thrive on these quests, find

them stimulating, enlightening. The act of reading multiplies and magnifies existence. But not for all. In Alice Munro's story "Carried Away" (*Open Secrets*, Alfred A. Knopf, 1994), the widow Grace wants her dead husband's borrowed books immediately returned to the library. Grace is a woman who, I assume, lived without books. She may not have known how to read, she may have been indoctrinated to be suspect of the audacious deed, or she may have authentically existed without awareness of transcendent art. In my discussion groups, we focused on Munro's subtle illumination of this startling detail, and its significance. She "painted" with words a reflection of the possible life without books. Humans exist in a variety of cultures, yet no culture is without forms of reflecting that existence. Brush-strokes, words, and notes of music record existence, and transform it into noted experience. Tales, epics, paintings, symphonies, novels—from rudimentary brush strokes. They are ours for the taking.

I suppose it is possible that one, like Grace, *can* float through the born-live-die program with nary a reflective, introspective, analytical thought, with never employing a painting, a symphony, a book, or a ballet, as a "thought machine." You would not be reading these musings, though, if you've never read the Bible—and thought about it, or *Goldilocks and the Three Bears*—and thought about it, or that you have never read a story by Chekhov or Ozick, or an essay by Montaigne, or a Shakespearean sonnet, without ending the reading with a sigh or thinking I see me, it is truly so. One *can* escape pondering the multifarious lenses through which existence can be viewed, I suppose. I am not sure how though, for once consciousness kicks in, a vast and awesome mental and emotional system thrives on active challenges. Only self-imposed avoidance energies, or controlled, mental restrictions, deny a healthy mind access to investigative resources.

We live in a time of possibilities. Not a profound thought; one could argue the point that this was always so. As evidenced by the legacy of our recorded history, human capacity for inventiveness and both effecting and resisting change illumines the complex life experiences of all persons. But our history repeatedly features societies molding individual powers by limiting free-thinking and access to information. Now, more than ever before, we are aware of the tenuous balance between the needs for an ordered society and the rights and liberties of diverse individuals, i.e. "humans," commingling globally. No longer do we live in the darkness of the middle ages, nor the isolationism of earlier twentieth century. No longer do we fear today's Galileo, Copernicus, or Jesus who challenges us to examine old beliefs by placing new, alien ways of thinking in our paths. As we move into this new paradigm of more unknowing, more acknowledged, chaos, we can reach for higher levels of thinking and being that connect us to new solutions, new responses. Living exclusively in previously circumscribed modes only limits creative energy and negates options for the future.

Human nature shows a need for order, at least an order from which to depart. Every time you read a book and share views of that book and the personal lives you bring to those views, you are journeying, one tiny step at a time, on a transformative path. Reading, always considered a stimulant for the mind, body, and soul, and reading and discussing en masse, offer the possibility of liberating the static self to move past fear into exciting realms of human consciousness and creativity.

One paragraph from the first edition of *The Reading Group Handbook* strongly articulates the optimum power of reading, and discussing: "The art of reading demands courage. In reading we challenge our belief system and activate a vulnerability to personal change—physical, moral, psychological, and social. If you do not want to change, don't read—or read only the same old stuff that has you stagnating in a puddle of your own beliefs. Those with the courage to encounter the truths of history and the forces of change, read on: Stretch your creativity."

Today, only a few years after the forming of those confrontational thoughts, the challenge resonates worldwide. We each have the choice to "dumb-down," close our minds and hearts, deteriorate creatively, politically, spiritually. Some will always find this the more comfortable route. Others will heed my words, the work of more visible influences than mine. Oprah Winfrey challenges millions of passive television watchers to READ, to use those brains, decipher words, enjoy word images, and think critically about same. I wish I could do that! I wish I could get millions to read those stories of startling, sobering social issues that we all know exist, and don't want to think about. "Make beautiful the ugly," are the wise words of Kenzaburō Ōe, 1994 recipient of the Nobel Prize for Literature (see 1995–1996 syllabus). As Oprah Winfrey stands as a model of the American success story for us, so do our writers who have come out of dark experiences, and through courage, resilience, and the gift of artfulness, reward us with tales that may hopefully see us through our own darkness. Francis Bacon, employing the words of Stoic philosopher Seneca, stated, "The good things which belong to prosperity are to be wished, but the good things that belong to adversity are to be admired."

I wish I could get millions to read something more challenging than the popular, and escapist, lowbrow mass market general fiction or romance. You, YOU, regardless of where you went to school, what your level or quality of education, *can* read anything you set your mind and will to tackle. The Industrial Revolution, the rise of the middle class, free and public access to books, and an increase in our leisure time afford us the opportunity to stretch past ourselves. Books are our steppingstones to otherness, and the selves that we yet have become. You can do it. Get past the fear.

The publishers, Oprah, Ray Suarez, the independent booksellers, and the superstores, the internet, and the millions of us who crave reading and discourse have revolutionized Americans' relationship to a book. A young mother enthusiastically once told me, "Book club is the best thing that ever happened to me. It saved my life." Another wrote to me, "I've become more confident! With two children, I *crave* it." And another, "I learn something from every book I read."

Start with the familiar, move past the fear to the new. Read other than the bestsellers, the titles marketed in your bookstore window, or the "hot" popular fiction that "everybody" is reading. Look for the hidden gems. Try a different genre—sci-fi, gay/lesbian, immigrant, essay, poetry, short story, classics, subversives from different eras, other religions' holy texts. Try other, other, other—not same, same, same. Even within other, exists same, because of the human factor. All writing is the story of how humans exist in their universe with each other, with their gods, their God.

This is what groupies rave about:

- "[Book group] guarantees that I read something challenging, different from my usual selections; provides intellectual stimulation ." Illinois

- "We laugh a lot and can relate some of our readings to our lives or feel the intellectual challenge of working through a more difficult work." California

- Exchanging ideas is the best way to keep growing. A few prejudices have disappeared." Washington

- "It's a wonderful learning experience. I have certainly changed my reading habits. I have read books I would never have picked off the shelf." Colorado

- "It's so much fun. This is the place where I am liked, accepted, and a valued member." California

- "I may have hated the book, but I learn so much about life and literature from the discussion." New York

- "Because of book group, I started doing some writing myself. We all have stories to tell." Minnesota

The last one suggests one of the highest levels of consciousness that reading groups can offer to you. Reading empowers each of us to transcend from the passive "listener" of story to the "hearer" and subsequently creator of story. Our lives, and the lives we hear about through daily communications are stories comprised of minuscule or sweeping brushstrokes. The next time someone tells you a story, write it down. Work on its design when the muse of creativity delightedly stings you. I continually find gossipy newspaper articles, and scraps of paper upon which I jotted down phrases, scenarios, bits of conversation. It's a beginning, my saving account for the future birthing of the story writer in me.

On the pages of this book are names of authors who found their voices. Here, I call up other venerable and courageous souls for speaking out, and creatively designing story for us: Homer, Herodotus, Plato, Mary Shelley, Alexis de Tocqueville, Jane Austen, Virgina Woolf, Margaret Mead, Franz Kafka, Arthur Miller, Zora Neale Hurston, Lady Murasaki, George Sand, Oscar Wilde, Tobias Wolf, Dorothy Allison, Tim O'Brien, William Maxwell, Sandra Benitez, Leslie Marmom Silko. And all the others, in all times and all places, who had to transcend silence, find their voice, and create it, for themselves and for others. You can too. Read. Be a courageous reader, and enjoy it. Mark Twain once said, "Courage is resistance to fear, mastery of fear—not absence of fear." That courage to work with and through the fear of reading challenging books, speaking your mind in a book group discussion, and perhaps getting down to writing something of your very own, is already within you. Let that truth be discovered.

As you read over this book and the title suggestions (limited as they are because of my limitations of knowing), I hope that you will take time to contemplate the significance of the simple yet mighty power of each word, the mighty act of reading, and the creative force of discussion. For you, in your own life as it touches others, may this conscious contemplation resonate in empowering, optimum experience that enhances the quality of your life. Thank you for reading my book.

APPENDIXES

The following appendixes are meant to be informative, helpful suggestions and in *no* way are to be considered complete. Many titles are included for thematic subject matter. The reader will find varying standards of literary merit.

Appendix A

SELECTED READING LISTS

Pulitzer Prize–Winning Authors, Fiction

AUTHOR	TITLE	YEAR
Booth Tarkington	The Magnificent Ambersons	1919
Edith Wharton	The Age of Innocence	1921
Willa Cather	One of Ours	1923
Sinclair Lewis	Arrowsmith	1926
(also Nobel Prize for Literature, 1930)		
Thornton Wilder	The Bridge of San Luis Rey	1928
Margaret Mitchell	Gone With the Wind	1937
John P. Marquand	The Late George Apley	1938
John Steinbeck	The Grapes of Wrath	1940
(also Nobel Prize for Literature, 1962)		
James Agee	A Death in the Family	1955
Allen Drury	Advise and Consent	1960
Harper Lee	To Kill a Mockingbird	1961
Shirley Ann Grau	The Keepers of the House	1965
Katherine Anne Porter	Collected Stories of Katherine Anne Porter	1966
Bernard Malamud	The Fixer	1967
William Styron	The Confessions of Nat Turner	1968

AUTHOR	TITLE	YEAR
N. Scott Momaday	*House Made of Dawn*	1969
Wallace Stegner	*Angle of Repose*	1972
Saul Bellow	*Humboldt's Gift*	1976
(also Nobel Prize for Literature, 1976)		
John Cheever	*The Stories of John Cheever*	1979
Norman Mailer	*The Executioner's Song*	1980
John Kennedy Toole	*A Confederacy of Dunces*	1981
John Updike	*Rabbit Is Rich*	1982
Alice Walker	*The Color Purple*	1983
William Kennedy	*Ironweed*	1984
Alison Lurie	*Foreign Affairs*	1985
Larry McMurtry	*Lonesome Dove*	1986
Peter Taylor	*A Summons to Memphis*	1987
Toni Morrison	*Beloved*	1988
(also Nobel Prize for Literature, 1993)		
Anne Tyler	*Breathing Lessons*	1989
Oscar Hijuelos	*The Mambo Kings Play Songs of Love*	1990
John Updike	*Rabbit at Rest*	1991
Jane Smiley	*A Thousand Acres*	1992
Robert Olen Butler	*A Good Scent From a Strange Mountain*	1993
E. Annie Proulx	*The Shipping News*	1994
Carol Shields	*The Stone Diaries*	1995
Richard Ford	*Independence Day*	1996
Steven Millhauser	*Martin Dressler: The Tale of an American Dream*	1997

50 Novels to Help Raise Your Moral Consciousness

(Compiled by Arthur Blaustein, University of California at Berkeley)

AUTHOR	TITLE
Isabel Allende	*The House of Spirits*
James Baldwin	*Another Country*
Sheila Ballantyne	*Norma Jean the Termite Queen*
Russell Banks	*Continental Drift*
Pat Barker	*Union Street*
Wendell Barry	*The Memory of Old Jack*
Saul Bellow	*Herzog*
John Cheever	*Falconer*

AUTHOR	TITLE
Robert Crichton	*The Secret of Santa Vittoria*
Robertson Davies	*A Mixture of Frailties*
E. L. Doctorow	*The Book of Daniel*
Harriet Doerr	*Stones for Ibarra*
Michael Dorris	*A Yellow Raft in Blue Water*
Ralph Ellison	*Invisible Man*
Louise Erdrich	*Love Medicine*
William Faulkner	*Intruder in the Dust*
Gabriel García Márquez	*One Hundred Years of Solitude*
Gail Godwin	*Mother and Two Daughters*
Günter Grass	*The Tin Drum*
Graham Greene	*The Honorary Consul*
Davis Grubb	*The Voices of Glory*
Ernest Hebert	*The Dogs of March*
Joseph Heller	*Catch 22*
John Irving	*The Cider House Rules*
Kazuo Ishiguro	*The Remains of the Day*
Nikos Kazantzakis	*Zorba the Greek*
Thomas Keneally	*A Family Madness*
William Kennedy	*Ironweed*
Ken Kesey	*One Flew Over the Cuckoo's Nest*
Maxine Kingston	*The Woman Warrior*
Milan Kundera	*The Book of Laughter and Forgetting*
Margaret Laurence	*The Diviners*
Ella Leffland	*Rumors of Peace*
Doris Lessing	*The Four-Gated City*
Bernard Malamud	*The Tenants*
Peter Matthiesen	*At Play in the Fields of the Lord*
Carson McCullers	*The Heart Is a Lonely Hunter*
Sue Miller	*The Good Mother*
Toni Morrison	*Beloved*
Alice Munro	*Lives of Girls and Women*
V. S. Naipaul	*A House for Mr. Biswas*
John Nichols	*The Magic Journey*
Joyce Carol Oates	*Them*
Tim O'Brien	*Going After Cacciato*
Walker Percy	*The Moviegoer*
Jayne Anne Phillips	*Machine Dreams*
Chaim Potok	*Davita's Harp*
May Sarton	*Kinds of Love*

AUTHOR	TITLE
Mary Lee Settle	*The Scapegoat*
Wallace Stegner	*Angle of Repose*
Robert Stone	*A Flag for Sunrise*
Amy Tan	*The Joy Luck Club*
Anne Tyler	*Celestial Navigation*
John Updike	*Rabbit Is Rich*
Kurt Vonnegut	*Jailbird*
Alice Walker	*Meridian*
Robert Penn Warren	*All the King's Men*
William Wharton	*Dad*

Law and Lawyers in Fiction

AUTHOR	TITLE
Louis Auchincloss	*I Come As a Thief; Powers of Attorney*
F. Lee Bailey	*Secrets*
Marion Borgenicht	*Undue Influence*
Jay Brandon	*Fade the Heat; Rules of Evidence*
Frederick Busch	*Closing Arguments*
Mary Higgins Clark	*The Cradle Will Fall*
Robin Cook	*Harmful Intent*
William J. Coughlin	*Death Penalty; In the Presence of Enemies; Shadow of a Doubt; Her Honor; The Twelve Apostles*
Henry Denker	*Outrage; A Place for the Mighty*
William Diehl	*Primal Fear*
J. F. Freedman	*Against the Wind*
Philip Friedman	*Inadmissible Evidence; Reasonable Doubt*
Andrew Greeley	*Love Song*
Vincent S. Green	*The Price of Victory*
Stephen Greenleaf	*Impact*
John Grisham	*The Client; The Pelican Brief; The Firm; A Time to Kill*
Ron Handberg	*Savage Justice*
George V. Higgins	*Defending Billy Ryan; Outlaws; Penance for Jerry Kennedy; Kennedy for the Defense; Mandeville Talent*
Clifford Irving	*The Trial*
Norman Katov	*Blood and Orchids*
Norma Klein	*The World As It Is*
John Lescoat	*Hard Evidence*

AUTHOR	TITLE
Paul Levine	*To Speak for the Dead; Night Vision*
Ronald Levitsky	*The Love That Kills*
John Martel	*Partners*
Steve Martini	*Compelling Evidence; Prime Witness*
Harold Mehling	*Assumption of Guilt*
John Jay Osborn	*The Associates*
James Patterson	*Along Came a Spider*
Richard N. Patterson	*Degree of Guilt*
Richard Powell	*The Philadelphians*
Barry Reed	*The Choice; The Verdict*
Nancy Rosenberg	*Mitigating Circumstances*
Grif Stockley	*Probable Cause*
Josephine Tey	*The Franchise Affair*
Robert Traver	*Anatomy of a Murder*
Scott Turow	*Pleading Guilty; The Burden of Proof; Presumed Innocent*
Dorothy Uhnak	*False Witness*
Gallantine Warfield	*State v. Justice*
Jerome Weidman	*Counselors-at-Law*
Shelby Yastrow	*Undue Influence*

Science Fiction

Although an often-disparaged genre, science fiction at its best embodies the highest literary standards of any other storytelling. It deals with people coming to grips with their lives and their times, just like other fiction, except that the context has been changed in some respect. Science fiction can be set in the past, present, or future, and the changes in the milieu described can be almost unnoticeable or obvious. Along with the development of character and the drama of narration, there generally is an idea or a series of extraordinarily thought-provoking ideas that makes readers sit back and reevaluate the way they relate to their own culture and world.

Some exceptional science fiction novels that are well known but not generally recognized as science fiction are:

AUTHOR	TITLE
Margaret Atwood	*The Handmaid's Tale*
Jean Auel	*Clan of the Cave Bear* (and sequels)
H. Rider Haggard	*King Solomon's Mines; She*
Aldous Huxley	*Brave New World*

AUTHOR	TITLE
George Orwell	*Nineteen Eighty-Four*
Upton Sinclair	*It Can't Happen Here*

The following stories, almost all of them classics in the field and constantly reprinted, range widely from the intensely personal to the universally significant, from humorous to somber. For reading, they range from merely engrossing to absolutely riveting.

AUTHOR	TITLE
Poul Anderson	*High Crusade*
Isaac Asimov	*The Gods Themselves*
Alfred Bester	*The Demolished Man*
Leigh Brackett	*The Long Tomorrow*
David Brin	*The Postman*
Orson Scott Card	*Ender's Game; Speaker for the Dead*
L. Sprague deCamp	*Lest Darkness Fall*
Robert A. Heinlein	*Citizen of the Galaxy; Double Star; The Moon Is a Harsh Mistress*
Zenna Henderson	*Pilgrimage; The People: No Different Flesh*
Frank Herbert	*Dune*
James P. Hogan	*Voyage from Yesteryear*
Daniel Keyes	*Flowers for Algernon* (Expanded from a prize-winning short story)
Ursula Le Guin	*The Dispossessed; The Left Hand of Darkness*
George R. R. Martin and Lisa Tuttle	*Windhaven*
Anne McCaffrey	*Dragonflight; The Ship Who Sang*
Walter M. Miller, Jr.	*A Canticle for Leibowitz*
Larry Niven and Jerry Pournelle	*The Mote in God's Eye*
Eric Frank Russell	*Sinister Barrier; Wasp*
Norman Spinrad	*Bug Jack Barron*
George Stewart	*Earth Abides*

Westerns

Westerns are the articulation of the American mythos. Whether they deal with the early frontier on the eastern seaboard, the upheavals of the opening of the frontier, or the tragedies of its closing, they epitomize the values treasured by American society. They starkly portray the battles of good against evil and the battles one waged within between one's better and worse instincts. These battles rage today. Many westerns tend to be formulaic, but the stories never tire in the retelling. The following "classics"—some of which helped originate the genre—not only immerse the reader in yesteryear, but make one ask both "How would I have done it then?" and "How should I do in today's world?" Some of these authors—Brand, Grey, Haycox, L'Amour—have been prolific, and readers captured by one of their novels have been known to devour their entire body of work. Be warned.

Andy Adams	*The Log of a Cowboy*
Thomas Berger	*Little Big Man*
Max Brand	*Destry Rides Again*
Walter van Tilburg Clark	*The Ox-Bow Incident*
James Fenimore Cooper	*The Deerslayer*
Zane Grey	*Riders of the Purple Sage*
Ernest Haycox	*The Adventurers; Bugles in the Afternoon*
Napoleon Augustus Jennings	*A Texas Ranger (The Story of Lee McNelly)* (Nonfiction, but reads like a novel). See also: Lee McNelly, *My Life As a Texas Ranger.*
Louis L'Amour	*Bendigo Shafter; The Daybreakers; Hondo; The Lonesome Gods*
Alan LeMay	*The Searchers*
Larry McMurtry	*Lonesome Dove*
Owen Wister	*The Virginian*

Mysteries in Historical Settings

AUTHOR	TITLE
K. K. Beck	*Death in a Deck Chair; Murder in a Mummy Case; Peril Under the Palms*
Gail Clark	*Dulcie Bligh; Baroness of Bow Street*
Lindsey Davis	*Silver Pigs; Shadows in Bronze; Venus in Copper*
P. C. Doherty	*Satan in Saint Mary's; The Crown in Darkness; A Spy in Chancery; Angel of Death; Whyte Harte; Serpent Among the Lilies*
Carole Nelson Douglas	*Good Night Mr. Holmes; Good Morning Irene*
Richard Grayson	*The Murder at Impasse Louvain; The Monterant Affair; Death of Abbé Didier; The Montmarte*

	Murders; *Crime Without Passion; Death en Voyage; Death on the Cards*
Robert Lee Hall	*Benjamin Franklin Takes the Case; Benjamin Franklin and a Case of Christmas Murder*
Ray Harrison	*Why Kill Arthur Potter?; Death of an Honorable Member; Death Watch; Death of a Dancing Lady; Counterfeit of Murder; Season of Death; Harvest of Death; Tincture of Death; Sphere of Death; Patently Murder*
J. G. Jeffreys	*Thieftaker; A Wicked Way to Die; The Wilful Lady; Conspiracy of Poisons; Suicide Most Foul; The Pangbourne Murders; The Tistlewood Plot*
Alanna Knight	*Enter Second Murderer; Blood Line; Deadly Beloved; Killing Cousins*
Alice Chetwynd Ley	*A Reputation Dies; A Fatal Assignation; Masquerade of Vengeance*
Peter Lovesey	*Wobble to Death; The Detective Wore Silk Drawers; Abracadaver; Mad Hatters Holiday; The Tick of Death; A Case of Spirits; Swing, Swing Together; Waxworks; Bertie and the Tinman; Bertie and the Seven Bodies*
William Marshall	*The New York Detective; Faces in the Crowd*
Edward Marston	*The Merry Devils; The Queen's Head; Trip to Jerusalem; The Nine Giants*
Elizabeth Peters	*Crocodile on the Sandbank; Curse of the Pharaohs; The Mummy Case; Lion in the Valley; Deeds of the Disturber; The Last Camel Died at Noon*
Ellis Peters	*A Morbid Taste for Bones; One Corpse Too Many; Monk's-Hood; St. Peter's Fair; The Leper of St. Giles; The Virgin in the Ice; The Sanctuary Sparrow; The Devil's Novice; Dead Man's Ransom; Pilgrim of Hate; An Excellent Mystery; A Raven in the Foregate; The Rose Rent; The Hermit of Eyton Forest; The Confession of Brother Haluin; The Heretic's Apprentice; The Potter's Field; The Summer of the Dane; A Rare Benedictine*
Francis Selwyn	*The Cracksman; Sergeant Verity and the Imperial Diamond; Sergeant Verity Presents His Compliments; Sergeant Verity and the Blood Royal; Sergeant Verity and the Swell Mob*

AUTHOR	TITLE
Leonard Tourney	*The Player's Boy Is Dead; Low Treason; Familiar Spirits; The Bartholomew Fair Murders; Old Saxon Blood; Knaves Templar*
Robert van Gulik	*The Emperor's Pearl; The Haunted Monastery; The Lacquer Screen; The Red Pavillion; The Willow Pattern; The Monkey and the Tiger; The Phantom of the Temple; Murder in Canton; The Necklace and the Calabash; Poets and Murder; The Chinese Nail Murders; The Chinese Maze Murders; The Chinese Lake Murders; The Chinese Bell Murders; The Chinese Gold Murders*

American Historical Fiction

AUTHOR	TITLE
Jane Adams	*Seattle Green*
Allen Appel	*Time After Time; Twice Upon Time*
Louis Charbonneau	*Trail*
Janet Dailey	*Great Alone*
Howard Fast	*Establishment; Immigrants; Second Generation; Immigrant's Daughter*
Jack Finney	*Time and Again*
Celia Holland	*Bear Flag*
John Jakes	*California Gold; North and South; Love and War; Heaven and Hell*
Anita Clay Kornfeld	*Vintage*
Larry McMurtry	*Lonesome Dove*
James Michener	*Centennial; Chesapeake*
Margaret Mitchell	*Gone With the Wind*
Katherine Neville	*The Eight*
David Nevin	*Dream West*
Belva Plain	*Crescent City*
Eugenia Price	*Savannah; To See Your Face Again; Before Darkness Falls*
Conrad Richter	*The Trees; The Fields; The Town*
Alexandra Ripley	*Charleston; On Leaving Charleston*
Kenneth Roberts	*Northwest Passage*
Fred Mustard Steward	*Glitter and the Gold*
James Alexander Thom	*From Sea to Shining Sea*
Herman Wouk	*Winds of War; War and Remembrance*

Foundations of Civilization

Here is an abbreviated list of those truly great books that are part of the foundation of our civilization and good for discussion.

Iliad and *Odyssey* by Homer
The Old and New Testaments
Comedies by Aristophanes
History by Herodotus
Meditations by Marcus Aurelius
The Divine Comedy by Dante
   Alighieri

Utopia by Sir Thomas More
Essays by Michel de Montaigne
Don Quixote by Miguel de
   Cervantes
The Faerie Queen by Edmund
   Spenser

On Politics and Politicians

FICTION

AUTHOR	TITLE
Jeffrey Archer	*Shall We Tell the President?*
Richard Condon	*The Manchurian Candidate; Winter Kills*
Maureen Dean	*Washington Wives; Capitol Services*
Allen Drury	*Advise and Consent; Come Nineveh, Come Tyre; Preserve and Protect*
Ward Just	*Jack Gance*
Michael Killan	*By Order of the President*
Fletcher Knebel	*Seven Days in May; Night of Camp David*
Jerzy Kosinski	*Being There*
Robert Mayer	*I, JFK*
William Safire	*Full Disclosure*
Muriel Spark	*The Abbess of Crewe*
Irving Stone	*The President's Lady*
Gore Vidal	*Burr; 1876: A Novel; Lincoln*
Irving Wallace	*The Second Lady*

NONFICTION

AUTHOR	TITLE
Stephen Ambrose	*Nixon: The Education of a Politician; Nixon: The Triumph of a Politician, 1962–72; Nixon: Ruin and Recovery, 1973–90*
Donald E. Barlett	*America: What Went Wrong*
Jim Becker	*Where's Dan Quayle?*
David S. Broder	*The Man Who Would Be President*
Clark Clifford	*Counsel to the President: A Memoir*
Blanche W. Cook	*Eleanor Roosevelt*
Richard B. Cramer	*What It Takes: The Making of American Presidents*
Robert Dallek	*Lone Star Rising: Lyndon Johnson and His Times*
David R. Farber	*Chicago, '68*
John Feinstein	*Running Mates*
Albert Gore	*Earth in Balance*
William Greider	*Who Will Tell the President?: The Betrayal of American Democracy*
Kathleen Jamieson	*Packaging the Presidency: A History and Criticism of Presidential Advertising*
Doron Levin	*Irreconcilable Differences: Ross Perot vs. General Motors*
Jacques Lowe	*The Kennedy Legacy*
David McCullough	*Truman*
Joe McGinnis	*The Selling of the President*
Porter McKeever	*Adlai Stevenson: His Life and Legacy*
Norman Mailer	*Some Honorable Men: Political Conventions*
Todd Mason	*Perot: An Unauthorized Biography*
Greg Mitchell	*The Campaign of the Century*
Hyman L. Muslin	*Lyndon Johnson: The Tragic Self*
Peggy Noonan	*What I Saw at the Revolution: A Political Life in the Reagan Era*
P. J. O'Rourke	*The Parliament of Whores*
Thomas Reeves	*A Question of Character: A Life of John F. Kennedy*
Arthur M. Schlesinger, Jr.	*The Disuniting of America*
Gail Sheehy	*Character: America's Search for Leadership*
Irving Stone	*They Also Ran*

AUTHOR	TITLE
Gil Troy	*See How They Run: The Changing Role of the Presidential Candidate*
Theodore White	*Making of the President, 1960; Making of the President, 1964; Making of the President, 1968; Making of the President, 1972*
Jules Witcover	*Crapshoot: Rolling the Dice on the Vice Presidency*

Midlife Readings
(Focused mostly on women)

NONFICTION

Developing a Twenty-first Century Mind, by Marsha Sinetar

Necessary Losses, by Judith Viorst

Women, Aging and Ageism, edited by Evelyn R. Rosenthal

Growing Older, Getting Better: A Handbook for Women in the Second Half of Life, by Jane Procino

Retrospect, by C. S. Jung

Old and Smart: Women and Aging, by Betty Nickerson

Look Me in the Eye: Old Women, Aging and Ageism, by Barbara McDonald with Cynthia Rich

The Phoenix Factor, by Dr. Karl Slaikey and Steve Lawhead

The Measure of My Days, by Florida Scott Maxwell

What Are You Doing with the Rest of Your Life?, by Paula Hardin

Late Show, by Helen Gurley Brown

The Change: Women, Aging and the Menopause, by Germaine Greer

In Full Flower: Aging Women, Power and Sexuality, by Lois Banner

The Fountain of Age, by Betty Friedan

Women Who Run with the Wolves by Clarissa Pinkola Estes

The New Old: Struggling for Decent Aging, by Nancy Williams

As We Are Now, by May Sarton (a memoir)

FICTION

Hot Flashes, by Barbara Raskin
Mr. and Mrs. Bridge, by Evan Connell
When I Am Old I Shall Wear Purple, edited by Sandra Martz
Only Morning in Her Shoes: Poems About Old Women, edited by Leatric Lifshitz
An Anthology of Literature on Growing Old, edited by Margaret Fowler and Priscilla McMuthchen
Memento Mori, by Muriel Spark
Tell Me a Riddle, by Tillie Olsen

"Sex Education," by Dorothy Canfield Fisher
"The Story of an Hour," by Kate Chopin
"Menesteung," by Alice Munro
"The Enormous Radio," by John Cheever
"The World of Apples," by John Cheever
Summer Before the Dark, by Doris Lessing
Henry and Cato, by Iris Murdoch
Consenting Adults, by Laura Hobson
She's Come Undone, by Wally Lamb

Children's Books

We can initiate with our children the same free-form discussions we have with our peers. Try it. Your kids will love it. You may, too. Secret of success: *Don't preach.* Listen and respect.

To guide you, the following titles are separated into three lists:

JY—Juvenile/youth books for children three to twelve years old
YA/E—Young adult/easier books for the 13-plus set
YA/C—Young adult/more challenging books for the 13-plus set

You as parents and teachers are the best judges of the appropriate choices.

JY: JUVENILE/YOUTH

Included here are children's books that young adults and older adults should read for a good foundation—as well as share with children.

Fables by Aesop
Peter Pan by J. M. Barrie
The Wizard of Oz by L. Frank Baum

The Secret Garden by Frances Hodgson Burnett

Alice's Adventures in Wonderland by Lewis Carroll

Alice Through the Looking Glass by Lewis Carroll

The Wind in the Willows by Kenneth Grahame

The Jungle Book by Rudyard Kipling

Just So Stories by Rudyard Kipling

Pippi Longstocking by Astrid Lindgren

Dr. Doolittle Stories by Hugh Lofting

Winnie-the-Pooh by A. A. Milne

Now We Are Six by A. A. Milne

The House on Pooh Corner by A. A. Milne

When We Were Very Young by A. A. Milne

Fairy Tales by Charles Perrault

Mother Goose Tales by Charles Perrault

A Child's Garden of Verses by Robert Louis Stevenson

Charlotte's Web by E. B. White

Stuart Little by E. B. White

The Little House Series by Laura Ingalls Wilder

Swiss Family Robinson by Johann Wyss

YA/E: YOUNG ADULT/EASY

Little Women by Louisa May Alcott

Dandelion Wine by Ray Bradbury

Wuthering Heights by Emily Brontë

Woman Hollering Creek and Other Stories by Sandra Cisneros

Robinson Crusoe by Daniel Defoe

Diary of Anne Frank by Anne Frank

Lord of the Flies by William Golding

Ordinary People by Judith Guest

The Chronicles of Narni by C. S. Lewis

Anne of Green Gables by L. M. Montgomery

The Adventures of Robin Hood by Howard Pyle

A Light in the Attic (poetry) by Shel Silverstein

Where the Sidewalk Ends (poetry) by Shel Silverstein

The Hobbitt by J. R. R. Tolkien

The Adventures of Tom Sawyer by Mark Twain

YA/C: YOUNG ADULT/CHALLENGING

Things Fall Apart by Chinua Achebe

The Canterbury Tales by Geoffrey Chaucer

Oliver Twist by Charles Dickens

Billy Bathgate by E. L. Doctorow

Ellen Foster by Kaye Gibbons

A Portrait of the Artist as a Young
Man by James Joyce
To Kill a Mockingbird by Harper
Lee
The Call of the Wild by Jack
London
Frankenstein by Mary
Wollstonecraft Shelley (try to
find the large edition illustrated
by Barry Moser)

Uncle Tom's Cabin by Harriet
Beecher Stowe
The Lord of the Rings by J. R. R.
Tolkien
The Adventures of Huckleberry Finn
by Mark Twain
Candide by Voltaire
The Color Purple by Alice
Walker

Fictional Works Featuring Male Protagonists

AUTHOR	TITLE
Russell Banks	Affliction
Pat Barker	Regeneration
Larry Brown	Dirty Work; Joe
Nelson DeMille	Word of Honor
Pete Dexter	Brotherly Love
Clyde Edgerton	Floatplane Notebooks
George Fraser	Flashman and the Dragon
Ernest Gaines	A Gathering of Old Men
Graham Greene	Monsignor Quixote
Dan Jenkins	Semi-Tough
Ted Jones	Grant's War
MacKinlay Kantor	Andersonville
William Kinsella	Shoeless Joe
Elmore Leonard	Stick
Norman Maclean	A River Runs Through It
Norman Mailer	The Naked and the Dead
Bernard Malamud	The Fixer
Richard Marius	After the War
Ed McBain	Downtown
Larry McMurtry	Anything for Billy
T. R. Pearson	Gospel Hour
E. Annie Proulx	Postcards
Patrick O'Brian	Master and Commander
Tim O'Brien	The Things They Carried

AUTHOR	TITLE
Paul Theroux	*Mosquito Coast*
Gore Vidal	*Lincoln*
Kurt Vonnegut	*Hocus Pocus*
Robert Penn Warren	*All the King's Men*
William Wharton	*A Midnight Clear*
Thomas Williams	*The Hair of Harold Roux*

Feminist Nonfiction

Composing a Life, by Mary Catherine Bateson

Feminism: The Essential Historical Writings, edited by Miriam Schneir

Women Writers at Work, edited by George Plimpton

The Writer on Her Work, Volumes I and II, edited by Janet Sternburg

Adam, Eve, and the Serpent, by Elaine Pagels

Literary Women, by Ellen Moers

The Female Eunuch, by Germaine Greer

The Natural Superiority of Women, by Ashley Montagu

Goddesses in Every Woman, by Jean Shinoda Bolen

Toward a New Psychology of Women, by Jean Baker Miller

The Dance of Anger, The Dance of Deception, and *The Dance of Intimacy,* by Harriet Goldgor Lerner

Womenspirit Rising, edited by Carol P. Christ and Judith Plaskow

Women's Rituals, by Barbara G. Walker

Writing a Woman's Life, by Carolyn G. Heilbrun

Life's Companion: Journal Writing as a Spiritual Quest, by Christina Baldwin

Gossip, by Patricia Meyer Spacks

The Female Imagination, by Patricia Meyer Spacks

In Transition, by Judith M. Bradwick

Women's Ways of Knowing, by Mary Field Belenky, Blythe McVicker Clinchy, Nancy Rule Goldberger, Jill Mattuck Tarule

Women's Voices in Hawaii, by Joyce Chapman Lebra (title supplied by Judy Robeck, Kihei, Hawaii)

Revolution from Within, by Gloria Steinem

No Man's Land: The Place of the Woman Writer in the Twentieth Century, Vols. 1 and 2, by Sandra M. Gilbert

The Madwoman in the Attic: A Study of Women and the Literary Imagination, by Sandra M. Gilbert and Susan Gubar

Reinventing Womanhood and
   Toward a Recognition of
   Androgyny, by Carolyn Heilbrun
Silences, by Tillie Olsen

A Vindication of the Rights of
   Women, by Mary Wollstonecraft
The Fountain of Age, by Betty
   Friedan

Fictional Works by Female Writers Featuring Female Protagonists

For too long the female consciousness has been repressed and suppressed by patriarchal domination. Now with increasing artistry and frequency, the drastic void and distortion of female images and models in literature are being repaired with care and skill, both by men and women. Many women writers, because of their traditionally marginal place in society, have claimed self-representation through a first-person voice—a common occurrence for the displaced or out-of-mainstream person. Many works by women are in the form of memoirs, diaries, letters, or they are novels that employ a first-person narrative voice. Below is a select list of works by women about women (not exclusively) that enlarges a woman's reflected vision of herself. You'll find repetition of some titles mentioned elsewhere. Look through other lists for more selections by women writers.

AUTHOR	TITLE
Louisa May Alcott	*Little Women*
Maya Angelou	*I Know Why The Caged Bird Sings* (and subsequent memoirs)
Margaret Atwood	*The Handmaid's Tale* and *Cat's Eye*
Jane Austen	*Pride and Prejudice*
Toni Cade Bambara	*Gorilla, My Love*
Simone de Beauvoir	*A Very Easy Death* and *The Woman Destroyed*
Mary Brave Bird (with Richard Erdoes)	*Ohitika Woman*
Charlotte Brontë	*Jane Eyre*
Emily Brontë	*Wuthering Heights*
Rita Mae Brown	*Rubyfruit Jungle*
Pearl S. Buck	*The Good Earth*
Rachel Carson	*Silent Spring*

AUTHOR	TITLE
Angela Carter	*Sleeping Beauty: And Other Favorite Fairy Tales*
Willa Cather	*My Antonia*
Kate Chopin	*The Awakening*
Sandra Cisneros	*House on Mango Street* and *Woman Hollering Creek and Other Stories*
Francesca Duranti	*Personal Effects*
Marguerite Duras	*War* and *Lover*
Eva Figes	*The Seven Ages* and *Waking*
Glückel of Hameln	*The Memoirs of Glückel of Hameln*
Emma Goldman	*Living My Life*
Mary Gordon	*The Rest of Life*
Shirley Ann Grau	*Nine Women*
Radclyffe Hall	*The Well of Loneliness*
Helen Keller	*The Story of My Life*
Maxine Hong Kingston	*Woman Warrior*
Harper Lee	*To Kill a Mockingbird*
Doris Lessing	*The Golden Notebook* and *Summer Before the Dark*
Anne Morrow Lindbergh	*Gifts from the Sea*
Beryl Markham	*West with the Night*
Paule Marshall	*Soul Clap Hands and Sing*
Carson McCullers	*The Heart Is a Lonely Hunter* and *The Member of the Wedding*
Margaret Mead	*Coming of Age in Samoa*
Susan Minot	*Folly*
Toni Morrison	*Sula; Beloved;* and *The Bluest Eye*
Lady Murasaki	*The Tales of Genji*
Anais Nin	*Diaries*
Cynthia Ozick	*The Shawl*
Emmeline Pankhurst	*My Own Story*
Christine de Pizan	*A Medieval Woman's Mirror of Honor* and *The Book of the City of Ladies*
Sylvia Plath	*The Bell Jar*
Adrienne Rich	*Of Woman Born*
Muriel Rukeyser	*The Life of Poetry*
Margaret Sanger	*Margaret Sanger: An Autobiography*

AUTHOR	TITLE
Sappho	*Sappho: A New Translation*
May Sarton	*Journals of a Solitude*
Mary Wollstonecraft Shelley	*Frankenstein* (Has a male protagonist)
Susan Sontag	*Illness as Metaphor* and *On Interpretation*
Gertrude Stein	*The Autobiography of Alice B. Toklas* and *Ida*
Anne Tyler	*Breathing Lessons* and *Dinner at the Homesick Restaurant*
Sigrid Undset	*Kristin Lavransdatter*
Alice Walker	*The Color Purple* and *Possessing the Secret of Joy*
Eudora Welty	*Delta Wedding* and *The Optimist's Daughter*
Virginia Woolf	*Mrs. Dalloway; To the Lighthouse;* and *A Room of One's Own*
Anzia Yezierska	*The Open Cage: An Anzia Yezierska Collection*

Short-Story Anthologies and Collections

1. ANNUAL AWARD-WINNING ANTHOLOGIES

Pushcart Prizes: Best of the Small Presses

The Best American Short Stories, series editor Shannon Ravenel, with annual guest editor

Prize Stories, The O. Henry Awards, edited by William Abrahams

Nebula Awards (science fiction)

Best Detective Stories of the Year, edited by Edward D. Hoch

2. REGULAR ANTHOLOGIES

New American Short Stories, edited by Gloria Norris

American Short Story Masterpieces, edited by Raymond Carver and Tom Jenks

The Best Short Story of the Modern Age, edited by Douglas Angus

The Signet Classic Book of Contemporary American Short Stories, edited by Burton Raffel

The Pocket Book of Short Stories, edited by M. Edmund Speare

Short Story Masterpieces, edited

by Robert Penn Warren and
Albert Erskine
Great American Short Stories,
edited by Wallace and Mary
Stegner
*The Norton Anthology of Short
Fiction,* edited by R, V, Cassill
The Nobel Reader, edited by
Jonathon Eisen and Stuart Try

*The Signet Book of British
Short Stories,* edited by
Frederick R. Karl
The Best of Tri-Quarterly, edited by
Jonathan Brent
The American Short Story, Volumes
1 and 2, edited by Calvin
Skaggs

3. COLLECTIONS

Transactions in a Foreign Currency,
by Deborah Eisenberg
A Visit from the Footbinder, by
Emily Prager
Self-Help, by Lorrie Moore
The Lone Pilgrim, by Laurie Colwin
Music for Chameleons, by Truman
Capote
*Unspeakable Practices, Unnatural
Acts,* by Donald Barthelme
Come Along with Me, by Shirley
Jackson
Emperor in the Air, by Ethan Canin
Where You'll Find Me, by Ann
Beattie
Something Out There and *Jump and
Other Stories,* by Nadine
Gordimer
The Old Forest and Other Stories, by
Peter Taylor

Goodbye, Columbus, by Philip Roth
Monkeys, by Susan Minot
The World Is a Wedding, by
Delmore Schwartz
The Magic Barrel, by Bernard
Malamud
The Portable Dorothy Parker
Blow-up and Other Stories, by Julio
Cortazar
*The Censors: A Bilingual Collection
of Stories* and *Open Door: Stories,*
by Luisa Valenzuela
The Elephant Vanishes, by Haruki
Murakami
*The Book of Seeing with One's Own
Eyes,* by Sharon Dubiago
Oriental Tales, by Marguerite
Yourcenar
The Infinite Passion of Expectation,
by Gina Berriault

4. GRAYWOLF ANNUAL

The small Graywolf Press in St. Paul, Minnesota, has bravely addressed multiculturalism, offering annual short fiction volumes with varying focuses:

The Graywolf Annual One: Short Stories, edited by Scott Walker

The Graywolf Annual Two: Short Stories by Women, edited by Scott Walker

The Graywolf Annual Five: Multi-Cultural Literacy, edited by Scott Walker

The Graywolf Annual Six: Stories from the Rest of the World, edited by Scott Walker

The Graywolf Annual Seven: Stories from the American Mosaic, edited by Scott Walker

The Graywolf Annual Eight: The New Family, edited by Scott Walker

The Graywolf Annual Nine: Stories from the New Europe, edited by Scott Walker

Beyond PC: Toward a Politics of Understanding, edited by Shawn Wong

Additional and Miscellaneous Short-Story Anthologies, All with Specific Focus

These anthologies were published in the last two or three years and are evidence of the growing interest in limited-focus volumes and in the proliferation of the short-story form. A reader can meet many writers and styles and perspectives on one topic by reading an anthology. Most of them contain detailed biographical notes on authors.

The Sleeper Wakes: Harlem Renaissance Stories by Women, edited by Marcia Knopf. Some powerful, colorful writing came out of Harlem in the 1920s and 1930s. This book contains an excellent, elucidating introduction and includes works of both noted and obscure writers.

The Mystery from Beyond, edited by Robert Weinberg, Stefan R. Dziemianowicz, and Martin H. Greenberg. Arranged in chronological order from the nineteenth century (Charles Dickens, Ambroise Bierce) to the contemporary (Joyce Carol Oates, Peter Straub, Clive Barker); twenty selections; a fine anthology.

The Year's Best Fantasy and Horror, Sixth Annual Collection, edited by Ellen Darrow and Terry Windling. About fifty stories by known major and minor writers; summation of 1992 fantasy and 1992 horror winners, with obituaries and essays on the sociopolitical place of horror and fantasy in the media.

Literary and Musical Rhythms

In 1993 the small Coffee House Press in Minneapolis published an enticing anthology—one of those things that you wish somebody would do. *Moment's Notice: Jazz in Poetry and Prose,* edited by Art Lange and Nathanial Mackey, fuses two or three art disciplines (depending on your perspective) and remarkably evokes the influence of jazz. No one will be surprised to find works by the likes of James Baldwin, Jack Kerouac, Amiri Bakara; but those of J. F. Powers and Michael Ondaatje and others will add delight.

Australian Literature: An Anthology of Writing from the Land Down Under, edited by Phyllis Fahrie Edelson. One example of the many national anthologies being published now that can introduce you to life in other countries.

The Schoolyard Game: An Anthology of Basketball Writings, edited by Dick Wimmer. Wimmer has put together excerpts and short pieces from known and lesser-known writers, all focused on a game that is fundamental to American society. Michael Jordan and Earl Manigault are subjects of two pieces.

The Best of the West: New Stories from the West Side of the Missouri, edited by James Thomas and Denise Thomas, introduction by William Kittredge. Territorial or regional anthologies are also blossoming onto library and bookstore shelves. Fifteen quality stories, biographical notes. Remarkable look at the western landscape.

The Faber Book of Gay Short Fiction, edited by Edmund White. This important collection of thirty-some stories by major and minor writers of the late nineteenth and the twentieth centuries helps to forge an identity, a recognition, and an overt acknowledgment of a fact of life as we know it today.

The Woman Who Lost Her Names: Selected Writings by American Jewish Women, compiled and edited by Julia Wolf Mazow, contains stories by well-known and not so well-known twentieth-century writers who depict the shaping of an identity that is pressured by a dominating culture and a time-driven consciousness.

Writing Our Way Home: Contemporary Stories by American Jewish Writers, edited by Ted Solotaroff and Ness Rapoport, contains twenty-some stories written in the last few decades that update the influence of the dominant culture on the disintegration of Jewish immigrants.

Territories of the Voice: Contemporary Stories by Irish Women Writers, edited and with an introduction by Louise DeSalvo, Kathleen Walsh D'Arcy, and Katherine Hogan, is a collection of writings by mostly well-known Irish women published in the United States.

Forgiveness: Ireland's Best Contemporary Short Stories, edited by Augustine Martin, is a collection that forms a fine portrait of the form and the people.

Flowers of Fire: Twentieth-Century Korean Stories, edited by Peter H. Lee, examines Korean history, politics, and the accompanying changes in style and sensibility.

The Forbidden Stitch: An Asian-American Anthology, edited by Shirley Geoklin Lim, Mayumi Tsutakawa, and Margarita Donnelly, includes stories spanning several generations, including Asian immigrants' passage from many distant lands and the clashes of multiple languages and cultures.

Note: Each of the last five titles has an illuminating foreword/introduction and informative authors' notes. The last title has a detailed bibliography.

Philosophy, Psychology, Biology—and More

Here is a partial list of writings that exemplify humanity's effort to define itself. It will aid you in the study of the history of life, the evolutionary process, and the nature of being.

AUTHOR	TITLE
Marcus Aurelius	*Meditations*
William Congreve	*The Way of the World*
Charles Darwin	*The Descent of Man* and *The Voyage of the Beagle*
Erasmus Darwin	*The Essential Writings of Erasmus Darwin*
Erich Fromm	*Man for Himself*
James Gleick	*Chaos: Making a New Science* and *Nature's Chaos*
Jane Goodall	*The Chimpanzees of Gombi: Patterns of Behavior*
Stanislav Grof	*The Holotropic Mind: The Three Levels of Human Consciousness and How They Shape Our Lives*
Thomas Hobbes	*Leviathan*

AUTHOR	TITLE
T. H. Huxley	*Evidence as to Man's Place in Nature*
Arthur O. Lovejoy	*The Great Chain of Being: A Study of the History of An Idea*
Rollo May	*The Courage to Create*
Mary Midgeley	*Beasts and Man: The Roots of Human Nature*
Desmond Morris	*The Biology of Art*
Erich Neumann	*The Origins and History of Consciousness*
	The Old Testament: Psalms
Plato	*The Republic*
Alexander Pope	*An Essay on Man*
Carl Sagan	*Cosmos*
Carl Sagan and Ann Druyan	*Shadows of Forgotten Ancestors*
Saint Augustine	*The Nature of Good*
Hippolyte A. Taine	*History of English Literature*
Henry David Thoreau	*Walden*
Mark Twain	*Letter from the Earth*
Edmund Wilson	*On Human Nature*
Kenko Yoshida	*Essays in Idleness (1130–1332)*

Early-Twentieth-Century Novels of the Spirit of Liberal Humanism

Brewing or gestating in the nineteenth century were concepts of evolution or revolution that were suppressed by the sociopolitical order dictating the elaborate application of the principle of continuity. The early twentieth century teemed with ideas that destroyed this concept and created a new one embracing inevitable change. This new vision now constitutes our concept of reality itself.

Traditional novel form and function of the earlier works of Jane Austen, Charles Dickens, William Thackeray, and even George Eliot were confronted by the intrusion of new, distinctive innovations that marked the arrival of the age of diversity, difficulty, and experiment.

Below is an abbreviated list of works by a few of those major writers daring to transform the old vision based on illusion to conform to changing events of their present and future. With little effort, a reader can find much commentary and analysis to aid group discussion of any of these works.

Joseph Conrad

The Nigger of the "Narcissus,"
   1897
Lord Jim, 1900
Nostromo, 1904
"The Heart of Darkness,"
   1910
"The Secret Sharer," 1910
Victory, 1915

E. M. Forster

Where Angels Fear to Tread, 1905
A Room with a View, 1908
Howards End, 1910
Passage to India, 1924

Virginia Woolf

Mrs. Dalloway, 1923
To the Lighthouse, 1927
Orlando, 1928
"A Room of One's Own," 1929
The Waves, 1931

The Years, 1937
Between the Acts, 1941

D. H. Lawrence

Sons and Lovers, 1913
The Rainbow, 1915
Women in Love, 1920
Lady Chatterley's Lover, 1928
Phoenix, 1936

James Joyce

The Dubliners, 1914
*Portrait of the Artist as a Young
   Man,* 1916
Ulysses, 1922

Aldous Huxley

Crome Yellow, 1921
Antic Hay, 1923
Point Counter Point, 1928
Brave New World, 1932
Eyeless in Gaza, 1936

Miscellaneous Nonfiction

These lists provide a smattering of informative books that you can find in the 800 division of the Dewey decimal classification. They can be a great asset to your discussion and education.

NONFICTION BOOKS IN THE MYSTERY GENRE

Hardboiled America, by Geoffrey O'Brien. Subtitled *The Lurid Years of Paperbacks,* O'Brien critiques and reexamines the tawdry suppliers of hours of reading pleasure. His checklist of what he sees as an ongoing cycle of American fascination with the genre dates from 1929 to 1958. Includes a good selected bibliography and an index. His look at the works of Dashiell Hammett, Ellery Queen, James Cain, et al., form a specialized history of our culture and will add to a discussion.

Murder in the Millions, by J. Kenneth Van Dover, studies the remarkable production and popularity of the writers Erle Stanley Gardner, Mickey Spillane, and Ian Fleming. Their fictional heroes Perry Mason, Mike Hammer, and James Bond became legends of our age.

The Lady Investigates: Women Detectives and Spies in Fiction, by Patricia Craig and Mary Cadogan. The authors trace the development of the female writers of detective fiction and the female detectives themselves from before the turn of the century. The icons Agatha Christie, Dorothy L. Sayers, Mary Roberts Rinehart, Carolyn Wells, Patricia Highsmith, and many others are featured.

EARLY (PRE–TWENTIETH CENTURY) WORKS BY AFRICAN-AMERICAN/BLACK WOMEN

In the nonfiction project *Written by Herself,* by Frances Smith Foster, attention is given to works lost in obscurity, notable among them *The Life and Religious Experience of Jarena Lee, a Colonial Lady* (1836); *Our Nig; or Sketches from the Life of a Free Black* (1859) by Harriet E. Wilson; and *Incidents in the Life of a Slave Girl* (1861), by Harriet Jacobs. This last work, subtitled *Written by Herself,* was republished in 1987 by the Harvard University Press and succinctly edited by Jean Fagan Yellin.

NONFICTION THEOLOGICAL LITERARY CRITICISM

This category sounds so dry, yet Robert McAfee Brown's *Persuade Us to Rejoice* is a highly useful supplement to the reading of the works of such writers as Alice Walker, Elie Wiesel, Alan Paton, Albert Camus, Ursula Le Guin. It sheds light on the powerful liberating force of their (and others') novels.

On Moral Fiction, by John Gardner. The author of the novels *October Light, In the Suicide Mountains, Grendel,* and almost twenty other fiction and nonfiction works, Gardner argues about the absence of moral quality in contemporary fiction. Notes and an index included.

Imagining Paris, by J. Gerald Kennedy. The author examines some of the American expatriates (Gertrude Stein, Henry Miller, F. Scott Fitzgerald, Ernest Hemingway, Djuna Barnes) and their writing during the first half of this century.

The Modern Movement, edited by John Gross. An excellent assemblage of essays and reviews about and by great figures of literary modernism:

W. B. Yeats, Wyndham Lewis, Ezra Pound, D. H. Lawrence, James Joyce, Virginia Woolf, Franz Kafka, T. S. Eliot, and more. Helps us to understand better some of our greatest writers.

Enduring Novels by American Writers

AUTHOR	TITLE
James Agee	*A Death in the Family*
Saul Bellow	*Seize the Day*
Thomas Berger	*Little Big Man*
Paul Bowles	*The Sheltering Sky*
Truman Capote	*In Cold Blood*
E. L. Doctorow	*Ragtime*
Ralph Ellison	*Invisible Man*
William Faulkner	*Absalom, Absalom!*
F. Scott Fitzgerald	*Tender Is the Night*
Dashiell Hammett	*The Maltese Falcon*
Joseph Heller	*Catch-22*
Ernest Hemingway	*The Sun Also Rises*
John Hersey	*The Wall*
John Irving	*The World According to Garp*
James Jones	*From Here to Eternity*
Harper Lee	*To Kill a Mockingbird*
Norman Mailer	*The Naked and the Dead*
Bernard Malamud	*The Assistant*
Carson McCullers	*The Heart Is a Lonely Hunter*
Toni Morrison	*Song of Solomon*
Vladimir Nabokov	*Lolita*
Joyce Carol Oates	*Them*
Edwin O'Connor	*The Last Hurrah*
Walker Percy	*The Moviegoer*
Sylvia Plath	*The Bell Jar*
Mordecai Richler (Canadian)	*St. Urbain's Horseman*
Budd Schulberg	*What Makes Sammy Run?*
Jean Stafford	*The Mountain Lion*
John Steinbeck	*The Grapes of Wrath*
John Updike	*Rabbit, Run*
Gore Vidal	*Burr*
Kurt Vonnegut, Jr.	*Slaughterhouse Five*
Eudora Welty	*Delta Wedding*
Thomas Wolfe	*Look Homeward, Angel*

U.S. Regional Authors

Readers in individual states and communities will be able to ascertain the names of local writers with help from librarians. Because local writers seem to unearth fascinating truths concerning area history, politics, and social customs, I'd be interested in copies of those lists, if you'd be so kind to send them to me.

NEW ENGLAND

Russell Banks
Linda Barnes (mystery)
J. B. Borthwick (mystery)
Nathaniel Hawthorne
Sarah Orne Jewett
Harry Kemelman (mystery)
John Knowles
Mary McGarry Morris

Charlotte McLeod (mystery)
Susan Minot
Katherine Page (mystery)
Robert B. Parker (mystery)
Cathy Pelletier
E. Annie Proulx
Virginia Rich (mystery)

MID-ATLANTIC

Louis Auchincloss
Paul Auster
Lawrence Block (mystery)
Jimmy Breslin
John Cheever
K. C. Constantine (mystery)
James Fenimore Cooper
Allen Drury
Tama Janowitz
William Kennedy

Bernard Malamud
Jay McInerney
Joyce Carol Oates
John O'Hara
Elliott Roosevelt (mystery)
Margaret Truman (mystery)
Anne Tyler
John Updike (Rabbit books)
Gore Vidal
Tom Wicker

MIDWEST

Nelson Algren
Ray Bradbury
Lillian Jackson Braun (mystery)
Robert Campbell (mystery)

Sandra Cisneros
Charles Cohen
Stuart Dybek
Joseph Epstein

Jon Hassler
Larry Heinemann
Eugene Izzi
Elmore Leonard
Ralph McInerny

Monica Quill (mystery)
Jane Smiley
Mark Twain
Jessamyn West
Larry Woiwode

SOUTH

Pinckney Benedict
Larry Brown
James Lee Burke (mystery)
Patricia Cornwell (mystery)
Harry Crews
Clyde Edgerton
William Faulkner
Fannie Flagg
Kaye Gibbons
Ellen Gilchrist
Gail Godwin
Barry Hannah
Joan Hess (mystery)
Carl Hiaasen
Josephine Humphries

Harper Lee
John Lutz (mystery)
John D. MacDonald (mystery)
Jill McCorkle
Toni Morrison
Flannery O'Connor
Walker Percy
Anne Rice
Anne River Siddons
Peter Taylor
Kathy Hogan Trocheck (mystery)
Elizabeth Dewberry Vaughan
Alice Walker
Eudora Welty

WEST

Alice Adams
Michael Allegretto (mystery)
Sarah Bird
Max Brand
Willa Cather
Emma Chizzet (mystery)
Carrie Fisher
Richard Ford
Judith Freeman
Tony Hillerman
Paul Horgan
Douglas C. Jones

Barbara Kingsolver
Louis L'Amour
Norman MacLean
Armistead Maupin
Cormac McCarthy
Larry McMurtry
Dan O'Brien
D. F. Ross
Walter Sattherthwai
John Steinbeck
Nathanael West

Not to Be Overlooked

Below is a multifarious list of authors not mentioned elsewhere in this text who may be of interest to you: known and unknown (at least as yet), highly stylized, postmodernist, beat generation, highly acclaimed. On your journeys through readings, you'll discover many more authors whose works are worth your time and energies. Again, I advise you to browse anthologies for new, emerging writers. Enjoy your discoveries and your readings.

Pam Houston
Steven Milhauser
Max Frisch
Alice Hoffman
John Casey
Harold Brodkey
Lee Smith
Martin Amis
Shelby Foote
Mark Helprin
Mavis Gallant
Kobo Abe
Bruce Chatwin
Manuel Puig
Ian McEwan
Verlyn Klinkenberg
E. M. Broner
Michael Tolkin
Louis Begley
Aleksandr Solzhenitsyn
Anthony Trollope
Gail Godwin
Joseph Epstein
William Burroughs
Ken Kesey
Reynolds Price
Denise Levertov
Robert Coover
Michel Tournier

Richard Brautigan
Irina Ratushinskaya
Douglas Copeland
Jeanette Winterson
Andrei Codrescu
Maxine Chernoff
Madison Smartt Bell
Claude Mauriac
Peter Ackroyd
Sean O'Faolian
Ishmael Reed
Toni Cade Bambara
Thomas McGuane
Georgia Savage
Eve Horowitz
Tess Gallagher
Beryl Bainbridge
William Carlos Williams
Vikram Seth
Rick Bass
Hortense Calisher
Esther Tusquets
William Kittredge
William Trevor
Sherwood Anderson
Joan Didion
Jorge Amado
Jack Kerouac

Mary Morris
Tom Robbins
Robert Bly
David Lodge
Paule Marshall
Bob Shacochis
Thomas Mann
Patricia Henley

Emily Prager
Jamaica Kincaid
Angela Carter
Pavel Kohout
Jeffrey Eugenides
Robert Olmstead
Pablo Neruda
Maxine Kumin

Banned Books

On February 26, 1962, President John F. Kennedy made the following remarks on the twentieth anniversary of the Voice of America: "We are not afraid to entrust the American people with unpleasant facts, foreign ideas, alien philosophies, and competitive values. . . . For, a nation that is afraid to let its people judge the truth and falsehood in an open market is a nation that is afraid of its people." Regardless of this statement, self-perpetuating ideals of conservative and liberal special-interest groups and individuals continually challenge public dissemination of certain books. Below is a partial list of books that are frequently attacked, considered dangerous, and/or banned in some communities. A more complete list can be obtained by writing to People for the American Way, Washington, D.C.

The Adventures of Tom Sawyer
Sleeping Beauty
Tarzan of the Apes
I Know Why the Caged Bird Sings
Just So Stories
The Mayor of Casterbridge
My House
Catch-22
Flowers for Algernon
A Raisin in the Sun
The Bible
Doctor Zhivago
Of Time and the River
All the King's Men

Catcher in the Rye
The Color Purple
Of Mice and Men
One Hundred Years of Solitude
The Handmaid's Tale
Grendel
Lord of the Flies
Death of a Salesman
A Farewell to Arms
Fear of Flying
Where the Sidewalk Ends
Sophie's Choice
Working
Gone With the Wind

APPENDIX B

SYLLABI FROM RACHEL'S READING GROUPS

"I cannot think of a greater blessing than to die in
one's own bed, without warning or discomfort, on
the last page of the new book that we most wanted
to read."

—*John Russell*

The lists below include mine and others' from around the country. The
titles are followed by brief commentary. Enjoy your reading!

MY NOVEL GROUP'S ANNUAL SYLLABI

1996–1997

Snow Falling on Cedars, by David Guterson (Harcourt Brace, hardcover,
1994; Vintage Books, paperback, 1995). As fast as a joke or cold germ
travels coast-to-coast by jet, so did the name of this, heretofore, little
known author and his sparse-selling novel. Word-of-mouth (book group
people are happy to take credit) catapulted *Snow* onto the bestseller list
and Guterson into the celeb world as a serious and serious-intentioned
writer who home-schools his children on one of the San Juan Islands in
the Pacific Northwest. *Snow*, a major contribution to Northwest regional
literature, explores the events and interpersonal relationships among the
residents of a fictional San Juan island (San Piedro) during the years surrounding World War II, coinciding with the grand design of the Japanese internment camps. Guterson's intensely humanistic vision unfolds
within the plot foundation of a three-day trial in which a Japanese fish-

erman is being tried for the murder of an Anglo fisherman. Old friendships, public and forbidden loves, war wounds, the powerful forces of the universe, and more, combine, creating a most satisfying read. Some will swoon over the beauty and richness of this novel; others will enjoy its philosophy and fine construction but feel authorial heavy-handedness. The informative Reading Group Guide from Vintage may still be available; call 1-800-793-BOOK.

Felicia's Journey, by William Trevor. (Penguin paperback, 1994). This psychological thriller engenders intense emotional response from every group and individual I assign it to. Many readers, having never read Trevor, some never having heard of him, found a masterful writer to intrigue them further with his many novels and short stories. *FJ* fits into the au courant exploration of Irish-English relations. Trevor depicts two main characters—young Felicia from a nameless rural Irish village who is at odds with portly ("nineteen and half stone"—276 lbs.!) Mr. Hilditch, a monstrous serial killer disguised as a good Samaritan in England's Midland. Trevor states in interviews that he focuses on personalities, nothing more; but readily admits that personality is formed by culture, religion, nationality, and family circumstances. Be prepared for a story that disturbs—and you're not sure why. A female book group participant reported having "invasion" dreams while reading this book.

The Wizard of Oz, by L. Frank Baum (Brimax Books, Bethleham, PA 1996). Not surprisingly, the 1900 children's classic has been read by far less than have seen the famous 1939 Victor Fleming film. The distinctions between text and film are notable and the reasons why it is considered to be greatly influential to our national psyche are engaging to discuss. There is much criticism, analysis, and history available to bring to discussions. But as an adult we have a choice to preserve the magical fantasy of our childhood tales, or to view them with adult discernment so as to better understand their effect and notoriety. I chose the latter, and 95 percent of those I met with enjoyed the discussion experience.

(Legend has it that when Baum was asked by his attentive young listeners for the name of the place where the Munchkins lived, he glanced over at the bottom drawer of a file cabinet alphabetically labeled O-Z, and created literary history.) ·

Peace on Earth, by Stanislaw Lem (A Harvest Book, Harcourt Brace, 1994). I earnestly thought that Lem's international stature would impress my groupies, that his ironic depiction of human folly would entertain, and that his moral and ethical philosophy would engage my readers. Still, the majority resisted this science fiction yarn featuring Lem's evolving spy hero, the astronaut Ijon Tichy, on his dangerous mission to the moon where the world's nations have deposited their superweapons, only to fear that "they" seem to be "doing their own thing" up there. Tichy's trip and what he experiences upon his return provide a vehicle for Lem's outlook on the absurdity of human behavior. Even though I experienced resistance to this text, intense discussions about politics, morality, and environmental issues flared. One woman made book-group history with an impassioned speech about morality and the future of the world.

Corelli's Mandolin, by Louis de Bernières (Vintage International, 1994). While a few readers did not like this book, it swept the votes for "best book of the syllabus." What is it about? A rich, complex novel such as this demands the glib answer, "Life," but that provokes frustration. *Corelli's Mandolin* is set on the Greek island of Cephallonia before, during, and after Mussolini's occupation and World War II. It depicts set patterns and irrevocable change of five mid-century decades. De Bernières whirls us about in life's dramatic extremes, and lulls us with moments of sweet respite. We ascend to cerebral heights of well-intentioned philosophy, history, education, medicine, technology; we play on hills of wit, whimsy, romance, sexuality, love, "joie de vivre"; we plummet to the craggy depths of sadness, bitterness, barbaric atrocity, cataclysmic change, and corrupt power.

Nightwood, by Djuna Barnes (A New Directions Book, 26th printing; original printing by this publisher 1961). Originally printed in 1936, this novel's plot centers on Robin Vote who marries Guido, has a child, leaves Guido, pairs up with Nora and then Jenny, leaving both, and ends up in a barn. That sounds simple enough, but Barnes's text is a dazzling, consternating fantasy representative of the experimental fiction emerging from the European (Paris) writers in the 1930s.

The reading of *Nightwood* created much reader frustration, ire directed toward me, and ultimately a discussion group sensation as we learned more about Barnes herself and were able to connect her biography to her text, which is said to be her masterpiece. Passages in the text rank with the finest of literature. You'll be underlining like crazy and wanting to read her discourses on love and desire and despair and more. My suggestion: research on her life and studies of the text previous to your reading will enhance your appreciation and understanding.

An American Women in a Chinese Hat, by Carole Maso (A Plume/Penguin Book, 1995). Maso's fourth novel tells the story of Catherine, a writer summering in Vence (Côte d'Azur, France), on a grant, 1988, the year Dukakis ran against Bush, marking the end of Reagan's administration. These last details are subtly threaded into Maso's text that explores androgyny, bisexuality, erotica, and AIDS, and compares the French culture to American politics. With an overt and confrontational self-consciousness, Catherine's anguished-writer-persona is reflected in her increasingly more complex first-person narrative voice. One wonders what to think of her, what Maso thought of her. The lyrical, poetic images are many and mighty. This book contemporizes some of Djuna Barnes's angst-filled existential thinking, and is much more accessible reading material. (Both books' settings are in France.)

Nostromo, by Joseph Conrad (Penguin Books, 1990). Even though my colleagues questioned my rationale when I included Conrad's 1904 masterpiece in the syllabus ("If you don't *have* to read it, why would you want to?"), I scheduled it after everyone had a chance to view the Masterpiece Theatre's Fall 96 production. The novel's Dickensian cast of characters, construction that shifted the novel from popular entertainment to one of high, carefully constructed art, and themes that would pervade twentieth-century literature, provides enough to sustain a great discussion. High school and college teachers employ it to explore questions of morality and personal integrity. A challenging, worthwhile selection.

The Riders, by Tim Winton (Scribner Paperback Fiction, Simon & Schuster, 1994). This prolific and popular Australian writer begins a "feel good" story about the anticipated, happy reunion of a family only to rip the rug right out from under Scully, the dad/husband, and from us, the readers, and turns it into a harrowing page-turner. Winton's writing is fresh, original, even graceful amidst its coarseness (many toilets in this novel—very corporeal). His vision of tenuous existence, necessary descents, and the difference between looking backward and moving forward, is infused with elements of religion and mythology, if you can find them. Put wife Jennifer under the file for Missing Persons and much discussion ensues along the lines of family relations and gender politics.

My Home Is Far Away, by Dawn Powell (Steerforth Press, 1995 reissue with Introduction by Tim Page; first published by Charles Scribner's Sons, 1944). When Terry Teachout reviewed this book and *The Diaries of Dawn Powell* in *The New York Times*, he began with, "Every decade or so, somebody writes an essay about Dawn Powell, and a few hundred more people discover her work, and are grateful. And that's it. Few American novelists have been so lavishly praised by so many high-powered critics to so little effect."

Dawn Powell's autobiographical novel is an outstanding literary find, and I commend Steerforth Press for committing their resources to its reissue. When an adult, in the 1940s, living in Greenwich Village, Powell stopped cranking out her urbane, comic "New York" novels to capture her childhood memories of Ohio before time and space irreparably damaged them. Readers will find popular book-group themes oozing out of her beautiful and resiliently humorous writing, and find this fifty-some-year-old book quite contemporary.

The Liar's Club, by Mary Karr (Penguin Books, 1995). Whereas Powell converted her childhood into novel form, Karr's memoir is a full frontal attack emanating from a dark, frozen defining moment that circles backward and around and through the assets and liabilities of being the daughter of her mother and her father in a Texas oil refining town. A snap-crackling tone and wit prevents Karr from weighing us down with her Gothic tale; instead we get a Texas-size dose of rebounding yarns that may, just may, exorcise the pain and capitalize on her parents' legacy. "[T]ruth was conspiring to assemble itself before me. Call it fate or grace or pure shithouse chance. I was being guided somehow into the chute that led down the dark corridor at the end of which truth's door would fly open."

1995–96

The Silent Cry, Kenzaburō Ōe. Ōe's Nobel Prize for Literature in 1994 brought him well-deserved attention in the United States. This 1967 masterpiece specifically noted by the Nobel committee was translated into English in 1974 and reissued by Kodansha in paperback in 1995. The novel is a particularly potent distillation of themes that haunt Ōe's early works. In this novel, the narrator, the father of a deformed son, confronts issues of personal, familial, and cultural identity.

Many group members appreciated this challenging book. Some research of Japan's history (the period of Meiji Restoration 1868–1912) and culture will help any discussion. Also a good map of Japan will show the island of Shikoku where the action takes place. Critical material: *The New Yorker*, 2/6/95; *Contemporary Literary Criticism [CLC]*, *Vol. 86 (last page of lengthy article has list of further resources material)*. Be prepared to read in Ōe's text what is called *grotesque realism*. (I believe the phrase describes itself well.) Page 229 of CLC explains the purpose of Ōe's grotesque image system. It has been said that Ōe works through the darkness to get to the light.

The Palace Thief, by Ethan Canin (Picador USA, 1994, $10). The promo blurb on the back of the book says, "Unforgettable." These four stories had every one of my discussion groups buzzing, and the stories resonated all year long. I often heard, "This reminds me of that Ethan Canin story we read," even though there is a decided focus on men and boys; both genders respond and identify with Canin's characters and conflicts. His writing moves us, although perhaps not to optimism.

The Stone Diaries, by Carol Shields (Penguin Books, 1995. $10.95). By now I think everyone has read this book, but if you have not, you may or may not be missing something special. My vote's not in. Shields's opening passage is worth the price of admission. It's highly inventive and thought-provoking and considered cutting-edge philosophy on untapped mind potential. As explored in Shields's tale of one woman's life from birth to death, readers can easily and intelligently recognize and personally identify with issues of this century's feminism, religion, and politics. The book is replete with details of ordinary lives, both male and female, and is intensely, deeply human and affirmative.

Othello, by William Shakespeare. I scheduled this to coincide with the end of the run of Chicago's wonderful Shakespeare Repertory performance. I facilitated the discussions of this still popular and enigmatic tragedy by working from the manuscript. I urged all to see the play, see the videos (Orson Welles's and Lawrence Fishburne's) and/or read Julius Lester's *Othello, a novel.* (The controversial Lester's revision of the original for young adults was a positive addition to the discussions.) As Iago represents the personification of evil, his character resonates for us in subsequent readings. Much contemporary fiction/lit. can be compared to *Othello.* (My suggestion: Read aloud the opening conversation between Roderigo and Iago; then compare that and the triangular relationship of Iago/Othello/Desdemona to the opening conversation and triangular relationship of Chad/Howard/Christine in Neil LaBute's 1997 film, *In the Company of Men.*)

"The Nose," and "The Overcoat," two of Nikolai Gogol's most famous stories are published in a Dover Thrift Edition and in a special Penguin edition, *Penguin 60's.* They are also highly anthologized, and in a collection with an excellent introduction, *The Overcoat and Other Tales of Good and Evil,* W.W. Norton, 1957. The three translations are slightly different; this was noted with interest. These stories written in the early 1830s and early 1840s respectively, served some of my readers as an introduction to Gogol's genius that marked a turning point in Russian literature. They were paired up with the next month's selection, a system that I have been trying for the last few years in the attempt to examine layers of time and literature as reflection of time and culture. (When the nameless narrator in *Feather on the Breath of God,* by Sigrid Nunez [HarperCollins,1995] mentions that her father reminded her of the little men in a Gogol or Chekhov story, my groupies had that reference as a common experience.)

Fording the Stream of Consciousness, by Dubravka Ugresic. (Written in 1988, originally translated in 1988 by Michael Henry Heim. Published in paperback as part of *Writings from the Unbound Europe* by Northwestern University Press, 1993.) I discovered Ugresic's work by reading her parody of "The Nose" included in Graywolf Press's *Stories from the New Europe*, 1992 ($11.00), entitled " A Hot Dog in a Warm Bun." *Fording* is, among other things, a seriocomic postmodernist examination of the difference between Eastern Europe and the West. An international writers' conference in Zagreb sets the stage for Ugresic's poignant, madcap, and multilayered novel that reads like a soap opera, a mystery, a survey of literature, an espionage thriller, a journal, and more. The skilled Ugresic stymies the reader's search for the novel's "truth," which may be her real objective.

Van Gogh's Room at Arles, by Stanley Elkin (Hyperion, 1992). Elkin died in May 1995, just as he was about to go on a publicity tour for his (posthumously award-winning) novel *Mrs. Ted Bliss.* Including one of his works in the syllabus is a way of paying homage to a writer; some say that this writer is so good that he'll never be popular. In three novellas, three separate protagonists are confronted with sudden changes in their political geography. Elkin presses the English language to brilliantly depict each experience. Elkin was a wizard of language. Parts of this book beg to be read aloud in the group. Readers will recognize the second novella as a parody of the royal family reminiscent of Lewis Carroll's in *Alice in Wonderland.* In my edit for *The New York Times'* advertorial "The Book Lover's Guide to Reading Groups" (June 22, 1997), I wrote of this book: "In Elkin's hands, the language sears indelible impressions for those who can bear the hilarity, the anguish, and convoluted landscapes."

Theory of War, by Joan Brady (Fawcett, 1993. $11.00). What a droll title for a seamlessly constructed, thoroughly engaging book that shocks the reader repeatedly. Brady's fictional reconstruction of her (white) grandfather's traumatic defining moment and its aftermath sit squarely in an unsentimental, realistic version of the development of our country from mid-nineteenth century to 1923. I was led to this book by some of you who sent in your reading lists. All of my groups in Chicagoland gave it an A+.

Paradise News, by David Lodge (Penguin Books, 1991. $10.95). Disguised as a "nerd-gets-a-life" story, this is not just another middlebrow quest novel. Lodge has skillfully designed an Arthurian-like fairy tale, or a Shakespearean-like romantic comedy, in which major and minor characters support, clarify, and celebrate Lodge's vision of the ambiguity of human conscience, and the struggle to reconcile spiritual and sensuous desires. Lodge manipulates us, like Dickens, right to the end, and we do not mind. We, like the protagonist Bernard Walsh, are better for the experience. We can all recognize Lodge's descriptions of Hawaiian "paradise" beyond the brochures when his English vacationers' expectations confront reality. (Lodge's novel *Therapy* received rave reviews. His many nonfiction books on literary criticism are worth your attention.)

Open Secrets, by Alice Munro (Alfred A. Knopf 1994). Although a good percentage of group members are not avid fans of short stories, I selected Munro's latest collection for the last meeting of the season and assigned only the first four stories. Why? Logically, Munro has only written one novel, so if one wants to read her works, one reads short stories. This is not force-feeding by any stretch of the imagination. Her work is state of the art. Other writers want to rub her belly, bask in her aura, learn the secrets of her magic spell-casting. Each story seduces, challenges, engages, and offers revelation in the ways of revelation. She writes of rural Canadian life in late nineteenth, early twentieth century with an archeologist's fervor; you savor the discovery and mystery of each shard. Read carefully the last sentence of the title story, and then begin the collection. Or don't. Start at the beginning, and work your way to that evasively revelatory sentence. (Let me hear from you.)

For some groups I facilitated discussions of:

A Place Where the Sea Remembers, by Sandra Benitez (Scribner, 1993. $10.00). This little gem quietly collects character studies of villagers of Santiago, Mexico. Their lives, while impoverished, ebb and flow with the fullest of life. A simple, fluid Benitez sentence has the intensity of a frame in a Bergman or Buñuel film. For those of you who vacation in Mexico (and those who don't), this book may be gently consciousness-raising. (Reading group guide available.)

Inside Mexico, by Paula Heusinkveld (John Wiley & Sons, $10.95). A helpful guide to the changing Mexican society.

Pride and Prejudice, by Jane Austen. Always a favorite and a must for any book group or individual uninitiated to the recent goddess of great novels transformed into sensational screen do's. Austen's novel was paired with, succeeded, or preceded Anna Quindlen's *One True Thing*. Quindlen's female characters discuss Elizabeth and Jane Bennett (the fictional sisters in Austen's nineteenth-century novel), which affords us the opportunity to see how authors and novels build on/from each other.

Rich in Love, by Josephine Humphreys (Penguin, 1987. $13.99). An engaging, contemporary, coming-of-age story told in first-person by a keen, wise high school girl thrust out of her "garden of Eden" when her mother leaves the family, and family home. The keen young woman still has a lot to learn. (Novel made into a movie available on video.) While Humphreys has not written the great American novel, this book highlights many cultural issues.

Bone, by Fae Myenne Ng (pronounced *"ing"*) (HarperPerennial, 1993. $11.50). Within San Francisco's Chinatown are individuals, members of families, who are holding secrets, hidden shames, hidden desires. The aftermath of a middle daughter's suicide is the catalyst for much soul-searching among the surviving family members, and the community.

The Music of Chance, by Paul Auster (Penguin, 1990. $10.95). You may know Auster's name from the movie *Smoke*. *The Music of Chance* has its own film version starring James Spader and Mandy Patinkin. This seemingly benign tale of a man who drives around after his life has taken a turn for the worse (his wife left him), gyrates into a suspense thriller of the darkest deepest, soul-searching dimensions, examining the roles of whim, chance, love, justice, and redemption. We look for the links to the totally unexplained mysteries of the Auster work.

History of the World in 10½ Chapters, by Julian Barnes (Vintage, 1990. $12). I'm always delighted when requested to discuss this book and have another chance to reread it. Barnes is a master linguist and stylist. His design, motifs, and vision for a better world (albeit slim), take the reader on a carnival ride of heart and soul and story and history.

Julip, by Jim Harrison (Simon & Schuster/Pocket Books, 1995. $12) These three novellas, like Elkin's, coalesce thematically in language and themes so subtly, that once the reader "sees" what Harrison has done, a newfound appreciation of his naturalist's vision emerges. The character Julip is a feminist treat. As a matter-of-fact, each main and secondary character is well sculpted. In my everyday life, these are not people I would ordinarily encounter. I appreciated Harrison introducing me to them.

Bastard Out of Carolina, by Dorothy Allison (NAL/Dutton, 1992). As evidenced by the ban of Angelica Houston's made-for-TV version of Bone Boatwright's coming-of-age story (and fictionalized biography of D. Allison), *Bastard* is a wrenchingly realistic portrayal of destructive forces within family structures. Allison's writing is visceral!! Beware. Yet there exists loving ties within the extended Boatright family.

The Pull of the Moon, by Elizabeth Berg (Random House, 1996. Hardcover $21.00). Nan and Martin were sweethearts, and baby boomers, and husband and wife of longevity. Then Nan turned fifty. This double epistolary (letters to Martin and private journaling) tracks Nan's trip that she takes, in her car, by herself, to nowhere on the map in particular. More correctly her journey is a journey to seek herself, the one beyond the wife and mother. Nan's present tense creates a soft suspense; both the reader and Nan are journeying into unknown territory filled with memories.

While Berg was on a publicity tour through Chicago, I discussed this book at Roberta Rubin's bookstore, *The Book Stall*, in Winnetka, IL—with Elizabeth in the room. Maybe I'll write a story about the experience—one day. She was quite receptive, and not yet 50.

1994–1995

The Music Room, by Dennis McFarland (Avon, 1990). This critically acclaimed novel and bestseller records the aftereffects of a brother's suicide that is announced on page 2. Martin Lambert, the surviving sibling, descends into a journey through memory to recovery. McFarland brings a Faulknerian family into the second half of the twentieth century. Everyone liked this book and was anxious to read his next book, *School for the Blind*, which came out about that time.

The Shipping News, by E. Annie Proulx (Charles Scribner Sons, 1993). This Pulitzer Prize–winner sent high school English teachers into spasms over Proulx's deletion of verbs and conjunctives, but this author is applauded for her ear for dialect as she depicts the speech patterns of Newfoundlanders. These craggy folk live among craggy nature. Much discussion focused on Proulx's main protagonist Quoyle and his "great damp loaf of a body." Quoyle challenged the readers' definition of hero, yet his admirable traits, not looks, win hearts. His odyssey is well constructed, rich and complex, and holds both the erudite and mainstream reader's attention. Plus, *The Shipping News* has, even though it chokes me to say it, a *happy* ending.

One woman came to her discussion with an entire page of notes on the meaning of knots, a significant leitmotif in the novel.

Retreat from Love, by Colette (Bobbs-Merrill, 1974, also Harvest Books international series). I wanted to "do" Colette, but now I'm sorry I picked this one. As the last in her Claudine series, and the first from under her husband's domination, the thin novel depicts dormant and emerging sexuality and love in a variety of forms. While the discussions were of value, several other of her books are more notable: *Mitsou*, 1919, *Cheri*, her 1920 masterpiece, or the beautiful 1922 *My Mother's House*.

The Spectator Bird, by Wallace Stegner (Doubleday, 1976). Anything by one of America's undisputed literary deans wins fans, and *TSB*, winner of 1977's National Book Award, is no exception. Stegner's concerns extend far past the development of the West into vast arenas of personal, social, and intellectual thought. In this novel, a retired literary agent, Joe Allston (updated from an earlier Stegner novel) looks back on his sixty-nine years, surveying life and contemporary civilization. The curmudgeon's cynical cogitations reveal Joe to be what Stegner once called himself, "a pessimistic meliorist." A postcard that arrives in the first chapter sets off a sequence of events, both of the present and of the *remembered* past, that forms the beauty of this novel. No reader will be disappointed.

The Master and Margarita, by Mikhail Bulgakov (1967 Harper & Row and NAL). A long-suppressed masterpiece of "writings from the drawer"; only published well after Bulgakov's 1940 death. In a reenactment of the Faustian legend, havoc and creativity, death and love, reign when the Devil visits the streets of Moscow in 1920. Bulgakov integrates first-century and twentieth-century history in this most engaging, enlightening fantasy. This is a "stretch" novel for the mainstream reader. Do your homework on Bulgakov for increased enjoyment and illumination. I was delighted to see this book as the featured title for some bookstore book groups around the country. It's singular.

The Robber Bridegroom, both the Grimm Brothers' tale and the novella by Eudora Welty (Harcourt Brace, 1942). In preparation for Atwood's bestseller, we discussed the unexpurgated Grimms tale and Welty's mid-century fantasy. One set in the woods of Old Europe, one set in Mississippi, these fantasy tales of bandits and fair maidens stand on their own, and aided our understanding of the next selection, *The Robber Bride*. This trio, written at different points within the past two centuries, provides a lens through which we could view evolving variations of themes and narrative techniques, and, especially, feminist applications.

The Robber Bride, by Margaret Atwood (Doubleday, 1993). This book made publishing history when Doubleday's vice president Marly Rusoff created the first Reading Group Guide to accompany it. Marly's vision hailed a revolutionary change in reading-group discussions by providing author info, probing questions, and plot synopses in pamphlet form, free to the public. (Most publishers have toll-free numbers or websites; call for info, or look for their ads in national newspapers. Or ask your local bookstore.)

Atwood's novel describes and updates the relationship between four college "girlfriends." Her examination of inter- and intra-gender power dynamics fascinates and instructs us. Use this book. Squeeze every ounce of insight out of it. Zenia, as character and archetype, transcends time and space, and may be unforgettable for you, as she is for so many of my groupies who keep bringing up her name in subsequent discussions of other titles.

Left Hand of Darkness, by Ursula LeGuin (1969 Ace Books, New York). This sci-fi masterpiece is set on an alien planet where all people are of one sex; a lone earthman is forced into intriguing identity dilemmas. Once you get past the obstacle of the alien names and cultural mores, LeGuin's work can be conceived as brilliant, important. Because of its sci-fi strangeness, some readers were repelled; most loved the opportunity to read and discuss. Also read her other masterpiece, *The Dispossessed.*

The Giver, by Lois Lowry (Houghton Mifflin, 1993). A seemingly Utopian fantasy that won several major young adult/children's literature awards will find its way into your heart and your soul. I invited all children over the age of ten to attend each discussion with their mothers (parents, in the case of coed groups). Lowry's book is ambiguous, enigmatic, provocative, and challenging, not in its narrative construct but in its ideas presented.

The Rest of Life, by Mary Gordon (Viking, 1993). Not everyone will like these novellas because Gordon's three protagonists mirror our emotional and cerebral selves so well that we can get the jitters. My short story groups and I pored over her pages, words, and ideas.

For some groups, I facilitated the discussion of:

The Fur Hat, by Vladimir Voinovich (Harcourt Brace Jovanovich, 1989). Exiled from the Soviet Union in 1980, Voinovich writes a satire with a human touch about an adventure writer who wants to belong to the Soviet Writer's Union—to get his hat.

Six Degrees of Separation, the book and film by John Guare (1990 Vintage). When an art dealer and his wife are "visited" by a young man purporting to be their son's friend, a series of events unfold in this powerful creation that confronts us with issues about truth, identity, justice, the meaning of art, greatness, and success. *Six Degrees* illuminates the tenuous contract we all have with the order we expect of life.

Too Loud a Solitude, by Bohumil Hrabal (Harcourt Brace, 1990). Finely balanced between pathos and comedy, this thin, mighty novel, set in old Czechoslovakia, seems analogous to the popular American film *Forrest Gump* in its depiction of what is important. One of Hrabal's obvious answers: BOOKS

Lost in Translation, by Eva Hoffman (Dutton, 1988). As an immigrant and refugee, Hoffman wrote this nonfiction that is both memoir and testimony to the human capacity to begin anew, reinvent oneself. Hers is crisp, brilliant writing. We live in the time of creative, heartfelt writings depicting immigration, dislocation, alienation, renewal. The first generation Americans are finding voices, as are the multiracial, multicultural young adult children of those innocents caught in the chaos of mid-century historical events.

1993–1994

A Thousand Acres by Jane Smiley

Symposium by Muriel Spark
  In preparation, I read and studied Plato's dialogue by the same name, written several thousand years ago.

Orlando by Virginia Woolf
  I put this in the syllabus as a follow-up to *A Room of One's Own*, not knowing that the film was being released the summer before. Coincidence.

Killing Orders by Sara Paretsky

Alice Through the Looking Glass by Lewis Carroll

The English Patient by Michael Ondaatje (Booker Prize winner)

The Portable Dorothy Parker (selected short stories and essays)

The Sound and the Fury by William Faulkner

Kitchen by Banana Yoshimoto

All the Pretty Horses by Cormac McCarthy

Alternatives: *Black Box* by Amos Oz
    The Lover by Marguerite Duras
    Frankenstein by Mary Wollstonecraft Shelley

Annotations

A Thousand Acres. Smiley dissects an Iowa farm family under a microscope in her Pulitzer Prize–winning dark vision of the American dream gone awry. Familiarity with story line of *King Lear* would help.

Symposium. Spark disguises her message about mortality and materialism in a splendidly crafted comedy of morals and manners set among affluent Londoners, with a mystery, a nonmystery, and a feminist perspective thrown in.

Orlando. Woolf's homage to her androgynous friend Vita Sackville-West is a fantastic and glorious escapade through history, society, literature, and gender.

Killing Orders. To study the genre, we read a Paretsky mystery with a Chicago setting, a feisty female detective, and a church connection with the underworld.

Alice Through the Looking Glass. Alice's trials and tribulations, real and unreal, took us back to childhood through adult eyes and showed us the brilliance of Lewis Carroll.

The English Patient. Ondaatje's language and story vie for attention in this post–World War II love story involving an English patient, a Canadian nurse, and a Sikh soldier.

The Portable Dorothy Parker. The mystique of the wisecracking queen of the Alonguin Round Table can be better understood after reading some of these selections that uncover her controversial ideas about women, love and sex, and her volatile personality.

The Sound and the Fury. This compelling story of the lust, incest, and suicide that led to the dissolution of an old southern family, the Compsons, has all the stylistic quirks of Faulkner, and it's worth it.

Kitchen. The young Yoshimoto has constructed two novellas on love (lost and regained) set in contemporary Japan that blend old and new traditions, and has been well received in her native country.

All the Pretty Horses. McCarthy's winner of the National Book Award tells in eloquent language of a young Texas rancher crossing the border down into Mexico, and his coming of age, with a romantic western twist. Knowledge of Spanish (or a Spanish-English dictionary at hand) would help.

Black Box. Oz, like Smiley, stunningly dissects a family with an entire epistolary narrative. This one is Israeli with even more "tsures" than Smiley's Cook family, because the Israeli population is a polyglot. Oz's family is a metaphor for the chaos in his native land.

1992–1993

Possession by A. S. Byatt
  An arduous, rewarding read that is fodder for university courses. Get out your mythology books and encyclopedias.
My Son's Story by Nadine Gordimer
  Gordimer, living and writing in Johannesburg, is a brave woman and the fifth to receive the Nobel Prize for Literature.
Heat and Dust by Ruth Prawer Jhabvala
  A simple read; a careful look reveals the integration of the Hindu belief in reincarnation and transmigration into the plotline. East meets West in India.

Howards End by E. M. Forster
Film was released about the same time and was discussed as a visual rendition of the novel that had been around for eighty years. Comparisons between these forms and the reasons for the film's production now were also discussed.

Louder Than Words, edited by William Shore
Great social consciousness–raising stories that were all donated; sales proceeds go to the nonprofit organization Share Our Strength. Part of the publishing industry's new interest in the community.

Ceremony by Leslie Marmon Silko
A story that allows us to see the sacred ideology and ceremony of Native Americans and their plight in America today.

A Room of One's Own by Virginia Woolf
Highly erudite language and brilliant essay form conveys today's feminist message. Written in 1928.

The Messiah of Stockholm by Cynthia Ozick
Ozick's tale is hilarious, seriously moral, highly complex, and enigmatic. Engenders great discussions of faith, belief, Jewish versus Christian doctrine, truth/fact versus fiction/story, self, and more.

Animal Dreams by Barbara Kingsolver
Probably the winner of the season. Highly accessible story exemplifying new fiction that is a tool for the author's social and political concerns. Better than soapboxes and soap operas.

The House on Mango Street by Sandra Cisneros
Tiny book of interesting hybrid genre packs a wallop. Watch Cisneros grow as a writer.

Annotations

Possession. In one regard, this is a double love story of two related women from different generations—one story about the repressed passions of mid-nineteenth-century England, and a modern story that requires an arduous journey to be taken before love can be freed from the shackles of misperceptions about the first. Byatt's best-seller and prize winner can be an intimidating reading challenge, but a diligent reader is rewarded with a richly designed English novel tapestry of love story, mystery, feminism, mythology, and more.

My Son's Story. A searing story of a man innocently pulled into politics, and a love affair that ruins his family. Gordimer's novel is a political allegory for the individual living under a corrupt, repressive government.

Heat and Dust. A modern Englishwoman seeks information about her errant grandmother, who married and went to India. In the search, their identities are fused.

Howards End. Forster's liberal humanist vision of the future for England in which different social classes and ideologies clash and unite. We are kept occupied reading about what happens to a valuable homestead and what it means to the members of the Schlegel and Wilcox families. Forster, as narrator, delightfully intrudes to comment on his characters as he takes them on their merry and not-so-merry way. Love, class prejudice, passion, murder, and more.

Louder Than Words. We read every selection in my short-story groups, but only the first three in the novel groups (Anne Tyler's "A Woman Like a Fieldstone House," Joyce Carol Oates's "Hostage," Lee K. Abbott's "Here in Time and Not"). Each revealed a social consciousness necessary for moral living in today's world.

Ceremony. Tayo, a half-breed Native American, returns from World War II having been taken prisoner in the Bataan Death March in the Philippines. But only his body has returned, not spirit. Silko's mystical tale has the aura of a sacred Native American story, and it tells of the young hero's return to his people and of the ritual ceremony required for return.

A Room of One's Own. Woolf's politically revolutionary 1928 essay may contain her obtuse, oblique language, but her message—"A woman must have a room of her own" and money of her own—is loud and clear. Discussion of her theories of androgyny within the essay led me to include *Orlando* in the 1993–1994 syllabus.

The Messiah of Stockholm. This is an exploration of the credibility of story and of literary and religious icons set in a quest tale of one isolated, lonely ne'-er-do-well, Lars Andemenning, who declares he is the son of Bruno Schulz, a real and noted Eastern European writer of phantasmagoria before being killed by a gestapo. Ozick's accessible story line contains twists and turns and enigmas. Her writings contain much intellectual and religious mystery, and in discussion of this one, I did a lot of talking.

Animal Dreams. Kingsolver's tale of return centers on the one sister, Codi Noline, who goes home to a small town in Arizona to care for her father, who is diagnosed with Alzheimer's. But the story intricately involves her sister, Hallie, who is only represented off-stage. Having her protagonist return home is the format Kingsolver employs to create a finely constructed, multifaceted love story with a happy, sappy ending. Native American philosophy, ecological issues, and concerns of "otherness" are threaded throughout.

The House on Mango Street. Cisneros, one of the new, fresh Chicano/a voices of the nineties, provides lyrical snippets that examine growing up poor,

Hispanic, and female. Imagery abounds and a careful reading provides extraordinary pleasure and insight.

1991–1992

History of the World in 10½ Chapters by Julian Barnes
  Oh, these English writers! First they become anal over form and fact, and then they rip the rules to shreds. Barnes's book is a perfect example of "You can't believe everything you read," but what do you do for comfort? He explores.
Ordinary Love and Good Will by Jane Smiley
  Great! Good for new groups.
Seize the Day and *Bellarosa Connection* by Saul Bellow
  His early novella that brought him acclaim and a most recent one that may redeem him as a woman-hater. But first you really have to love his sense of humor.
Jasmine by Bharti Mukherjee
  Looking like and reading like supermarket fluff, Mukherjee can find her way into your heart and mind and reincarnations. East meets West in America.
Absalom, Absalom! by William Faulkner
  If you are ever going to read Faulkner as an adult, do it together and do your research.
The Things They Carried by Tim O'Brien
  He'll carry away your heart.
Several stories by Guy de Maupassant
  I copied and distributed some of Maupassant's short stories and connected the discussion to timely impressionist art. Realism versus romanticism.
The Elegy of Lady Fiametta by Giovanni Boccaccio
Solomon Gursky Was Here by Mordecai Richler
The Hearts and Lives of Men by Fay Weldon
  Fun, feminist, and humanist.

Annotations

History of the World in 10½ Chapters. Barnes's antinovel provokes questions about the nature of history, story, and fiction in relation to the individual and time and space. Indeed, ten chapters and a parenthetical partial one comprise the novel exposing Barnes's superior stylistic skills. A bawdy, beautiful seriocomic novel by one of the new and exciting English stylists.

Ordinary Love and Good Will. Following *Age of Grief,* for which Smiley gained a deserved reputation as master of the novella form, these two distinct but intricately related novellas examine separate modern American families and the challenge of the individual in society. Smiley's male and female characters and coursing events mirror our literary archetypes, and offer much to discuss. Smiley explores two hauntingly meaningful words—duty and desire.

Seize the Day and *Bellarosa Connection.* Reading an early novella that brought him fame and a recently written and fully stylized one, we were able to discuss separately and connectedly the journeys of Bellow's fumblingly human, male protagonists—each approximately the age Bellow was when he wrote them. Tommy Wilhelm of *Seize the Day* and the unidentified narrator of *Bellarosa Connection* afford us clues to Bellow's private and creative soul.

Jasmine. Mukherjee's swiftly reading novel reflects her own knowledge and experience of growing up female and Hindu, and the culture clashes she herself encountered when she came west. The protagonist (Jasmine, Jane, and more) lives through various incarnations in this picaresque tale; her decisions and actions in India and the United States raise illuminating controversy in discussion.

Absalom, Absalom! One of Faulkner's more difficult narratives teaches much about language, history, family secrets, the heritage of the South, and the workings of the mind. The Harvard freshman Quentin Compson learns about himself and the Old South through the unraveling of the story of his hometown's mythic (or legendary) figure, Thomas Sutpen.

The Things They Carried. These stories are about war, specifically the grotesque, bizarre, incredible Vietnam War. But don't let that subject matter frighten you away. O'Brien's magical storytelling skills sweep these tales through the actual to the allegoric and metaphoric, ultimately examining the moral, ethical, and spiritual wars within us all. One of our all-time favorites; a book that changed our lives!

Two arcane stories by Guy de Maupassant. I copied and distributed these; we examined his style, intent, and the connection of these literary pieces to the accompanying effusion of and hidden messages in impressionist art. "A Country Excursion," one of the stories, is a delightful and poignant tale of exactly what the title describes—a special afternoon outing for a family of poor, hardworking city dwellers that had unanticipated excitement and passion for the middle-aged mother and her blossoming daughter after they met some sophisticated men. This tale encompasses universal truths about the transitoriness of life, passions, and the societal limitations imposed on females.

The Elegy of Lady Fiametta. This new translation of the fourteenth-century writer's work caught my eye on a bookstore shelf and led my groupies and me on an adventure into what is considered to be the first psychological novel in a modern language, and a milestone in feminist literature. Authored by a man, it is a ribald romance story, a study of the Italian Renaissance court and church, and a sensitive, bittersweet portrayal of a woman's confines.

Solomon Gursky Was Here. Declared public enemy number one in Canada, Richler is a most controversial writer, and his picaresque novel is consternating, hilarious, moral, religious, mythical, and more.

The Hearts and Lives of Men. Weldon hasn't really written one bad book. Each is inventive, entertaining, and bitingly clever in depicting modern times and male-female relations. This one takes on the art world, the class system, and a woman's destiny (fated or self-determined), and carries it off with an intrusive maternal narrative voice that leads your way.

1990–1991

Jane Eyre by Charlotte Bronte
   Great for summer reading. What a role model this female is!
The Shawl by Cynthia Ozick
   Unforgettable!
Wedding Song by Naguib Mahfouz
   We traveled into modern Egyptian lives and found ourselves. The 1988 Nobel Prize for Literature recipient. Anything Mahfouz has written is worthy of your time. Get ready to be swept away by his language.
Tracks by Louise Erdrich
   Part of the tetralogy she's writing about her Chippewa heritage. Both powerful and enjoyable.
The Remains of the Day by Kazuo Ishiguro
   Read it and love it, and then you'll read everything else he wrote.
If Not Now, When? by Primo Levi
   The multifaceted journey of raggedy, brave partisan fighters in World War II.
What We Talk About When We Talk About Love by Raymond Carver
Henry and Cato by Iris Murdoch
   Once you're into her books, you could become a fanatic fan.
The Mambo Kings Play Songs of Love by Oscar Hijuelos
   Pulitzer Prize winner, 1990. Novel far superior to the movie.

Fierce Attachments by Vivian Gornick
  Intense mother-daughter relationship allows for examination of it and yours.

Annotations

Jane Eyre. This is a great summer book for anytime reading or rereading. Brontë gives voice to an admirable female role model who took us proudly into twentieth-century literature written by and about women.

The Shawl. One of Ozick's most accessible works is also an unforgettable reading experience, and an honored member of my all-time favorite list. Not just a Holocaust story, it is representation of life at its cruelest, and at its most hopeful.

Wedding Song. Mahfouz is the first Egyptian to win the Nobel Prize for Literature (1988). Anything he has written is worthwhile, and is usually translated brilliantly.

Tracks. This is part of a tetralogy about Erdrich's Chippewa heritage, and is a heartrending tale of a female protagonist among her people and her land as they are caught in the vise of modernity. Powerful and enjoyable.   ·

The Remains of the Day. Don't just see the movie, read this extraordinary book about a traditional English butler's allegiance to duty and his weeklong journey to self-revelation. Discussion led to illusions we all live by. This book may lead you to read others of Ishiguro's.

If Not Now, When? A tour de force examining human inventiveness, fortitude, and survivorship.

What We Talk About When We Talk About Love. Carver, the master of minimalism, is said to have not only scraped the flesh from the bone but sucked out the marrow. These spare stories reflect the hard edge of life, the baseness of it. Yet Carver, more than Robert Altman in his movie *Short Cuts,* based on Carver's stories, incorporated more of a presence of hope, affirmation, and tenderness amid the dark. It is there in most stories; we just have to find it, or else I'm just pretending it's there because I need to.

Henry and Cato. What a tapestry of intelligence and inventiveness she weaves. Once you're into her books, you could become a fanatic fan. Some of my groupies beg for more and drool endlessly over what they read of hers.

The Mambo Kings Play Songs of Love. This Pulitzer Prize winner (1990) solidly placed the Latino writers on the American literary map. This poignant novel is far superior to the movie and reflected for us so finely the entrée of Latin Americans into North America. Part of the landscape of American history.

Fierce Attachments. This memoir of Gornick's own relationship with her mother allowed us to examine it—and ours. For many of my groups the discussion of this book was a groundbreaking event in our internal dynamics.

1989–1990

Love in the Time of Cholera by Gabriel García Márquez
A Sport of Nature by Nadine Gordimer
A River Runs Through It by Norman Maclean
Sappho, a new translation by Mary Bernard
Light and *Waking* by Eva Figes
Pride and Prejudice by Jane Austen
Crossing to Safety by Wallace Stegner
The Human Factor by Graham Greene
A Theft by Saul Bellow
Billy Bathgate by E. L. Doctorow

1988–1989

Middlemarch by George Eliot
The Handmaid's Tale by Margaret Atwood
Monkeys by Susan Minot
If on a Winter's Night a Traveler . . . by Italo Calvino
Confessions of a Mask by Yukio Mishima
Later the Same Day by Grace Paley
A Bend in the River by V. S. Naipul
Eye of the Heart, Latin American stories edited by Barbara Howes
A Late Divorce by A. B. Yehoshua
Hotel Du Lac by Anita Brookner

Some Other Books I Have Discussed

Black Box by Amos Oz
Sleeping Arrangements by Laura Cunningham
The Painted Bird by Jerzy Kosinski
    Holocaust literature; a blend of art and real life
The Storyteller by Mario Vargas Llosa
Mrs. Dalloway by Virginia Woolf
To the Lighthouse by Virginia Woolf

Native Son by Richard Wright

Invisible Man by Ralph Ellison

Desert Rose by Larry McMurtry

Siddartha by Hermann Hesse

Cat and Mouse and *The Tin Drum* by Günther Grass

The Unbearable Lightness of Being by Milan Kundera

The Book of Laughter and Forgetting by Milan Kundera

The Bridal Canopy by S. Y. Agnon

The Hotel New Hampshire by John Irving

The World According to Garp by John Irving

Chronicle of a Death Foretold by Gabriel García Márquez

Final Payments by Mary Gordon

Moon Tiger by Penelope Lively

White Noise by Don DeLillo

Shiloh and Other Stories by Bobbie Ann Mason

The Whiteness of Bones by Susanna Moore

My Old Sweetheart by Susanna Moore

The Manticore and *Fifth Business* by Robertson Davies

What's Bred in the Bone by Robertson Davies

Ellen Foster by Kaye Gibbons

Sauce for the Goose by Peter DeVries

Deliverance by James Dickey

Switch Bitch by Roald Dahl

Iron and Silk by Mark Salzman

Nineteen Eighty-Four by George Orwell

The Great Gatsby by F. Scott Fitzgerald

The Real Thing, a novella by Henry James and a play by Tom Stoppard

Beloved, Sula, and *The Bluest Eye* by Toni Morrison

The Women of Brewster Place by Gloria Naylor

The Crying of Lot 49 by Thomas Pynchon

A Chain of Voices by André Brink

Waiting for the Barbarians by J. M. Coetzee

Ironweed by William Kennedy

Lovingkindness by Anne Roiphe

The White Hotel by D. M. Thomas

Death Comes for the Archbishop by Willa Cather

Stones for Ibarra by Harriet Doerr

Memento Mori by Muriel Spark

Women of Crisis by Robert and Jane Coles

   Robert Coles is a prize-winning social scientist; anything by the Coles would be an asset to your reading.

A Thousand Cranes by Yasunari Kawabata
  1968 Nobel Prize for Literature
The Lover and *War* by Marguerite Duras
In My Mother's House by Kim Chernin
Age of Innocence by Edith Wharton
Tell Me a Riddle and other stories by Tillie Olsen
Interview with a Vampire by Anne Rice
  Many fell in love with this and went on to read other works by the author.
Three Lives by Gertrude Stein
  A cubist experiment in language.
Gifts from the Sea by Anne Morrow Lindbergh
Even Cowgirls Get the Blues by Tom Robbins
  A feminist and philosophical frolic, it topped the charts for a while among my groupies.
Jitterbug Perfume by Tom Robbins
Summer Before the Dark by Doris Lessing
The Golden Notebook by Doris Lessing
The Female Man by Joanna Russ
  Radical feminism.
Persuasion by Jane Austen
Parallel Lives by Phyllis Rose
The Fanatic Heart, stories by Edna O'Brien

Three Syllabi

The following three syllabi are suggested lists for beginning, intermediate, and advanced readers or group participants. Each list contains three groupings arbitrarily arranged and sprinkled with various themes, styles, and complexity for each level.

LIST 1

FOR BEGINNERS

Group A

The Awakening, Kate Chopin
Heat and Dust, Ruth Prawer Jhabvala
Anywhere But Here, Mona Simpson
American Appetites, Joyce Carol Oates
In the Land of Dreamy Dreams, Ellen Gilchrist
Anagrams, Lorrie Moore

How to Make an American Quilt, Whitney Otto

Lovingkindness, Anne Roiphe

Animal Dreams, Barbara Kingsolver

Cold Sassy Tree, Olive Ann Burns

Group B

Ordinary Love and Good Will, Jane Smiley

To Kill a Mockingbird, Harper Lee

The Object of My Affection, Steve McCauley

Pride and Prejudice, Jane Austen

Stones for Ibarra, Harriet Doerr

Billy Bathgate, E. L. Doctorow

The Group, Mary McCarthy

The Robber Bridegroom, Eudora Welty

The Famished Road, Ben Okri

My Old Sweetheart, Susanna Moore

Group C

Excellent Women, Barbara Pym

84, Charing Cross Road, Helene Hanff

A Woman of Independent Means, Elizabeth Forsythe Hailey

All Creatures Great and Small, James Herriot

My Name Is Asher Lev, Chaim Potok

A Summons to Memphis, Peter Taylor

Fifth Business, Robertson Davies

The Lives and Loves of a She-Devil, Fay Weldon

Eve's Tattoo, Emily Prager

LIST 2

INTERMEDIATE

Group A

So Long, See You Tomorrow, William Maxwell

Madame Bovary, Gustave Flaubert

Love in the Time of Cholera, Gabriel García Márquez

Ironweed, William Kennedy

Epitaph for a Small Winner, Machado de Assis

The Remains of the Day, Kazuo Ishiguro

The Beast in the Jungle, Henry James

Herzog, Saul Bellow

Song of Solomon, Toni Morrison

The Painted Bird, Jerzy Kosinski

Group B

"The Death of Ivan Ilych," Leo Tolstoy

Mariette in Ecstasy, Ron Hansen

The Left Hand of Darkness, Ursula Le Guin

Invisible Man, Ralph Ellison

The Music Room, Dennis McFarland

Tracks, Louise Erdrich

Strange Fits of Passion, Anita Shreve

Illumination Night, Alice Hoffman

Harmony of the World, Charles Baxter

Before and After, Rosellen Brown

Group C

The English Patient, Michael
  Ondaatje
All the Pretty Horses, Cormac
  McCarthy
A Child in Time, Ian McEwan
The Passion, Jeannette Winterson

Paris Trout, Pete Dexter
*I Been in Sorrow's Kitchen and
  Licked Out All the Pots,* Susan
  Straight
Joe, Larry Brown
Violence, Richard Bausch

LIST 3

ADVANCED

Group A

The Volcano Lover, Susan Sontag
Possession, A. S. Byatt
*History of the World in 10½
  Chapters,* Julian Barnes
The Waves, Virginia Woolf
Absalom, Absalom!, William
  Faulkner
Lolita, Vladimir Nabokov
The Faerie Queen, Edmund
  Spenser
The Periodic Tables, Primo Levi
Gravity's Rainbow, Thomas
  Pynchon
The Messiah of Stockholm, Cynthia
  Ozick

Group B

Immortality, Milan Kundera
July's People, Nadine Gordimer
*Hard-Boiled Wonderland and the
  End of the World,* Haruki
  Murakami

The Name of the Rose, Umberto
  Eco
Friday, Michael Tournier
Native Son, Richard Wright
King Lear, William Shakespeare
Slaughterhouse Five, Kurt Vonnegut
Solomon Gursky Was Here,
  Mordecai Richler
Dream Tigers, Jorge Luis Borges

Group C

Falconer, John Cheever
The Stranger, Albert Camus
Mr. Mani, A. B. Yehoshua
Canopus in Argos: Archives, Doris
  Lessing
Surfacing, Margaret Atwood
Buddenbrooks, Thomas Mann
Executioner's Song, Norman Mailer
Wedding Song, Naguib Mahfouz
Counterlife, Philip Roth
Collected Stories, Katherine Anne
  Porter

APPENDIX C

SYLLABI FROM GROUPS AROUND THE COUNTRY

𝒯ollowing are lists of reading group syllabi from around the country, sent to me by questionnaire respondents. Any book listed by multiple groups is indicated by an asterisk (*), and I have tried not to repeat these titles.

• FROM NANCY FEINGOLD, CHICAGO

Paris Trout by Pete Dexter
Malcolm X by Alex Haley
Geek Love by Katharine Dunn
  Group favorite.
Possession by A. S. Byatt*
  Group favorite.
Maus I and II by Alan Spiegelman
  Group favorite.
John Dollar by Marianne Higgins*
Jazz by Toni Morrison*
  Felt it was overrated.
Immortality by Milan Kundera*
  Sparked argument over Kundera's sexist views.
Philadelphia Time by John Edgar Wideman

Vox by Nicholson Baker
Kitchen God's Wife by Amy Tan*
Mating by Norman Rush*
Middle Passage by Charles Johnson*
Mariette in Ecstasy by Ron Hansen*
The Beet Queen by Louise Erdrich
Because It Is Bitter, Because It Is My Heart by Joyce Carol Oates

• FROM KAREN GREEN, SPOKANE, WASHINGTON

Cold Sassy Tree by Olive Burns*
  We loved it.
Beloved by Toni Morrison*
  Very intriguing and emotional.
A Yellow Raft in Blue Water by Michael Dorris*
Life and Death in Shanghai by Nien Cheng*
I Heard the Owl Call My Name by Margaret Craven
At Risk by Alice Hoffman*
  AIDS issues. Great discussion.
Damage by Josephine Hart*
Fried Green Tomatoes at the Whistle Stop Cafe by Fannie Flagg*
  Many groups mentioned this book. Many shared the food and the
  movie together.
Scarlett by Alexandra Ripley
Borrowed Time by Paul Monette*
  AIDS biography.
The Eleventh Hour by Graeme Base
  Fun. We did this with our kids and opened the result page together.
The River Why by David James Duncan
Circle of Friends by Maeve Binchy
Book Case by Stephen Greenleaf
Mists of Avalon by Marion Zimmer Bradley*
Cannibal in Manhattan by Tama Janowitz
The Road from Coorain by Jill Kerr Conway*
  A very popular book club book.
Mrs. Caliban by Rachel Ingalls*
A Prayer for Owen Meany by John Irving
The Education of Little Tree by Forrest Carter*
  Intense reaction.
Mary Reilly by Valerie Martin*

• **FROM MADONNA HAYES, WEST MILFORD, NEW JERSEY**

Rebecca by Daphne du Maurier
Childhood's End by Arthur C. Clarke
Savages by Shirley Conran
The Prince of Tides by Pat Conroy*
   Conroy has a true gift for storytelling. One coed group chose to dis-
   cuss this on five summer evenings, dividing the book by chapter.
The Hunt for Red October by Tom Clancy
The Shell Seekers by Rosamund Pilcher
Kane and Abel by Jeffrey Archer
Daughter of Time by Josephine Tey
Clan of the Cave Bear (and others) by Jean Auel*
Lonesome Dove by Larry McMurtry*
How to Make an American Quilt by Whitney Otto*
   Good book group book.

• **FROM MARJORIE MACLEAN, LANGLEY, WASHINGTON**

An Episode of Sparrows by Rumer Godden
Plain and Simple by Sue Bender
The Crucible by Arthur Miller
Obasan by Joy Kogawa
The Rain God by Arturo Islas
The Spectator Bird by Wallace Stegner
World's Fair by E. L. Doctorow
The Milagro Beanfield War by John Nichols
The Haj by Leon Uris
Old Goriot by Honoré de Balzac
The Promise by Chaim Potok*

• **FROM ANONYMOUS, EUGENE, OREGON**

Biography of My Father by Margaret Truman*
I Will Fight No More (Chief Joseph) by M. Beal
The Book of Job
An American Tragedy by Theodore Dreiser
Short stories by Anton Chekhov

• From **Penny Reick, Winnetka, Illinois**
("Friday Morning Theology Group")

The Chalice and the Blade by Raine Eisler
Befriending the Earth by Thomas Berry, C.P.
Loving the Torah More Than God? by Frans Jozef van Beeck, S.J.
The Book of J by David Rosenberg
Belonging to the Universe by Christopher Mooney
A World of Grace edited by Leo O'Donovan
The Gnostic Gospels by Elaine Pagels
Closer to the Light by Melvin Morse, M.D.
Object Lessons by Anna Quindlen
A Circle of Quiet by Madeline L'Engle
The Artist of the Floating World by Kazuo Ishiguro
Indian Giver by James Welch
Cure for Dreams by Kaye Gibbons
The Bean Trees by Barbara Kingsolver*

• From **Shirley Erwin, Hartland, Wisconsin**

Wild Swans by Jung Cheng*
Housekeeping by Marilyn Robinson*
The Secret History by Donna Tartt
Living Your Dreams by Gayle Delaney
Names of the Mountains by R. Lindberg
The Way of Life by Lao Tzu
Preparing for the Twenty-first Century by Paul Kennedy
The Most Beautiful House in the World by Witold Rybczyenski

• From **Rena Cohen, Highland Park, Illinois**

One Hundred Years of Solitude by Gabriel García Márquez*
Illumination Night by Alice Hoffman*
The Counterlife by Philip Roth*
Disturbances in the Field by Lynne Sharon Schwartz
The Dark Wind by Mark Hillerman
Haakon by C. F. Griffon
  Written by the mother of a group member. She attended the meeting, and it was quite interesting because the book is about a homosexual, which the author isn't. She was primarily interested in the problem of tolerance.

Oscar and Lucinda by Peter Carey
A Vision of Light by Judith Merkle Riley
    Good read and we learned some history, but not much to discuss.
Cat's Eye by Margaret Atwood
Crime and Punishment by Fyodor Dostoyevsky
Heart Mountain by Gretel Ehrlich
The Uses of Enchantment by Bruno Bettelheim
    We all read the introductory material, which sets out his thesis. Then,
    each was assigned a chapter relating to a specific fairy tale.
Aunt Julia and the Scripwriter by Maria Vargas Llosa
    My choice because I loved the movie *Tune in Tomorrow* so much. But
    guess what? Here's one case where the movie had more to say than the
    book.
Lucy by Jamaica Kincaid
    A good book group book.
Seventh Heaven by Alice Hoffman
Midnight's Children by Salman Rushdie
The Sea, The Sea by Iris Murdoch
There Are No Children Here by Alex Kotlowitz*
East Is East by T. Corraghesan Boyle

•**From Sarah Simpson, Lombard, Illinois**

Their Eyes Were Watching God by Zora Neale Hurston*
Lakota Woman by Mary Crow Dog
I Know Why the Caged Bird Sings by Maya Angelou*

•**From Jeane Lumley and Jolynn Huffman, Parker, Colorado**

Fair and Tender Ladies by Lee Smith
The Good Times by Russell Baker
California Gold by John Jakes
Simon's Night by Jon Hassler
Outer Banks by Anne River Siddons
The Picture of Dorian Gray by Oscar Wilde
    Great book club book.
Blue Highways by William Least Heat Moon
How the Garcia Girls Lost Their Accents by Julia Alvarez*
Old Jules by Mari Sandoz
    (Jean and Jolynn's group put together a 5″-by-8″ pamphlet in which
    members' names, addresses, and phone numbers are listed. The

agenda lists date, time, book, hostess, who supplies the refreshments, and who leads the discussion. Very impressive.)

• FROM MARCI WHITNEY-SCHENCK, UNIVERSITY OF CHICAGO
ALUM BOOK GROUP

The Trials of Socrates by I. F. Stone
Spring Snow by Yukio Mishima
March of Folly by Barbara Tuchman
King, Warrior, Magician, Lover by Robert Moore
   About the men's movement.
Lolita by Vladimir Nabokov
   Controversial. Groups love or hate it.
The Trial by Franz Kafka

• FROM MEREDITH MULLINS, MELBOURNE, FLORIDA

Hamlet by William Shakespeare
Nicholas and Alexander by Robert Massie
Bone People by Keri Hulme
   Gets mixed reviews from groups.
The Diary of Anne Frank
To the Scaffold by Carrolly Erikson
Lady Chatterley's Lover by D. H. Lawrence
The Yearling by Marjorie Rawling

• Elizabeth Bluhm used to be in a coed group in New York in the late 1980s. She remembered the sparks that flew the night they discussed *The Red and the Black* by Stendhal. This book engenders a radical split between those who hate it and those who love it.

• FROM BEVERLY PIRTLE, HUNTINGTON BEACH, CALIFORNIA

The Woman in White by Wilkie Collins
The Rag Doll Plagues by Alejandro Morales
Death of an Angel by Alejandro Morales
Angle of Repose and *Collected Stories* by Wallace Stegner
Revolution from Within by Gloria Steinem
No Room of Their Own, edited by Ida Rae Egli
Schindler's List by Thomas Keneally*
Composing a Life by Mary Catherine Bateson
   Great book.

The First Man in Rome by Colleen McCullough
Iron John by Robert Bly

• **FROM THE NATIONAL COUNCIL OF JEWISH WOMEN, CHICAGO AREA**

Can't Quit You Baby by Ellen Douglas*
The Oxherding Tale by Charles Johnson
To Know a Woman by Amos Oz*
The Family Moskat by I. B. Singer
The Bluest Eye by Toni Morrison
To Dance with the White Dog by Terry Kay
Bastard Out of Carolina by Dorothy Allison
Anagrams by Lorrie Miller

• **FROM MADELAINE SARGENT, MENASHA, WISCONSIN**

Bonfires of the Vanities by Tom Wolfe
The Man Who Mistook His Wife for a Hat by Oliver Sacks
    Good read.
Bingo by Rita Mae Brown
    Brown writes good books for discussion.
The Yellow Wind by David Grossman*
Lost in the Cosmos by Walker Percy

• **BASKING RIDGE LIBRARY SERIES, NEW JERSEY**

The Shadow Lines by Amitav Ghosh
In Custody by Anita Desai
Patterns in Childhood by Christa Wolf
The Beggar by Naguib Mahfouz
Cracking India by Bapsi Sidwa*

• **FROM KATHY LAWS, FLOWER MOUND, TEXAS**

The Train to Estelline by Jane Roberts Wood
Seven Habits of Highly Effective People by Stephen R. Covey*
Backlash by Susan Faludi*
You Just Don't Understand by Deborah Tannen*

•FROM ANONYMOUS, ILLINOIS

The Bookmaker's Daughter by Shirley Abbott
God's Pocket and *Paris Trout* by Pete Dexter
Entered from the Sun, The Succession, Death of the Fox, trilogy by George
    Garrett
Dickens by Peter Ackroyd
War Against Public Life: Why Americans Hate Politics by E. J. Dionne
The Gold Bug Variations by Richard Power
You Can't Go Home Again by Thomas Wolfe
The Tax Inspector by Peter Carey
Brazzaville Beach by William Boyd

•FROM CAROL MCKEGNEY, PETALUMA, CALIFORNIA

The Bridges of Madison County by Robert Waller
Waiting to Exhale by Terry McMillan

•FROM JUDY ROBECK, MAKAWAO, HAWAII

God Is Red by Vine DeLoria
Huna by Enid Hoffman
Nana I Ke Kumu by Pukui Haertig Lee
City of Joy by Dominique La Pierre
Sleeping with Soldiers by Rosemary Daniell
Temple of My Familiar by Alice Walker*

•FROM CLETA SCHMITT, WOODBRIDGE, VIRGINIA

Blind Faith by Joe McGinness
Garden of Eden by Ernest Hemingway
My Antonia by Willa Cather
The Witching Hour by Anne Rice
    General disgust.
Twice Shy by Dick Francis
    Did not engender a good discussion.
Out of Africa by Isak Dinesen
Possessing the Secret of Joy by Alice Walker
    Controversial.
The Killer Angels by Michael Shaara
    Discussed by couples and a big success.

Representative Titles from My Mother's (Helen Weiss's) Group (Drexel Hill, Pennsylvania)

Please keep in mind that my mother never graduated from college, only took classes at Johns Hopkins University for two years before marrying in 1940. It was a time when women were not allowed on campus until after 4:00 P.M. (so as not to be a distraction). Many times when I ask her about a title I've recently discovered, I hear her say, "Oh, we did that years ago." Perhaps you, too, will adopt incorrect but ever-so-appropriate usage of the verb *did* to describe the activity of your reading group.

AUTHOR	TITLE
William Barrett	*Irrational Man* (nonfiction)
John Barth	*Lost in the Funhouse*
Samuel Beckett	*Watt*
Saul Bellow	*Mr. Sammler's Planet*
Anthony Burgess	*Abba Abba*
Carlos Castenada	*Tales of Power*
Don DeLillo	*Libra*
E. L. Doctorow	*Loon Lake*
William O. Douglas	*Points of Rebellion* (nonfiction)
Umberto Eco	*The Name of the Rose* and *Foucault's Pendulum*
George Eliot	*Middlemarch*
Louise Erdrich	*Love Medicine*
John Fowles	*Daniel Martin*
Carlos Fuentes	*The Old Gringo*
William H. Gass	*Omensetter's Luck*
Hermann Hesse	*Demian*
Henry James	*Portrait of a Lady* and *The Ambassadors*
James Joyce	*Portrait of the Artist as a Young Man*
Franz Kafka	*The Castle*
Jerzy Kosinski	*The Devil Tree*
Milan Kundera	*The Joke*
Doris Lessing	*The Memoirs of a Survivor*
Eric V. Lustbader	*French Kiss*
Naguib Mahfouz	*Palace Walk*
Bernard Malamud	*The Tenants* and *The Fixer*

AUTHOR	TITLE
André Malraux	*The Conquerors*
Thomas Mann	*Death in Venice*
Wright Morris	*The Field of Vision*
Anaïs Nin	*The Diary of—* and *Ladders to Fire*
Marge Piercy	*Summer People*
Robert Pirsig	*Zen and the Art of Motorcycle Maintenance*
Plato	*The Great Dialogues of Plato*
Carl Sagan	*Dragons of Eden* (nonfiction)
J. D. Salinger	*Franny and Zooey*
William Shakespeare	All works
Alan Sillitoe	*The Storyteller*
Isaac Bashevis Singer	*The Magician of Lublin*
Wole Soyinka	*The Bacchae of Euripides*
Gertrude Stein	*Ida*
Laurence Sterne	*Tristram Shandy*
Josephine Tey	*The Daughter of Time*
Dylan Thomas	*Under Milk Wood*
Alexis de Tocqueville	*Democracy in America* (nonfiction)
Anne Tyler	*Earthly Possessions*
John Updike	*Roger's Version*
Kurt Vonnegut Jr.	*Hocus Pocus*
Virginia Woolf	*Jacob's Room* and *The Waves*
Gary Zukav	*The Dancing Wu Li Masters*
Beowulf	

Appendix D

SOURCES FOR REVIEWS, CRITICISMS, AND AUTHOR INFORMATION

$\mathcal{M}$any books are reviewed in magazines and newspapers. Some libraries subscribe to these periodicals and/or have them available on microfilm. You need to know the author, title, and year (sometimes month) of publication; then check the following sources for citations.

1. General indexes for book reviews:
   a. *Reader's Guide to Periodical Literature*. Listed by year, starting with 1900. There are book reviews in the back, listed alphabetically. Most major magazines are indexed.
   b. *Book Review Digest*. Listed by year, starting with 1920. Excerpts from selected reviews are included, along with other citations.
   c. *Book Review Index*. Indexes a wide range of publications.
   d. *New York Times Index*. Indexes by year, starting with 1925. Reviews are listed under "Book Reviews," and by title under "Book Reviews—Title Index."
   e. Your city may have an index for your local paper. Ask your reference librarian.

2. Other sources found in some libraries; usually located in the reference section:

a. Authors: Critical and Biographical References
b. *Reader's Advisor*
c. *Reader's Catalog*
d. The library computer system, Infotrac, will print out magazine citations when you code in the author or title of the book (only for contemporary books); you can then retrieve the information from the magazines (if your library has them) or from coded tapes (again, if your library has them). Ask the librarian to help you. Some libraries will honor requests and retrieve copies of articles through an interlibrary network system.
e. Good reviews are available in *Publishers Weekly, Library Journal, Kirkus Reviews,* and other industry publications.

CRITICISM ON BOOKS OR AUTHORS

If your author or book has withstood the test of time, there may be published criticism available. Search in the catalog file for author, genre, or subject matter. Ask your librarian to familiarize you with your library's catalog and shelving system. The 809 classification covers literary criticism. Browse through and see what you can find. Even general ideas can generate specific applications.

Here are some important sources of criticism:

a. *Contemporary Literary Criticism* (CLC) and *Twentieth-Century Literary Criticism* (TCLC), both published by Gale, often contain numerous articles on the author and her/his works. Check the index volume under author or title; the last volume entry is the most recent. If you are looking for information on an earlier work, check earlier entries including *Nineteenth-Century Literary Criticism* and *Literature Criticism from 1400–1800.* I have found the Gale series very useful in reviewing criticism. In using it, however, you should be aware of the following hints:

- If the author's death date is after December 31, 1959 (for example, William Faulkner), or the author is still living (for example, Mary Gordon or Barbara Kingsolver), turn to *Contemporary Literary Criticism.*
- If the author died between 1900 and 1959 (for example, Willa Cather, Mark Twain, or Virginia Woolf), use *Twentieth-Century Literary Criticism.*
- If the author died between 1800 and 1899 (for example, Nathaniel Hawthorne or George Sand), use *Nineteenth-Century Literary Criticism.*

• If the author died between 1400 and 1799 (for example, Daniel Defoe or Jonathan Swift), turn to *Literacy Criticism from 1400 to 1800*. One exception is William Shakespeare, who is covered by *Shakespearean Criticism*.

• From antiquity through 1399 (for example, Dante, Homer, or Virgil), turn to *Classical and Medieval Literature Criticism*.

Gale also publishes a *Children's Literature Review* and a *Short Story Criticism*.

b. *Contemporary Authors* (CA) often contains numerous articles on the author and her/his works. Check the index volume under author or title; the last volume entry is the most recent. If you are looking for information on an earlier work, check earlier entries.

c. *Library of Literary Criticism* is arranged by author and time period, with reviews of books written between A.D. 680 and 1904.

d. *Masterplots*; *Masterplots II, Short Stories Series*; *Masterplots II, American Fiction Series*; *Masterplots II, British and Commonwealth Fiction Series*. These volumes summarize plot, character, theme, style, and technique.

e. Magill publishes a series of sets of criticism:

• *Critical Survey of Short Fiction*

• *Survey of Science Fiction Literature*

• *Critical Survey of Long Fiction*

• *Survey of Contemporary Literature*

• *Survey of Modern Fantasy Literature*

f. *Novelists and Prose Writers* (1979), *Contemporary Novelists* (1986), Dramatists (1979), Poets (1979). These provide brief biography and commentary, and list works and suggested reading lists for each author.

g. *Dictionary of Literary Biography* (DLB). Use the index for the latest or multiple entries.

h. *Twentieth-Century Authors*, a biographical dictionary.

i. *Something About the Author* (SATA).

j. Private, university, and newspaper publications have reviews and criticisms. *Sewanee Review, Hudson Review, Wilson Library Journal, American Literature, Modern Fiction Studies, New York Review of Books, Village Voice Literary Supplement*, etc., are names of a few.

k. Several libraries (municipal and university) around the country subscribe to *Reading Women*. If you, your library, or your group would like to subscribe, send $29.00 to Reading Women, Box 296, Winnetka, IL 60093, or ask for our information packet before subscribing. *Reading Women* reviews only quality fiction already available in paperback, and presents commentary and analysis to aid book groups with their discussion. It acts as a guide to book selection and improved critical thinking. *Reading Women* has no advertising in its eight pages, and is proud to be thriving.

1. Several other sources of guidance have crossed my path. I list them here for your information.

- *American Institute of Discussion* (AID). Daniel Blanchard, president, has developed an interdisciplinary approach to the arts; volunteer moderators coordinate community groups. For information, write to American Institute of Discussion, Box 103, Oklahoma City, OK 73101. AID has groups in Oklahoma, Missouri, Texas, Arkansas, and Louisiana. Training in how to moderate a discussion would be an asset to your group dynamics.

- *The Women's Review of Books,* Wellesley College Center for Research on Women, Wellesley, MA 02181, includes newly published hardcover nonfiction feminist criticisms; also contains advertising.

- *The Bloomsbury Review.* A mainstream, progressive publication offering essays, reviews, and interviews on a wide range of books, authors, and subjects. Includes advertising. Write to: 1028 Banock Street, Denver, CO 80204.

- *The Minnesota Women's Press.* Distributed free in the Twin Cities area; for-profit organization, reasonable subscription rates, objectively reported women's local and national issues; has book and film columns, advertising. Press operates the Bookshop and the Women's Library at same address: 771 Raymond Avenue, St. Paul, MN 55114. Store specializes in women's books and conducts the Salon and Book Groups. Call 612-646-3968.

- *A Common Reader* is a free 5"-by-8" sales catalog with about 100 pages of newsprint offering multifaceted book selections with informative descriptions. It also has a table of contents. Offers hardcover and paperback listings. Write to: 141 Thompkins Avenue, Pleasantville, NY 10570, or call 1-800-832-7323.

- *The Quality Paperback Book Club* offers slightly lower prices on their paperback editions, which are sometimes available before public release. Write to: Customer Service Center, Box 8813, Camp Hill, PA 17012-8813, or call 1-800-348-7128.

ABOUT BOOK GROUPS

Recently, Harpo Productions, Inc. (Oprah's company) and Starbucks, the coffee-brewing corner meeting place, agreed to carry Oprah's monthly book selections for sale in every Starbucks store. Stop in. Pick up and read the copy on one of their paper cups; the words testify to the progressive humanism that sustains the book group movement. In huge print float the words by Gustave Flaubert (author, in nineteenth century France, of *Madame Bovary*): "Read in order to live." Around these words, in smaller size type reads the community connection: "Reading provides hope, discovery, and opportunity. The Starbucks Foundation, with support from Oprah's Book Club, is working to unlock these possibilities. All proceeds from the sale of the Oprah's Book Club selection at Starbucks are donated to The Starbucks Foundation to support literacy in local communities. Join the fight for literacy. Help others discover hope and opportunity." The epigraph to E.M. Forster's novel *Howards End* is " . . . only connect." Reading groups are not just all the rage, they are our hope for a better future.

Other events and modes of communication have spread the good news about book groups. Several books were published after mine, either specifically for and about reading groups or generic to today's booklovers. Some are listed here:

- Auchincloss, Louis. *The Book Class.* Houghton Mifflin, Boston, 1984.

- Dodson, Shireen. *The Mother-Daughter Book Club.* HarperPerennial, New York, 1997. Dodson's book is causing a sensation, creating a special movement within the larger one that can only bring improved relationships and communications between the parties in this primal and primally important duo. Grab your daughter—and start a club.

- Laskin, David, and Holly Hughes. *The Reading Group Book.* Penguin, New York, 1995.

- Pearlman, Mickey. *What to Read: The Essential Guide for Reading Group Members and Other Book Lovers.* HarperCollins, New York, 1994.

- Saal, Rollene. *The New York Public Library Guide to Reading Groups.* Crown, New York, 1995.

- Santmyer, Helen Hooven. " . . . And Ladies of the Club." Berkley, New York, 1985.

- Slezak, Ellen, ed. *The Book Group Book.* Chicago Review Press, 1993, New York, 1995.

BOOK GROUP PUBLICATIONS

Reading Group Choices: Selections for Lively Book Discussions. Paz & Associates, Nashville, Tennessee, 1995, 1996, 1997, 1998. Each booklet lists 26 books selected by an advisory board and includes author biography, summary, and discussion questions. (800-260-8605. dpaz@pazbookbiz.com)

Reverberations, the newsjournal of the Association of Book Group Readers and Leaders. Annual membership $18. P.O. Box 885, Highland Park, IL 60035

Reading in Company: Starting a Reading Group. Pamphlet, Arizona Center for the Books. P.O. Box 34438 Phoenix, AZ 85067-4438

An Introduction to Shared Inquiry. The Great Books Foundation, 35 East Wacker Drive, Suite 2300, Chicago, IL 60601-2298 (800-222-5870)

RESOURCES FOR THE BOOKLOVER

Adler, Mortimer J., and Charles Van Doren. *How to Read a Book.* Touchstone (Simon & Schuster) Originally published in 1940, this guide revolutionized thinking about reading and caused people to think past mechanics to comprehension and construct.

American Audio Prose Library, Inc. Collection includes readings by and interviews with over 132 contemporary writers. P.O. Box 842 Columbia, MO 65205 (800-447-2275).

Barthes, Roland. *The Pleasures of the Text,* translated by Richard Miller. Farrar, Straus and Giroux. An obtuse little treasure to open minds to new ways of perceiving your relationship with a reading experience, New York, NY, 1994.

Bauermeister, Erica; Larsen, Jesse; Smith, Holly. *500 Great Books by Women, A Reader's Guide.* Penguin, New York, NY, 1994.

Birkerts, Sven. *The Gutenberg Elegies: The Fate of Reading in an Electronic Age.* Fawcett Columbine, New York, NY, 1995.

Burns, Eric. *The Joy of Books, Confessions of a Lifelong Reader.* Prometheus Books, Amhurst, NY, 1995.

Corey, Melinda, and George Ochoa. *Literature: The New York Public Library Book of Answers.* Simon & Schuster, New York, NY, 1993.

Denby, David. *Great Books, My Adventures with Homer, Rousseau, Woolf, and Other Indestructible Writers of the Western World.* Simon & Schuster, New York, NY, 1996.

Flynn, Elizabeth A., Schweickart, Patrocinio, eds. *Gender and Reading, Essays on Readers, Texts, and Contexts.* The Johns Hopkins University Press, Baltimore, MD, 1986.

Furman, Laura, Standard, Elinore, eds., *Bookworms, Great Writers and Readers Celebrate Reading.* Carroll & Graf, New York, NY, 1997.

Gilbar, Steven, ed. *The Open Door; When Writers First Learned to Read.* David Godine, Inc. in association with The Center of the Book in the Library of Congress, Washington, DC, 1989.

Glaspey, Terry W. *Great Books of the Christian Tradition, and other books which have shaped the world.* Harvest House Publishers, Eugene, OR, 1996.

Gross, Jacquelyn. *Make Your Child a Lifelong Reader.* Jeremy Tarcher, Inc., New York, NY, 1986.

Kanigel, Robert. *Vintage Reading. From Plato to Bradbury, A Personal Tour of Some of the World's Best Books.* Bancroft Press, Baltimore, MD, 1997.

Kimmel, Margaret Mary, Elizabeth Segel. *For Reading Out Loud! A Guide to Sharing Books with Children from Infancy to the Teens.* Dell, New York, NY, 1991.

Krashen, Stephen. *The Power of Reading, Insights from the Research.* Libraries Unlimited, Inc., Englewood, CA, 1993.

Manuel, Alberto. *A History of Reading.* Viking/Penguin, New York, NY, 1996.

Morris, Evan. *The Book Lover's Guide to the Internet.* Ballantine/Random House, New York, NY, 1996.

Nell, Victor. *Lost in a Book: The Psychology of Reading for Pleasure,* Yale University Press, New Haven CT, 1988, 1990.

Pennac, Daniel. *Better Than Life.* Coach House Press, Toronto, Ontario, Canada, 1994.

Perstein, Jill S., ed. *Out of the Mold, Independent Voices Breaking Out of the Mold.* American Booksellers Association, Tarrytown, NY, 1997. Published in celebration of independent bookselling and National Independent Bookstore Week, this anthology of essays, stories, poems, graphics, promotes thinking about reading and creativity. (ABA number is 800-637-0037 for more info)

Raabe, Tom. *Biblioholism: The Literary Addiction.* Fulcrum, Golden, CO, 1995.

Schwartz, Lynn Sharon. *Ruined by Reading, a Life in Books.* Beacon Press, Boston, MA, 1996.

Segal, Jeanne, Ph.D. *Raising Your Emotional Intelligence.* Owl Books/Henry Holt, New York, NY, 1997. I particularly like this book as an aid to the discussion process, for it helps teach us how to approach experience from above and below the neck.

Wagner, Patricia Jean, author and editor. *The Bloomsbury Review Booklover's Guide, A Collection of Tips, Techniques, Anecdotes, Controversies & Suggestions for the Home Library.* The Bloomsbury Review, 1996.

WEBSITES

Evan Morris's book listed above, *The Book Lover's Guide to the Internet,* introduces you to the most expansive format for the concept of reading groups. The internet has exploded with attention given to the movement. Most publishers, bookstores, on-line booksellers, and organizations focused on literacy and reading have websites on the internet. Even some authors have their own websites.

The frustration with a book as limited as this one is the lack of space to compile complete lists, yet that task is an impossible one since as we inhale and exhale internet history is being made, things are in constant flux.

Here are some websites worth a visit, to constitute a beginning: All begin with http://www.

Booksellers

amazon.com
books.com
B&N.com

About Books and Authors

nytimes.com/books
greatbooks.com : Great Books Foundation
ala.org : American Library Association
bookweb.org : American Booksellers Assoc.
pantheon.cis.yale.edu/david/it.html (no www.; a site relating to Amer. lit. with links to others
bookwire.com : Includes the electronic version of the book publishing industry newsletter, *Publishers Weekly,* with links to many more sites
imgnet.com/auth/ : author's sites and more
oprahshow.com

Publishers

bdd.com
chronbooks.com

randomhouse.com
godine.com
harpercollins.com
penguin.com
hmco.com

On AOL, try these keywords

barnesandnoble
BC (BooksCentral)
TBR (TheBookReport)
Oprah
books

APPENDIX E

GLOSSARY OF LITERARY TERMS

These terms, definitions, and examples are intended to enrich your discussion.

Allegory. A narrative that makes coherent sense on the literal level and also has a second, correlated design. Allegories are historical, political, or based on ideas, so that characters have to represent abstract concepts. Nadine Gordimer's *My Son's Story* is an allegory for the politics in South Africa. The third book of Swift's *Gulliver's Travels* is an allegorical satire directed toward philosophical and scientific pedantry.

Allusion. Reference within a story to an event, person, place, or another literary work. A. S. Byatt's *Possession* is full of allusions to English, Norse, French, Celtic, and Germanic mythology, much of English literary history, and rural superstitions.

Ambiguity. Story, character, language, and action that evoke conflicting meanings and convey diverse attitudes and feelings. In an era when writing reflects sociopolitical confusion, more and more ambiguity is found in our fiction.

Anachronism. A reference to an object, event, or person that is misplaced in time with the historical period being depicted. An example would be if, in E. M. Forster's *Howards End* (1910), Helen Schlegel took Leonard Bast's Sony Walkman from the Beethoven concert instead of his umbrella.

Analogical. Beyond the literal meaning of a text is the revelation of, or search for, higher spiritual meaning. This is considered the highest level of text interpretation (the others being *literal, allegorical,* and *moral,* in that order). Most of Muriel Spark's novels afford this level of interpretation, specifically *Memento Mori* and *Symposium.*

Anticlimax. An event that loses importance by occurring after the action has been resolved. In *So Long See You Tomorrow,* by William Maxwell, we learn of the murder in the first pages. The murder is anticlimactic to the rest of the book.

Antihero. A protagonist who is distinguished from the classic hero by his or her flaws and inability to perform heroic deeds. Traditionally, heroes were of a special status, such as kings, noblemen, or princes; ordinary men were designated as antiheroes. Willy Loman in Arthur Miller's *Death of a Salesman,* or Macon Leary in Anne Tyler's *Accidental Tourist,* could be viewed as antiheroes.

Archetype. Themes, images, or characters that are variations of patterns established long ago and that have universal application. Father-son conflicts, a wicked stepmother, descent into an underworld, the return of the conquering hero are all examples of archetypes.

Catharsis. Literally, a purgation or emotional cleansing that can be experienced by fictional characters in plays, books, and films—and even by the readers/audiences and authors/playwrights—after having undergone emotionally traumatic events. Authors are sometimes said to be compelled to write as a form of catharsis, or working out and expiating the burden of painful memories. A catharsis should bring a sense of illumination and/or redemption. Sympathetic readers/audiences love the vicarious connection with fictional characters and authors.

Character. A character may be only "part of the scenery" or represent an ethical or social evaluation of the period. An author "uses" a character in relation to motivation, action, and change. The discussion usually scrutinizes the character's credibility and dimensionality. Each character in E. M. Forster's *Howards End* represents a mindset of the time and is used by Forster to move his vision along instead of acting as living reproductions. On the other hand, I remember reading something Anne Tyler said—that she is looking forward to being in heaven so she can find out how her characters turned out.

Climax. The point of highest interest and intensity in the plot; the apex that controls the balance (the denouement) of the rise and fall of action. In Forster's *Howards End,* the murder/death of Leonard Bast could be argued as the climax.

Closure. The sense of completion or resolution at the end of a book that usually affords an emotional satisfaction and sense of fulfillment on the part of the reader. Loose ends are tidily tied up. Closure or "closed" texts are in opposition to "open" texts that create an often disturbing sense of irresolution and incompleteness. The contrast between and reasons for "open" and "closed" texts makes for good discussion.

Comedy. Usually entertains and amuses us, and comforts us with the knowledge that no disaster causes permanent damage and that all will end happily. Comic forms are romantic, comedy of manners, farces, and satires. Depending on the sophisticated wit of the author, comedies can be high (intellectual, very verbal) or low (base, earthy, ribald). Comic relief breaks the tension of serious drama or tragedy.

Conflict. Interaction that creates tension in a story, usually between characters, values, doctrines, times, and space. Traditionalists consider conflict to be paramount in a story. Experimentalists have sometimes deleted it. Characters, families, events, etc., are specifically designed in opposition or alignment with others for contrasts and comparisons. In Smiley's *A Thousand Acres,* the Clark, Cook, and Ericson families and individual members can be compared and contrasted.

Connotation. A suggestive, associated meaning of a word as opposed to its denotation or explicit meaning. Connotation can cause ambiguity.

Deconstruction. Scholarly thought and elaborate theory involving language and meaning by which a text can be unraveled word by word and studied for its significance. Deconstruction can be interpreted as academic play, literary terrorism, or advanced mode of criticism. Notable philosophers whose writings fall into this category are Jacques Derrida, Jonathan Culler, Paul de Man, and Ferdinand de Saussure.

Dystopia. Literally, "bad place." The opposite of utopia, or the ideal situation or "good place." Marge Piercy's *Woman on the Edge of Time,* George Orwell's *Nineteen Eighty-Four,* and Aldous Huxley's *Brave New World* are dystopian novels. James Hilton's *Lost Horizon* is a modern utopian novel. Dystopian novels paint reality darkly; utopian novels are literary representations of imaginary places or exaggerated manifestations of the author's society.

Epigraph. A quotation at the beginning of the book or chapter that heralds the author's focus or theme.

Epilogue. A concluding section added to a novel or story, usually bringing a sense of closure; sometimes jumping forward in time.

Epiphany. In a religious sense, a "manifestation" that signifies God's presence. In a secular experience, an epiphany occurs when a character has a sense of revelation, an enlightenment—one of those moments when troubling things become clarified or events of life become connected in new revelatory ways. The devoted butler, Mr. Stevens, has his epiphany in *The Remains of the Day* during the closing pages of the novel. It took a six-day journey for him to have it. (Do you think that Ishiguro is implying that on the seventh day he rested?) James Joyce, in the mid-twentieth century, adapted the term to the secular experience in his novel *Portrait of the Artist as a Young Man* to signify the sudden revelation that occurs while observing a commonplace object—and that object too takes on an appearance of radiance.

Figurative language. General term covering often lyrical language used in nonliteral ways. Hyperboles, metaphors, symbols, similes, and others fit this category.

Folklore. The legends, superstitions, tales, songs, proverbs, riddles, spells, nursery rhymes, customs, rituals, and the pseudoscientific lore explaining natural forces. Mostly passed down orally as opposed to in written language. Byatt's *Possession* combines folklore with literature.

Hero. Usually the principal character in a text who exhibits virtuous qualities and distinguishes himself or herself with courage, abilities, and noble deeds. I include "her-self" in this definition. Heretofore women have been given the place of heroines, or helpmates, in mostly male-created literature. Progressive humanist perspectives include the woman as the main character of her life or story, as the man would be of his, and as such she is called upon to exhibit those same qualities—whether in the same or different circumstances, and whether determined by biology or otherwise. Gender-blind analysis would apply to *antihero* also.

Imagery. A vague critical term referring to the use of language that activates any or all of the five senses. Particular figurative language molds metaphors and similes (which are symbols in the reader's mind) in ways that emphasize and convey the author's vision or intent. Distinct images created with words are intended to evoke specific visceral and emotional reactions.

Irony. The subtly humorous distinction between what is portrayed and what is actually the case. Rooted in Greek comedy when an *eiron* was a "dissembler," irony intends to imply a meaning other than the one ostensibly asserted. An example of verbal irony is found in the opening sentence of Jane Austen's *Pride and Prejudice*: "It is a truth universally acknowledged that a single man in possession of a good fortune must be in want of a wife." (The irony being that it is the woman depicted by Austen who is the fortune hunter.) Structural irony sustains the duplicity throughout, as in Jonathan Swift's essay "A Modest Proposal," in which a well-meaning but insanely rational economist's solution for overpopulation in time of famine is turning the children into gastronomic delights! The style can be understated or overstated in the author's manner of writing. The understatement can be so skillful that ambiguity concerning authorial intent is created, as in *The Remains of the Day* by Kazuo Ishiguro.

Local color. Details of a particular region, place, and time period such as dress, customs, language, dialect, flora, and fauna. These details give a sense of authenticity to a novel or short story. Rudyard Kipling's *Kim* (1910) and the highly anthologized short story "The Revolt of 'Mother' " by Mary Wilkins Freeman (1852–1930) are two examples of fiction noted for local color.

Motif (and leitmotiv). Recurring elements, incidents, or complex images used by the author to convey the theme. *Leitmotiv* is sometimes used interchangeably with *motif*, but is better thought of as the author's abstract doctrine or persuasion. Motif in *The Adventures of Huckleberry Finn* would include the water/river, the raft, and the land. Twain explores society, morals and prejudices, personal choices, and freedom accordingly.

Mythology. Legend and folklore often concerning supernatural beings. The study of mythology as structure, religion, and rationale for social customs is paramount to literary analysis. We cannot separate mythology from the way we view ourselves today. Guides to the myths are useful ancillaries for reading groups. Some myths have recurred so frequently in various times and cultures that they have embodied archetypes—essential elements of the human experience. Heroes, villains, "shrews"; cycles of birth, death, and rebirth; actions of falling in love, hatred, feuding, forgiving; symbols of the sun, snakes, and woods appear in varying forms, but remain archetypal. Comparative studies of mythologies, especially those of C. G. Jung, hypothesize the presence of a "collective unconscious" believed to be the primitive source of these archetypes, myths, and symbols.

Naturalism. Connected with realism as a literary movement and defined in the nineteenth century, naturalism deals with a picture of life in ways more visceral than realism and is influenced by Darwinian biology. Its thesis centers on humans behaving solely as creatures of nature, with no connection to religious or spiritual precepts of behavior. Humans are considered higher-order animals whose characters are products of two kinds of natural forces: heredity and environment.

Oxymoron. The combining of two terms that transcend sense and logic. Examples: loving hate, joyful pain, cold as hell, or *Pagan Rabbi* (a novel by Cynthia Ozick, who is noted for her thought-provoking oxymorons, among other things). A well-known oxymoron in political satire: military intelligence.

Paradox. Related to oxymoron, this is a self-contradictory, absurd, yet seemingly reconcilable and rational statement. One of the most famous is the conclusion of John Donne's sonnet, *"Death, Be Not Proud"*: "One short sleep past, we wake eternally/ And death shall be no more;/ *Death shall not die.*"

Parody. A literary work intentionally styled to mockingly imitate, ridicule, or exaggerate to a satirical point the writing style of another work or author's works.

Pathos. Using the passions, suffering, or deep feelings in a text to evoke intense emotional responses from the reader. King Lear's speech to Cordelia upon their reconciliation (*King Lear* IV, 7, 59ff) is a famous example of pathos.

Poetic justice. In the framework of morality, a term to signify just and proportionate rewards and punishments in relation to a character's vice or virtue. This can be discussed in opposition to the naturalistic idea of a tragic flaw.

Realism. Fiction that gives the illusion of reflecting life as it seems to the reader. "So realistic," we say. "That's the way it really is." (Or *really* is as the reader sees it.)

Regional novel. A general term, like local color, to indicate a story that represents a specific region of the country. In some cases, the influential essence and spirit of the land or region transforms it into a character, if not the main character, of the novel. Appendix A includes a listing of some regional writers. An example of a regional novel: My community, the stretch of suburbia north of Chicago called the North Shore, has been reflected in the novels of Charles Cohen. *Silver Linings* (1988), *Those Lake Views* (1990), and *Silver Balls* (soon to be released) are satirical looks at the foibles and mores of present-day suburbia.

Romanticism. Fiction that fosters the limitless capacities and aspirations of humans (men, for the most part, since its nineteenth century conception), and presents characters and life in larger, more splendid dimensions. Romance pictures elements, action, and character as we want them to be, rather than as they are.

Semiotics. The study of language as made up of certain coded "signs," and the diverse meanings conveyed by specific words and the arrangements of words. This area of study is connected to deconstruction in that it breaks down the literary arts into their smallest common denominator—words.

Sensibility. Implies a response or feeling associated with a particular culture or moral code, as in "feminist sensibility" or "macho sensibility."

Stream of consciousness. A narrative technique that divulges the workings of a character's mind—the mental process of intermingling memory, ideas, and sensory responses without logical differentiations. To accurately effect this, conventional syntax and punctuation are usually abandoned. *As I Lay Dying* by William Faulkner, *Portrait of the Artist as a Young Man* by James Joyce, and *Mrs. Dalloway* by Virginia Woolf are apt examples.

Symbol. From the Greek *symbolon*, meaning "mark," "token," or "sign." A symbol is something that represents something by inference, analogy, association, or is contrived in fiction by the author. In *Howards End*, Leonard Bast's raggedy umbrella is his crucial link to the social stratification of the gentleman. He clings to this illusion of himself by carrying an umbrella, tattered as it is. When Helen Schlegel carelessly takes his "treasured identity," he desperately runs after it. Helen, on a much higher social rung, absent-mindedly takes others' umbrellas constantly. Forster uses the umbrella to symbolize class stratification, its membership qualifications, and how an individual's identity may be superficially tied to mere objects. Many symbols—white, lion, mouse, lily, snake—exist by tradition and convention and stories told over and over again. Many symbols are invented or created by modern writers. Some writers, such as Katherine Anne Porter, are known for their heavy-handed use of symbolism, and readers search for them in texts.

Tetraology. Four separate texts comprising a planned unit. *Trilogy* denotes a series of three related texts.

Tragedy. A term broadly applied to works that are serious in nature and turn out disastrously for the main character. A tragic hero is neither entirely good nor entirely bad, and usually exhibits what is called a tragic flaw, which is commonly seen as the human concept of hubris or pride. Pride, self-centeredness, and blindness to others visit misfortunes on characters. These misfortunes can end disastrously (tragedy) or happily (comedy).

Tragicomedy. This term implies mingling of tragic and comic elements in a variety of ways. Discovering these ways makes for good group discussion.

Transcendental. A metaphysical term pertaining specifically here to potential reader response of moving beyond one reality (your own) into another's (the life of fiction).

Verisimilitude. Denotes the author's achievement of the illusion of reality and truth by his or her skillful use of all elements.

Zeitgeist. From the German for "time spirit." The spirit or intellectual atmosphere of an age or period.

ADVICE FROM QUESTIONNAIRE RESPONDENTS

$\mathcal{Y}$ou have heard it from me in these preceding pages—now hear advice from reading group veterans around the country.

A true story. "Our book club was participating in an annual overnight retreat at the lake home of one of the members. We all agreed that a good beginning for the weekend was to write—in this case an incident or memory of bonding we had experienced with our mothers. (In the group, we had read and discussed many pieces of literature that dealt with mother-daughter relationships and issues.)

"I watched as the others wrote. Everyone was intense and serious; one wept profusely. No one spoke. Following the writing and dinner, we arrived at the "moment of truth" when we would read our work round-robin at the table.

"The amazing part of our experience as we shared the incidents with our friends were the universals that we felt. The specifics may have been quite different (one wrote of shopping for clothes with her mother; another of baking on special occasions; several described the experience of looking into mirrors and seeing their mothers' faces reflected there), but the generalities were the same: We all had unique experiences of bonding with unique mothers—bonds that would not be broken as long as *we* went on living. And we all suffered the pain of watching our mothers change and grow old.

"The stories were poignant. There wasn't a dry eye among us. This was a rare and invaluable opportunity to listen and communicate with my peers. I will never forget the warmth and unity I felt at sharing those moments with my friends and fellow book club members, who were now somehow even closer than before." —Sandy Brown

Some true feelings. "Sometimes I would read the assigned stories—loving them, hating them, often sure I had not understood a word of their meaning. But when the book group met, something Rachel would say or a question she would ask would suddenly spark a response I was not even consciously aware of, as if it had come from some remote part of me without my knowledge or consent, and I realized for the first time in my midthirties that I was smart.

"This continued awareness ignited my most serious evaluation of 'the feminine role.' Our bimonthly short-story group made clear the overwhelming universality of women's angst down through the generations, personified and chronicled via the written page. The literature we read helped me to better understand my mother and ultimately to know exactly who I was becoming.

"In the subsequent years, the book group evolved into a safe and secure place to learn about others, both fictional and real, as well as ourselves. The skills I practiced there aided me in the complete life change I was about to embark upon in my mid-forties. The skills and awareness I had used in defining literature, I took to further exploration and self-development in less conventional arenas of study." —Marla Gassner

Some history. "I can't imagine life without a book group. We've belonged to one during all but five years of our forty-three-year marriage, and those five years were dull intellectually. As life changed, our group changed. Members have died, divorced, remarried, had children and grandchildren, moved away, or lost interest, but the core group has remained supportive, kind, and adaptable to changing interests. One group vignette: We had an 'affluence' party after reading *The End of Affluence*—posh menu, evening dresses, and black tie. We were all financially secure and feeling rosy. Within the next two years, men were laid off, two companies went down the tubes, and the stay-at-home wives were back in the workforce. Now twelve years later everyone has reestablished new careers and is doing well again except for one couple. They did not recover and dropped out. The rest of us tried hard to keep them 'in,' but they couldn't handle the situation. I feel we failed in support, but we did try." —Anonymous

Here are a few additional comments:

- "Give it a try! It's nice to have a reason to read and an opportunity to share."

- "Do it—it's a great asset to life! Reading is wonderful; sharing is even better."

- "Do it! All women! Hire a leader!" —Marla Green

- "Find people who enjoy a good debate, but who also respect the opinions of others." —Nancy Feingold

- "If starting a group, be informal yet structured enough to keep discussion on track. If joining, come with an open mind and a commitment to reading the books." —Pat McDowell

- "Do it today. It is a wonderful, healthy activity and one that we can share with our friends and families. Don't allow your group to get too chatty. Try to discuss issues." —Karen Green

- "Be sure you are aware of the books the group reads. If organizing a group, be sure everyone understands your format." —Madonna Hayes

- "An open attitude is essential. A sense of humor is essential. You need a willingness to listen, share, and preserve confidentiality, and you need an interest in others—what they have to say—and a nonjudgmental standpoint." —Judy Denenberg

- "The initial membership should be diverse, since there will be a lot of change. Old friends do not always make the best book club members." —Barb Loevy

- "Be careful about choosing your members." —Anonymous

- "A reading group should have a focus and an agreed-upon format." — Sarah Simpson

- "Even if you only start with three people, do it. Your group can grow and change for the benefit of all. Be open to all opinions and be ready to challenge yourself." —Barb Alexander

- "If you want to talk books, stay away from going in with friends. Have a facilitator to control the flow and direction of questions. Choose someone with an excellent sense of group dynamics." —Jacquie Kohn

- "Having a leader is crucial and the leader should pick the books. So it's important to agree with the leader's taste in literature." —Kathy Sackheim

- "Do it! Very special experiences with very special people who need not be your bosom buddies. In fact, my closest friends are not in any of my three groups." —Anonymous

- "Don't take it too seriously. Enjoy the natural process of digressing from the topic." —Carol McKegney

- "Keep it small and simple. Keep it lively. Don't read long books each time. Diversify the types of books. Learn about other cultures. Look to classics for inspiration and illumination, too." —Shirley Erwin

- "Visit once or twice before committing yourself to the group." —Bonnie Phemister

- "Join! It's great fun. Don't make refreshments too big of a chore for the host/hostess." —Carol Kaplan

- "We value and treasure our differences as a source of richness, and our choice of reading material is always secondary to our commitment to nourishing the relationships among our group members. We feed each other's souls." —Penny Reick

And because many questionnaires were answered *en groupe* with members' knowledge and input, many said that they appreciated this opportunity. As Penny Reick wrote, "It has been an enriching exercise for our group to define and articulate who we are to each other. Thank you for this opportunity."

Author's note: Many great writers took no writing classes and attended no writing workshops. They learned to write by reading. Remember this as you embark on your new reading group experience—one that will have its own story, and one that many ignite creative writing energies within you. Enjoy!

If interested in a pamphlet on:

- improving group dynamics
- improving leadership skills
- improving critical reading skills

Rachel Jacobsohn is available for presentations, workshops and seminars. She can be contacted at 847-266-0431 or e-mail: rachelj@interaccess.com, or write for a brochure to P.O. Box 885 Highland Park, IL 60035.

READING WOMEN CUMULATIVE INDEX

Back issues are available for $6 ($3 for Prepublication Edition). Volume I, Number 4, is available in photocopy only.